"I have known and admired Bob Roberts for years. He is a leader in the movement to convert belief to action and proclamation to credible demonstration. Roberts is bold. He is adventurous. And he's biblical. He is a consummate connector. *Real-Time Connections* forges a new path as Christianity addresses a globalized world. It is well worth reading."

—BOB BUFORD, founder, Leadership Network,
author, *Halftime* and *Finishing Well*

"Bob Roberts has done it again in *Real-Time Connections*. He's written a book that is readable, honest, and powerful. It's a book for everyone! It offers real-life answers to how followers of Jesus around the world can partner with God as he changes nations through their everyday lives. This book is unique in that it deals with the mega-issues of our planet yet brings them home (literally) by compelling us to be involved. I loved it!"

—CARL MEDEARIS, author,
Muslims, Christians, and Jesus

REAL-TIME CONNECTIONS

REAL-TIME
CONNECTIONS

Linking Your Job to God's Global Work

BOB ROBERTS JR.

ZONDERVAN®

ZONDERVAN.com/
AUTHORTRACKER
follow your favorite authors

We want to hear from you. Please send your comments about this book to us in care of zreview@zondervan.com. Thank you.

ZONDERVAN

Real-Time Connections
Copyright © 2010 by Bob Roberts Jr.

This title is also available as a Zondervan ebook. Visit www.zondervan.com/ebooks.

This title is also available in a Zondervan audio edition. Visit www.zondervan.fm.

Requests for information should be addressed to:
Zondervan, *Grand Rapids, Michigan 49530*

Library of Congress Cataloging-in-Publication Data
  Roberts, Bob, 1958 - .
    Real-time connections : linking your job to God's global work / Bob Roberts Jr.
      p. cm.
    Includes index.
    ISBN 978-0-310-27717-0 (softcover)
    1. Evangelistic work. 2. Great Commission (Bible) 3. Employees—Religious life.
  4. Globalization—Religious aspects—Christianity. 5. Roberts, Bob, 1958 - I. Title.
  BV3793.R63 2009
  248'.5—dc22   2009026493

Published in association with the literary and marketing agency of C. Grant and Company.

Cover design: Rob Monacelli
Interior design: Cindy LaBreacht

Printed in the United States of America

10 11 12 13 14 • 20 19 18 17 16 15 14 13 12 11 10 9 8 7 6 5 4 3 2

To NorthWood Church

THIS IS OUR STORY

In '85 we began a journey together in starting our church —
    And you graciously followed a very young and
        inexperienced pastor
      Who was an average preacher at best.
In '92 we continued a journey together as we stumbled into the
        kingdom —
    And you graciously followed a young and broken pastor
      Who was hungry for God finding Jesus as enough.
In '95 we continued a journey together into the world —
    And you graciously followed a naïve and globally ignorant
        pastor
      Who was burdened for Vietnam yet not knowing how to
        help them.
In '01 we continued a journey together of teaching and
        mentoring churches and people —
    And you followed a visionary connecting pastor of
        churches, people, and nations
      Who had more vision and opportunity than resources or
        processes.
In '08 we continued a journey together of scalability and redefini-
        tion of everything —
    And you followed a pastor putting the west behind and the
        east before us
      Who finally was finding vocabulary engagement for the
        twenty-first century.

In '10 we continue a journey together never knowing where it will
take us —
Yet following wherever he leads, obeying what he says,
Abandoned to our friend, Savior, Friend, brother — Jesus
In the midst of an ever-increasing adventure of the
unexpected.

──────────────────────O

CONTENTS

ACKNOWLEDGMENTS

There is no way I could do what I do apart from my wife, Nikki, who walks with me every step of this journey. This ministry has not just changed others, but probably us most of all.

Tom Williams, who really knows English and grammar: you were awesome, patient, and insightful. I couldn't have done this without your focused dissection again and again. Thanks also everyone that worked on this book: Ryan Pazdur, Verlyn Verbrugge, Paul Engle, and especially Chris Grant.

To all the staff at NorthWood, but particularly the Glocal Impact Office, which helps mobilize people, and Matt Wellborn, who drives our New Members Base Camp helping people engage their vocations from day one.

FOREWORDS

When Jesus gave us the Great Commission, it was a call to every disciple and every church to take the whole gospel to the whole world. We must not just focus on our own family and communities.

You may have never considered yourself a minister, but the Bible clearly teaches that every believer is called to full-time service, or ministry, through their local church. Regardless of your work or career, God wants to use your spiritual gifts, heart, abilities, personality, and experiences to serve him by serving others. Ministry wasn't set aside for only a select few. God has a unique purpose, place, and role that only you can fulfill. When God saves you, he also sets you apart for service. This book is an excellent guide to help you discover your part in God's great plan for history.

Bob Roberts has been a dear friend, coworker, and partner in ministry for over twenty years. We have served together and prayed for each other, even when we were ministering on opposites sides of the globe. So I can promise you this: what you are about to read is no mere theory, written by someone who just wanted to write a book. Everything in this book has been field-tested in all kinds of situations. Over the past fifteen years, Bob has trekked all over the planet, sharing the love of Jesus, meeting needs, training leaders, and planting churches. He is a veteran of ministry that you should listen to and learn from. His passion and compassion are contagious!

I love many things about Bob — his authenticity, his passion for God and others, and his great sense of humor. But what I admire most is his unselfishness. Years ago, Bob made a strategic decision that most pastors never make: to invest more time in helping other churches instead of spending all his time on growing his own church.

Just as Saddleback Church did years earlier, Northwood Church intentionally decided that instead of seeking to be the largest church, they would focus on being a multiplying church — one that plants new churches and supports other churches in the start-up phase. I believe that is what Christ wants every church to do, but models are hard to find. With human bodies, the ability to reproduce is the evidence of physical maturity. In the same way, truly mature churches give birth to baby churches. In Saddleback's case, we even have great-great grandbaby churches, and in Northwood Church's case, they have helped plant over 120 other churches around the world! That's reproduction! That's maturity! That's unselfishness!

Your church and every local church must have a global vision. But even churches that understand our global responsibility often feel paralyzed by the enormity of the task, not knowing how or where to start. What we need are simple, grassroot models of how to connect with unbelievers and share God's love as Acts 1:8 commands: in Jerusalem (your hometown), in Judea (your county, state, or province), in Samaria (witnessing cross-culturally with people who live in your area but are different from you), and to the ends of the earth. *Real-Time Connections* shows you how to do this.

I especially recommend this book for all individuals and congregations participating in the P.E.A.C.E. Plan (Planting churches & promoting reconciliation, Equipping servant leaders, Assisting the poor, Caring for the sick, and Educating the next generation). This is a wonderful text to inspire, challenge, and equip yourself and others to fulfill the Great Commandment and the Great Commission.

You're not holding this book by accident. God wants to use you to help change the world.

> — RICK WARREN, founding pastor — Saddleback Church;
> author of the *Purpose Driven Life*

F aith is a bridge over fear. On the other side of that bridge is a land full of people seeking partnership. And all around us is a world crying out in pain.

Bob Roberts is a bridge-builder. He has forged true friendships with people who have deep differences. He knows from experience that unlikely partnerships can alleviate unspeakable pain. This book is the architecture of the bridge, the story of Bob's travels, and an invitation to potential companions.

Like a lot of Americans from a generation ago, Bob was once afraid of the people of Vietnam. But after a deep search in his Scriptures, Bob decided that fear wasn't the way Jesus approached other human beings. So he went to Vietnam, met some people, and discovered that God was at work there too. Bob encouraged some of the members of his church to visit Vietnam, and behold, they discovered the same thing. Today, Bob's church has some amazing programs going with people in Vietnam — exchange programs, service programs, programs that connect real people with real people.

Some years back, Bob discovered he had an even greater fear: Muslims. It's a fear that a lot of Americans share. In recent surveys, about 40 percent of Americans said that they thought Islam was connected with violence. The group most likely to have a negative view of Muslims was evangelical Christians. Bob didn't think that was right. In the example of Jesus, he found a way of building a bridge over this new fear. Bob traveled to the other side, to places like Afghanistan and Gaza, and found friends and partners committed to ending the pain in the world.

I live in Chicago and spend a good deal of time in places like New York City, San Francisco, and Washington, D.C. I hear an awful lot of prejudice against evangelicals in some of the circles I run in. There are plenty of people who think that every evangelical wants to subordinate women, launch wars against Muslims, and force everyone to attend their church. "You can't talk to those evangelicals," some of my friends warn me. "You can only try to defeat them."

But here's the thing: I've known hundreds of evangelicals over the years, and I can count the bad experiences I've had on one hand. The evangelicals I know are warm, intelligent people, committed to living their lives according to a higher calling — a calling I admire, even if I don't share it entirely. When I hear someone make an ignorant or bigoted statement about evangelicals, I speak up. How could I not? These are my friends being insulted, some of the best people I know.

In fact, I am a Muslim who believes the American evangelical movement is among the greatest hopes for humankind. Your community has the courage of its convictions. When you believe in something, you act on it, and those actions bring new life to many millions of people — from AIDS orphans in Africa to women forced into brothels in Southeast Asia. I am awed and humbled by your work, Bob, and inspired by the inspiration you find in your faith.

I am not a candidate for conversion. Islam is my home; it is deep in my heart and long in my history. What I am is an open-hearted, ever-willing partner. I am one of the people on the other side of fear. We can walk together, learn from one another, and be unlikely partners in the alleviation of unspeakable pain. I know that you will feel compelled to invite me into the fullness you have found in your faith. I respect that. I will respond with a smile. I will tell you that I understand what you mean when you talk of truth, love, and mercy — this is what I get from Islam. If our discussion veers toward heaven, we may have some different views. When we speak of earth, I am confident that we will find a great deal in common, including the belief that God put us here to be stewards of his creation. We will have to decide whether we were meant to argue about heaven — a kingdom where God reigns — or partner together on earth.

In an era in which people from different religions are interacting with greater frequency and intensity than ever before, faith can be a bubble that separates us from those who are different, a barrier that heightens tensions between religions, a bludgeon that seeks to intimidate and dominate, or a bridge that connects us in a spirit of respect and partnership. The Holy Qur'an says that God made us different nations and tribes so we might come to know one another. This is the architecture for the bridge of partnership in Islam. As I was crossing over that bridge, I met Bob Roberts. And now he is a friend for life.

Bob's book — his life really — asks a simple, direct question. Are evangelical Christians willing to build a bridge over the fear of other faiths and cross to the other side, the land of partnership and possibility?

> — EBOO PATEL is an Indian American, a Muslim, a sociologist, and the founder and leader of the Interfaith Youth Core, a Chicago-based institution building the global interfaith youth movement.

CHAPTER 1

Rethinking the Great Commission

"These who have turned the world upside down have come here also..." ACTS 17:6

I was watching the Olympics on television when I saw something that made me stop and think. It began with an ad for Coca-Cola, celebrating the 122-year history of the soft drink. I still find it amazing that when I travel all over the world — from deserts to jungles to some hole in the wall in the middle of nowhere — no matter where I go I can always find a Coke! The Coke ad was followed by a commercial celebrating the hundred-year anniversary of General Motors, offering everyone the employee discount for purchasing a vehicle. Like Coke, which has become a global phenomenon, the automobile has become an indispensable reality, the primary mode of transportation all over the world. As I was sitting there watching these ads, it suddenly hit me—if Coke and GM can engage the world, why can't we as Christians, with the power of the Holy Spirit and the powerful motivation of the Great Commission?

THE CHURCH IN THE WEST VERSUS THE FIRST-CENTURY CHURCH

Centuries ago, the chief driver of global engagement was the church. Christians, because of God's unique work in their lives, not only have human hearts that grieve over suffering, but the Holy Spirit that lives within them, empowering them to fulfill what Christ has called them to do in the Great Commission and the Great Commandment. But world transformation isn't just something for pastors and religious professionals to talk about as they inspire others to join a church or join a program. For the world to be transformed by Jesus it will take every one of us; every follower of Jesus Christ is gifted by God and called to impact the world, right where they are. It's time for us to turn the world upside down!

Far too often, when the church in the West thinks about the rest of the world, she lacks creativity and insight. Church leaders have no problem coming up with creative and innovative ways of doing church in their own backyard; yet when asked to engage in global missions, they default to a colonial response. The truth is, if we are honest with ourselves, we really don't understand the world we live in. We have not fully grasped the reality of the changing world, this new phenomenon we call "globalization." Churches in the West are stuck in a mind-set that puts them at the center of everything God is doing. And though we use words like missional and emergent, when it comes to engaging our brothers and sisters in other nations we operate from archaic, outdated models of cultural engagement. For all of our focus on reinventing the church, perhaps we just need to get back to the basic teachings of Scripture and respond to what God has called us to do — make disciples.

That first-century church turned the world upside down. The first disciples took the Great Commission, given to them by Jesus, and went to the farthest reaches of the known world. They traveled to the east and to the west, from Spain to India, and went to the north and to the south, from Britain to Africa. The generations between that first-century explosion and our own have dreamed of fulfilling the Great Commission, but actual achievement of that dream has been limited by tools and time.

Today we have the means to do what no generation has ever done. In addition to the empowering presence of the Holy Spirit, we have jet planes and the internet. The opportunities for travel and communication between people and nations are unprecedented. For the first time in history, all the necessary elements, divine and human, are present to enable us to take the gospel to every person throughout the world. Fulfilling the Great Commission is no longer simply a question of potential — the possibility of completion is real. Completion is now a matter of obedience and dependence on God's Spirit.

Though we have the *potential* to turn the world upside down, much like those first disciples, we will first have to turn our own thinking upside down and take a fresh look at how they accomplished their task. In the years between their time and ours, the process of evangelism has undergone some radical changes, distorting our understanding of God's mission in this world. What is the Great Commission? How was it meant to be fulfilled? What would it look like if every follower of Jesus were to take it seriously? We need to rethink the answers to questions such as these.

We need to ask the most elementary questions all over again. Do we really know what the Great Commission is? What would it look like if it were fulfilled? How do we fulfill it? Is it a program where churches gather funds to send missionary pastors and their families to preach the gospel in foreign countries? What is the relationship between the church and the government, and how does this affect our thinking about the Great Commission? Is church planting the best way to fulfill the Great Commission?

FULFILLING THE GREAT COMMISSION

That's a lot of questions! Let's begin by taking a fresh look at the Great Commission, reading it as if we had never read it before:

> Jesus came to them and spoke to them, saying, "All authority has been given to me in heaven and on earth. Go, and make disciples of all nations, baptizing them in the name of the Father and of the Son and of the Holy Spirit, teaching them to observe all things that I commanded you. Behold, I am with you always, even to the end of the age." (Matthew 28:18 – 20)

The essence of the commission that Jesus gave to his disciples is to "go, and make disciples of all nations." "Go" is in a Greek grammatical construction that denotes "as you are going." It suggests that being a follower of Jesus is something we do *naturally*, on a regular basis. It's not referring to a special "missionary mode" that we turn on in certain situations. Jesus expressed this part of the Great Commission to define a way of life for his followers, a mind-set to inform their understanding of what it means to be his disciples. Disciples are always in a state of readiness to engage in this mission.

The second part of that phrase refers to making disciples. But what does it mean to "make disciples"? And what is meant by the phrase "all nations"? If we can find biblical answers to these two questions, we are well on our way to understanding Jesus' Great Commission.

To find what it means to "make disciples," we turn to the book of Acts, which recounts the disciples' fulfilling the Great Commission. It is helpful to study the Gospels if you want to understand discipleship, but the book of Acts gives us a unique understanding of what it looks like when the teachings of Jesus are reproduced in the lives of his followers. How did the making of disciples *actually happen* in the early church?

In Acts 1 – 10 the New Testament church stays narrowly focused on two geographic areas: Jerusalem and Judea. Then, in Acts 11:19 – 26, something changes that takes our understanding of Jesus' commission and the process of making disciples to a new level. Several men, most likely businessmen of some type, find themselves on the run as persecution breaks out in Jerusalem. These men, from Cyprus and Cyrene, wind up in Antioch. As they settle into making a life in this new city, working and making a living, they also start telling others about Jesus. Eventually, a church develops in Antioch — a missionary church that ends up sending out the first missionaries to the Gentile world, Paul and Barnabas (Acts 13:1 – 4). These two missionaries take the gospel to many unreached places. And just a few chapters later they find themselves returning home to Antioch, having "turned the world upside down."

What did Paul and Barnabas do that changed the world and turned everything "upside down"? In Acts 17 Luke gives us an early understanding of the Great Commission and how these first disciples understood and practiced it.

> Now when they had passed through Amphipolis and Apollonia, they came to Thessalonica, where there was a Jewish synagogue. Paul, as was his custom, went in to them, and for

> three Sabbath days reasoned with them from the Scriptures, explaining and demonstrating that the Christ had to suffer and rise again from the dead, and saying, "This Jesus, whom I proclaim to you, is the Christ." (Acts 17:1 – 3)

The Jews at Thessalonica did not merely believe with their heads, they took Paul's words to heart. So many turned to Christ that others became disturbed and caused a civic uproar. They rounded up Paul, Silas, and those who had hosted them and took them before the city leaders.

The point here is not that preaching the gospel causes trouble (though, of course, it sometimes does). The point is that making disciples leads to a noticeable change in the community. In Matthew 25, Jesus taught his disciples to feed the hungry, give water and clothing to those in need, provide shelter for the homeless, and seek justice for those who are oppressed. In Acts 2 we see the disciples living out a new way of life as they share their finances, food, and resources with one another. Throughout Acts there are miracles of healing, deliverance from demons, and other such signs. This is a *different* kind of community and it has a *different* kind of impact on the cities and towns where it exists. These early Christians have a message to believe, but they also live out a compelling model of God's love before a world that is watching them. We know that historically, at least one Roman emperor, Julian, emperor from AD 360 to 363, used the example of Christians to inspire a return to polytheism, urging his own followers to serve one another like the Christians served each other and those in their communities.

Sadly, in many of our communities, we do not see this kind of impact. Rarely does our evangelism lead to deep changes in our neighborhoods and cities. I believe this is due to the fact that much of our evangelism is focused on making *converts* instead of *disciples*. There's a big difference between a convert and a disciple. Making a convert is often a hit-and-run proposition. The goal in *conversion*, as it is typically understood, is to get someone to say, "I accept Jesus in my heart," and to be baptized. Once that goal has been accomplished, we tend to move on to the next person, assuming that our job is done. This leads to a shallow and superficial understanding of what conversion is. Though we may talk about life change and may preach a gospel that focuses on radical transformation, we often settle for redefining conversion to simply mean that someone has changed their religious views.

That's why I prefer to talk about *making disciples*. Making a disciple requires more than just getting a person to say certain words or to perform a religious ritual. It requires a deep conversion of the heart that ultimately turns one's life upside down and sets him or her in an altogether different direction. Mere conversion is not the goal of evangelism; it is simply the starting point for the process of discipleship. Getting people to convert to Christianity is not the way to complete the Great Commission; conversion is simply the beginning of a lifelong process of change and transformation.

In the book of Acts we find disciple making in almost every chapter. And note that the heroes of the early church — the apostles Peter, James, and Paul — often went into a city with the idea of serving the people. Their goal was to make disciples. While they certainly went to present a message, that was not their only focus. They also came to meet the needs of the people in that community. Throughout Acts the early church ministered the love of God to people: healing the sick, raising the dead, and collecting money for poor or persecuted saints. Such activities were not simple afterthoughts or a prelude for teaching the gospel; this was an essential part of their mission — to meet people's needs and to demonstrate the love of God through acts of service.

The message that the apostles preached demanded a specific response to the challenges of life. It would have been hypocritical to preach a gospel of love for God and for their neighbor, to teach about the life of Jesus, and not practice it as well. Serving wasn't simply a devotional response tied to a form of worship; it was a life-encompassing obedience to *verbally* tell others about the good news and *physically* share that good news through practical acts of service. My point is this: anytime we travel down an either-or path that pits telling people about God's love against sharing that love with them, we have an incomplete witness, which will never allow us to complete the Great Commission.

These early disciples were not trying to be creative or original; they were simply following the teaching of Jesus: to do good works before others so they could see the nature of their Father in heaven (cf. Matthew 5:16). Acts of service were done to give people a better picture of God and to make them more receptive to the gospel when it was preached. People came to Jesus for healing, and he healed them and then used those opportunities to share the good news with hearts that were now open and receptive to his message.

Recently, I had the opportunity to sit at the top of the Mount of Olives in the apartment of the Grand Mufti of Jerusalem — the highest Islamic official in that city. We spoke to each other about our longing for peace in the Holy Land. We agreed that a war pitting one religion against another would be seen as a failure of all three of the great monotheistic faiths.

I went on to ask him if he would be willing to partner with Jews and Christians to do humanitarian projects together. I emphasized that none of us would compromise our convictions. I wasn't suggesting that we accept a weak relativism or implying that all faiths are somehow the same. On the contrary, we should each passionately hold to our faith and live it out. I told him that I felt that God should be seen through our behavior and our life, not by our rhetoric and posturing. He agreed with me. Then I told him, "You know that as a Christian, I want the whole world to be Christian. I want to baptize everyone — even you!" He responded, laughing, "Yes, and you know I want the whole world to be Muslim."

Was I compromising my Christian principles by making this offer? Was I suggesting, even implicitly, that what we believe is unimportant? Not at all! I was simply showing this man, who has very different and often opposing beliefs about God, that Christians are truly interested in serving others.

What if people saw who God was by our posture of servanthood and our lifestyle of compassionate care? I'd like to propose a new contest, similar to the contest between Elijah and the priest of Baal on Mount Carmel, between people of different religious views. But instead of a hostile confrontation involving sacrificial bulls, buckets of water, and fire from heaven, what if we challenged them to outdo us in love, service, and sacrifice? What if our primary witness to God was through sacrificial deeds of kindness instead of the righteous rhetoric that seems to dominate the discussion? If we were to begin our outreach with acts of love and service to our communities and neighborhoods and then move toward an explanation of our message, how much more effective might our evangelism be?

I've seen this approach work throughout the world. In fact, I'm not sure it's possible to see authentic community transformation any other way. If all a church wants is a few converts who will start a few isolated churches, then the traditional approach works just fine. But if we are looking for real transformation that begins with individual disciples of Christ and spreads outward, changing entire communities, we need to change our thinking about how to fulfill the Great Commission.

THE GOSPEL OF THE KINGDOM

The Great Commission is not just about changing lives, as important as that is; it's about changing the world. It's about transforming people in such a way that they cannot help but transform their families, their neighborhoods, their cities, and their countries. But this way of thinking about the Great Commission raises two questions that we need to address. First, is the seed of the gospel, when planted in the heart of an individual, sufficient in and of itself to transform a person? I believe it is. Both church history and the biblical witness testify to the fact that the gospel carries within itself sufficient power to transform individuals.

That leads us to the second question. If the gospel is sufficient to change individuals, is that same seed of the gospel, when planted in the heart of a community, sufficient in and of itself to transform an entire community? Again, I believe it is. This is what we see when we read the book of Acts, and again it has been confirmed by both biblical and church history.

The key to this wider, viral transformation of the community is in restoring the context of the gospel of the *kingdom*. Many have come to understand the gospel narrowly, in only personal, individual terms. True, the gospel is a gospel of personal salvation; but it is so much more than that. In Matthew and Luke there are four times where the message of salvation is referred to as the "gospel of the kingdom" (Matthew 4:23; 9:35; 24:14; Mark 1:14 KJV). While salvation of individual people is certainly included in the kingdom message that Jesus preached, the larger question is: What did Jesus redeem through his work on the cross? The gospel of the kingdom of God is something that we are to preach to all peoples and all creation. It is the reconciliation of "all things" to God. Revelation 14:6 describes it as an *eternal* gospel that will be preached to all nations, tribes, and tongues. The gospel of the kingdom of God is the good news that God has established his rule and reign in all things. It's about more than just my eternal destiny; it's about God's larger work in history and creation.

I think this is an important distinction for us to make. Let me explain the difference. If my gospel focus is exclusively on salvation, my focus tends to be on getting people to believe certain things. When a convert mouths the right belief statement, we think our work is done. They are saved because they have accepted the gospel and believed in Christ. But if my focus is on the gospel of the *kingdom*, I look at the Great Commission through a wider lens. My focus is still on sharing a message with someone to get a believing convert, but that no longer is my goal, my endgame. It becomes the starting point for a much larger mission, namely, to transform the individual and to reproduce transformation that brings change to an entire community. But the gospel of the kingdom enlarges our vision to the redemption and reconciliation of all things to God (see Colossians 1:20).

In my home church of NorthWood in Keller, Texas, we refer to this as "Kingdom In — Kingdom Out." *Kingdom In* is the way we talk about our personal relationship with God. It's about accepting Christ, receiving him into our lives, and becoming a functioning member of his kingdom as it exists on earth. *Kingdom Out* is how we refer to our relationships with other people and our calling in this world. It's all about my love for God overflowing from a grateful heart into the hearts and lives of other people, drawing them into the joy I have experienced through his grace.

FOUR COMMON MISUNDERSTANDINGS

This focus on making *converts* who assent to a specific belief instead of *disciples* who live transformed lives is just one of the ways we have misunderstood and misapplied the teaching of the Great Commission. There are other errors we must address — errors that affect our understanding of the *scope* of the Great Commission, the *means* by which it will be accomplished, and the *focus* of our efforts. Here are four additional common misunderstandings of the Great Commission that we must rethink.

MISUNDERSTANDING 1:
The Great Commission Begins in Matthew.

Rethink it: The Great Commission begins in Genesis.

As we've just been discussing, the Great Commission is really about the kingdom of God. The kingdom is a way of referring to the rule and reign of God over all things, his sovereign authority over the cosmos. The kingdom of God is bigger than a specific location or time in history; it has origins in the beginning of all things. In Genesis 1 God creates human beings and gives them dominion, the authority to rule, over this world. We are to be stewards of all that God has given us, responsibly managing God's creation. All too often we fail at this task, falling into sin and applying a system of laws, offerings, and sacrifices.

God graciously helps human beings to learn to acknowledge their sin and gives them hope that we can be brought back into fellowship with him. Much of the Old Testament looks forward toward the ultimate sacrifice that God's Son will one day make to redeem all people. At one point, early in the book of Genesis, God gives Abraham a promise that through him all nations — or peoples and tribes — will be blessed (Genesis 12:1 – 3; 17:3 – 8). Notice how Paul sees the gospel when he connects his message to the promise God made to Abraham:

> The Scripture foresaw that God would justify the Gentiles by faith, and announced the gospel in advance to Abraham: "All nations will be blessed through you." (Galatians 3:8)

Paul and the apostles saw Jesus as the fulfillment of the Old Testament. In everything that Jesus did and said, he was bringing fulfillment and direction to God's purposes in creation and his work with the people of Israel. In other words, Jesus didn't come up with the Great Commission on the spot! When Jesus commanded his disciples to disciple the nations, he was harking back to Abraham. Paul, the apostle to the Gentiles, notes that the blessing of the nations is the *gospel*, the same gospel that Jesus commands to be taught and preached in the Great Commission. Paul's message in the synagogues, his message of hope for the Gentiles, was not a radically new message. It was simply that Jesus was the Messiah — the Christ who fulfills all of God's promises to Abraham and his purposes with the people of Israel.

Many Christians have a faulty picture of the early church. There is a mistaken notion that after Jesus rose from the dead and gave his disciples the Great Commission, the Jewish people rejected the gospel and the early church was largely dominated by Gentile believers. While it is true that a majority of the Jewish people did come to reject the gospel, Christianity began as a Jewish movement to Jesus. In Acts a great number of Jewish people followed Jesus. In its early chapters, the door opened for other Jews to enter the kingdom, and the early church saw an explosion of evangelism throughout the Jewish nation. Later, whenever Paul visited a town and looked for a way to share the gospel, he began in the Jewish synagogue.

This Jewish zeal to spread the gospel is not as strange as it may seem. Of all people, these Jewish followers of Jesus understood that Christianity was not a new religion — it was a continuation of God's work, beginning in Genesis. Christianity initially emerged, not as a full-blown religion, but as a sect of Judaism. To truly grasp the intention and scope of the Great Commission, we must recognize that Judaism already had a global view of God's purposes. When the first disciples preached the gospel, they were often careful to emphasize the call of Abraham and of Moses and the tide of Jewish history leading to its culmination in Christ. They wanted their listeners, both Jewish and Gentile, to recognize that God's purposes in Christ went all the way back to the creation.

I often remind people that the Great Commission, this call to make disciples of the nations and bring the message of God's kingdom to the world, is first given to us, not in Matthew 28, but in

Genesis 12. It's given to a man named Abram, who lives in a pagan country. God spoke to him:

> Now Yahweh said to Abram, "Get out of your country, and from your relatives, and from your father's house, to the land that I will show you. I will make of you a great nation. I will bless you, and make your name great. You will be a blessing. I will bless those who bless you, and I will curse him who curses you. *In you will all of the families of the earth be blessed.*" So Abram went, as Yahweh had spoken to him. Lot went with him. Abram was seventy-five years old when he departed out of Haran. (Genesis 12:1 – 4, emphasis added)

Notice that God calls Abram out of his lifelong homeland to go to an unknown land, where he will become the father of a great nation. Why Abram? What was there about this man that attracted God's favor? We know that Abram was not always a model of godliness and perfection. He could be dishonest at times, was prone to lie when governed by his fears, and would even take matters into his own hands when his faith in God wavered. Yet in his grace, God chose this man. He was obviously adventuresome and courageous, willing to pull up stakes and head out for a place he had never seen.

Seen through the lens of God's redemptive purposes, it is difficult to overemphasize the impact of Abram's move, leaving his homeland to go where God would lead him. In many ways, his move launched the greatest movement of all time, a movement that has shaped national boundaries, changed economic realities, affected foreign policies, and determined military strategies for much of world history.

Abram's move also initiated the greatest religious movement of all time. Three major world religions claim Abraham as a "father" for their faith. He is the indisputable father of monotheistic religion. But here's the kicker: the greatest religious movement of all time began, not with a priest, a preacher, a monk, or a religious leader, but with a businessman. You see, Abram was not a religious professional; he was a highly successful cattleman. As a Texan, I can relate to that! Even by Texan standards, though, Abram had a big dream, a dream that would find its fulfillment in the Great Commission.

MISUNDERSTANDING 2:
Preachers Are the Key to the Great Commission.

Rethink it: Disciples, ordinary followers of Jesus, are the key.

When Abram received his call from God, he packed up his family and his belongings and moved from his homeland, following God's leading to the geographical spot we now know as the Holy Land. When Abram arrived, what was the first thing he did? Did he head for a synagogue, a temple, or a church? No, because none of these things existed at that time. Notice what he does instead:

> Yahweh appeared to Abram, and said, "I will give this land to your seed." He built an altar there to Yahweh, who appeared to him. He left from there to the mountain on the east of Bethel, and pitched his tent, having Bethel on the west, and Ai on the east. There he built an altar to Yahweh, and called on the name of Yahweh. (Genesis 12:7 – 8)

The first thing Abram did was to build two altars. Do you get the picture? There was no religious infrastructure, and yet he responded to God with both personal worship and public obedience.

By *personal worship* I mean that Abram expended the effort to recognize and honor God with his altars. His worship was not dictated by external factors or requirements, but flowed out of a personal response to God's provision. By *public obedience* I mean that when God called Abram or asked him to do something, he listened and did it. For example, in Genesis 13 God tells Abram to walk through the land and promises him that every place he sees will be his. What is Abram's response to God's command? Verse 18 tells us that Abram did what God commanded and then built yet another altar in Hebron at the oaks of Mamre. Obedience and worship flowed together in his life. Abram is not only a model of faith, but gives us a picture of the ultimate disciple — one who obeys not from law or duty but from the heart.

For Abram, knowing God was a very personal experience (Kingdom In), yet it was also a very public and demonstrative way of life (Kingdom Out). In Genesis 14 we read that Abram's nephew Lot was captured by a combined army of four regional kings, who attacked his home city, Sodom. Abraham raised his own army and defeated the kings, rescuing Lot. After the battle, Abram gave to Melchizedek, the king and priest of Salem, a tenth of everything he owned. He also returned the captives he had taken and all the spoils of war to the king of Sodom, saying, "I have sworn to the Lord, God Most High, possessor of heaven and earth, that I will not take a thread or a sandal thong or anything that is yours, for fear you would say, I have made Abram rich" (14:22 – 23). Abram trusted God in all that he did. His faith was a visible witness of his dependence on God.

Abram's faith is even more amazing when we consider the fact that he never saw God's promise fully realized. It would be more than seven hundred years before the promise would be fulfilled and Abram's descendants actually established a nation in the Promised Land. But Abram wasn't one to focus on immediate results; he believed that the promise was true, and he remained true to that vision through simple obedience to God.

There is much we can learn from the example of Abram as we consider the Great Commission. When Jesus told his followers to go into the world and make disciples, he wasn't just talking to religious professionals. He was referring to people like Abram — men and women who love God and are willing to go when he calls. The type of people whom Jesus wants for his commission are people who are ready to worship him anywhere, people who will serve others and affect the world and its future with their present obedience. Jesus did not give his commission to recruit converts to a cause; he called for disciples, men and women transformed after the pattern of Abram.

MISUNDERSTANDING 3: The Church Is Where We Focus Our Efforts to Fulfill the Great Commission.

Rethink it: Society is where disciples should engage the world.

I love the church. I pastor a church, I believe in the church, and I help start churches. But Jesus makes it clear that we are to make disciples of "all nations." When our efforts to spread our faith are limited to the four walls of a building or we spend all of our time and effort on a specific group of Jesus followers, our ministry is restricted and it never reaches the masses. The only way for disciples to cultivate a viral faith is for them to focus their efforts outside the church and learn to engage society.

In Genesis 17 we encounter Abram again. He is now ninety-nine years old. He has been a faithful disciple, and God wants to confirm his covenant with him once again. The covenant is so expansive and far-reaching that God decides to change his name from Abram, which means "exalted father," to Abraham, which means "father of many." The terms of the covenant explain the reason for the change:

> "As for me, behold, my covenant is with you. You will be the father of a multitude of nations. Neither will your name any more be called Abram, but your name will be Abraham; for the father of a multitude of nations have I made you. I will make you exceeding fruitful, and I will make nations of you. Kings will come out of you. I will establish my covenant between me and you and your seed after you throughout their generations for an everlasting covenant, to be a God to you and to your seed after you. I will give to you, and to your seed after you, the land where you are traveling, all the land of Canaan, for an everlasting possession. I will be their God." (Genesis 17:4–8)

In this passage, God tells Abraham that he will be "father of a multitude of nations." Historically, most people only recognize two nations or people groups who have descended from Abraham through his sons, Isaac and Ishmael. So in what sense can Abraham be considered a father to *many* nations? The writings of the New Testament help us to see that the fulfillment of this promise comes through Jesus. Jesus, the descendant of Abraham, is the one who establishes the kingdom of God that overrides the boundaries of nations and reunites humankind to fellowship with God.

This passage makes it clear that the context for God's fulfillment of the Abrahamic call was the *nations*, which can be roughly translated as family groups, tribes, and tongues; this isn't our modern concept of a nation-state. In other words, the focal point of God's work in the world is not the church or the temple; it is the nations. The nation forms the grid on which God works out his plan of redemption. The vision for transformation was never intended to be limited to a few individuals cloistered in churches indulging a private, feel-good, "Jesus and me" religion. From the beginning, with the Abrahamic covenant and continuing through the Great Commission, the basic focus of Christianity is social and national transformation.

Each nation is really a society in itself, and together, the societies of all nations — those in the Old Testament, those of the New Testament, and those of today — are composed of the same fundamental building blocks: groups of people who work within the society, functioning in their own areas of expertise, or "domains." I typically focus on the following eight domains: economics, education, health, communication, society, science-technology, agriculture, and governance. Each domain impacts the social order at the level of the individual, the family, the tribe, the city, and the nation.

Everyone within a nation functions within one or more of these domains, whether they lived in the twelfth century BC or the twenty-first century AD. These core structures of a society don't change. People working in these eight areas fill the basic needs of society; they are the ones that keep things functioning. When God called Abraham and promised to "bless the *nations*" through him, this was a promise to bring transformation and blessing to entire people groups, not just individuals. And when Jesus continued God's work in bringing fulfillment to the Abrahamic covenant, he was giving a call to ordinary people, to affect society at the deepest level by making disciples who would transform every nation. In other words, the Great Commission is not simply a call to recruit people into the Christian faith; it is a command to engage in discipleship in every domain of a society in such a way that the nation is transformed.

Do you see how this turns our common understanding of the Great Commission on its head? The Great Commission isn't really about getting people to come listen to a preacher who has a call to do "religious work"; it's a call to those who are engaged in the eight domains of society — the everyday followers of Jesus who work in education, art, government, economics, and agriculture. Transformation and change won't come about because we have more preachers and churches; it will happen as ordinary believers engage in discipleship within the domains in which they have been placed.

DISCIPLE + SOCIETY = GREAT COMMISSION

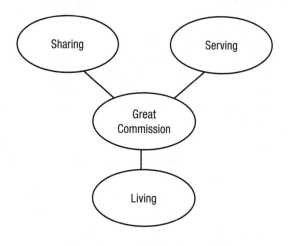

PREACHER + CHURCH = GREAT COMMISSION

This concept is particularly applicable today, because many countries do not allow professional missionaries or preachers. Some missiologists refer to these as closed countries, countries that are closed to professional missionaries and open missionary activity. Admittedly, I do find that there are many nations who are nervous about allowing religious organizations in. Some mission organizations have recognized this and have begun programs that try to "reformat" missionaries into businessmen. But is this really the best way? Instead of taking a "religious professional" and teaching them to do something they have never done, why not just take a businessman and teach them what it means to be a disciple?

After all, if we truly understand discipleship in the biblical sense, part of being a disciple is loving God, serving others, and sharing the good news with those who have not heard it. While many countries are nervous about religious professionals, I have found that lay Christians are often welcomed when they come with an idea that can improve a given domain of society. Builders, teachers, engineers, and many other occupations that function within the domains of society are welcomed almost anywhere in the world. A person can use his or her job in just about any country as an opportunity to fulfill the Great Commission. They won't be preaching sermons, but they will be loving and serving people and looking for opportunities to talk about Jesus in ways that are as normal as talking about the weather or the ball game. Shifting the focus of the Great Commission from religious professionals to everyday disciples of Jesus changes everything—and in a good way.

But how does this transformation and change really happen? How does the blessing given through Abraham reach other nations? Jesus himself gave us the answer. He ministered to people at the point of their deepest needs. He made God winsome to people by showing his love through his care. And this is exactly what he enjoins every believer to do in Matthew 25:

> "Then the King will tell those on his right hand, 'Come, blessed of my Father, inherit the kingdom prepared for you from the foundation of the world; for I was hungry, and you gave me food to eat; I was thirsty, and you gave me drink; I

was a stranger, and you took me in; naked, and you clothed
me; I was sick, and you visited me; I was in prison, and you
came to me.'

"Then the righteous will answer him, saying, 'Lord, when
did we see you hungry, and feed you; or thirsty, and give you a
drink? When did we see you as a stranger, and take you in; or
naked, and clothe you? When did we see you sick, or in prison,
and come to you?'

"The King will answer them, 'Most assuredly I tell you,
inasmuch as you did it to one of the least of these my brothers,
you did it to me.'" (Matthew 25:34 – 40)

The significance of this passage is enormous. Notice that Jesus'
basis for judgment is not whether a person is religious. It's not how
many Scriptures he can quote or how many people he can get to
say the sinner's prayer. It's not the number of notches he has on his
convert belt, how often he goes to church, or whether he believes in
premillennial post-tribulationism, predestination, or eternal secu-
rity. The one question that matters to Jesus is: Have you loved people
enough to minister to them? That is how we follow Jesus as his disciples. That is the true mark of a Christian.

In the Old Testament, which is the record of authentic religion
before Jesus came, the laws that described godly behavior were written on stone tablets for the nation of Israel to read and follow. These
laws were intertwined with the elaborate religious infrastructure of
Judaism. But in the New Testament, which is the record of our relationship to God after the sacrifice of Jesus, we are told that God's
laws are now placed within the heart of the redeemed individual.
This means that the kingdom of God is no longer defined by the bor-
ders of a single nation or the real estate of a specific place. It crosses
the geographic boundaries of nations, establishing its rule in the real
estate of every heart committed to God. The concept of God's people
has shifted significantly. No longer are we citizens of a literal nation-
state; now we are kingdom disciples.

This means that God loves not only our nation and those that have
endorsed Christianity; he loves all the *nations* — whether they are
pagan, Islamic, Jewish, Hindu, or Buddhist. If you want to participate

in the Great Commission to change the world, you already have the first qualification necessary. You are a part of a society, and you have a vocation that functions in a particular domain within society. As a disciple of Christ, you have the power within your hands to bring transformation to those within your domain through your own expertise, knowledge, and participation in that domain's activities. That is the key to changing the world — not sending professional missionaries to make converts and build churches.

The cross not only reconciles us as individuals, but it brings reconciliation to "all things." Once again, we must avoid seeing these truths in conflict with one another. I have found that many Christians believe the purpose of redemption through Christ on the cross is simply about reconciling that individual to God. While this is true, it isn't the *full* truth. The New Testament clearly shows us that redemption goes beyond God's work of redeeming individuals.

> The creation itself also will be delivered from the bondage of decay into the liberty of the glory of the children of God. For we know that the whole creation groans and travails in pain together until now. (Romans 8:21 – 22)

Here Paul informs us that not only will we human individuals be reconciled to Christ, but that the "whole creation" groans in anticipation of reconciliation. God's full purpose is the restoration of all things to their original perfection. When Jesus made his triumphal entry into Jerusalem, he said if the people didn't cry out, the rocks would cry out. More than individuals are involved in reconciliation; everything God created anticipates it, animate or inanimate. To miss this crucial fact is to relegate faith to a private, individualized realm Jesus never intended.

Paul reaffirms this idea in his letter to the Colossians:

> For by him were all things created, in the heavens and on the earth, things visible and things invisible, whether thrones or dominions or principalities or powers ... For all the fullness was pleased to dwell in him; and through him to reconcile all things to himself, by him, whether things on the earth, or

things in the heavens, having made peace through the blood of his cross. (Colossians 1:16 – 20)

Then in his second letter to the Corinthians, Paul ties the message of reconciliation to the Great Commission:

But all things are of God, who reconciled us to himself through Jesus Christ, and gave to us the ministry of reconciliation; namely, that God was in Christ reconciling the world to himself, not reckoning to them their trespasses, and having committed to us the word of reconciliation. We are therefore ambassadors on behalf of Christ, as though God were entreating by us. (2 Corinthians 5:18 – 20)

Are you beginning to see that the scope and vision of the Great Commission goes beyond individual conversions? Here Paul tells us that this ministry of reconciliation is to be our ministry. We are God's ambassadors, having been reconciled ourselves and now commissioned to carry his message of reconciliation to all creation. Society itself is to be reconciled — not just individual people, but the societal infrastructures that hold nations together.

Even the use of the term *ambassador* underscores this idea. It is a political term denoting one who carries information from one nation to another. The measure of the disciple is that he or she takes up the cross and follows Christ into the world to all nations or societies. If you want to change the world, you need to understand that you are an ambassador and God has called you to be a minister of reconciliation within the domain of society where you have been placed.

MISUNDERSTANDING 4: Only Certain People or Groups Are Allowed to Participate in the Great Commission.

Rethink it: The barriers that separate people come down in the church, starting with our witness to the world.

The barrier between Jews and Gentiles was not the only one that needed to come down before the Great Commission could be fulfilled. It was only one of three great distinctions that seriously divided people in the early days of the gospel. The other two were the divide between slaves and free men, and the division between men and women. Paul tackles all three of these barriers, with care, but also with truth. His writings and his actions make it clear that all the boundaries that divide people and exclude them from God's grace and love must come down.

I've often wondered: How did the early church produce so many disciples so quickly? Most contemporary church models for discipleship suggest that you put people in a small group and pour solid teaching into them, and they will naturally begin to multiply other disciples. You simply repeat the process with each new convert. But does this really work? In just a few short chapters of Acts we see these early disciples already transforming the world around them.

How did this happen so quickly? One of the things we need to consider may go back to their initial decision to follow Christ. For many of those early disciples, the decision to follow Jesus was made in a hostile environment. Following Jesus meant that they could die; by contrast, our decision today involves becoming nice people. The original disciples also understood that this was a long-term commitment, a shifting of priorities that involved putting self second, serving God and loving neighbors first.

In the contemporary Western church we tend to think that discipleship produces a nice, neat, doctrinally sound, perfectly balanced way of life. Jesus offers us an *improvement* on our already good life. But early followers of Jesus weren't looking at the decision to follow Jesus in terms of life improvement — for them Jesus was life itself. Following him meant more than adding something new to their existing identity; it involved the death of the old life and a resurrection into a completely new identity. It was an invitation that anyone could respond to, even the rejects of society.

In Old Testament Judaism, women were excluded from the inner court of the temple, relegated to one side of the Jewish synagogues, and they received no formal education. No special ritual was required for Jewish girls, as for boys, to enter the Jewish community. But the book of Acts notes that several women were indispensable cogs in the workings of the New Testament church. Acts 17 records three instances of women following Jesus: "not a few of the chief women" (v.4); "many ... prominent Greek women" (v.12); and "a woman named Damaris" (v.34).

Women appear to be pillars in the church in several other passages. Mary, the mother of John Mark, hosted a church in her home (Acts 12:12); Lydia was an influential woman in the church at Philippi (16:14 – 15); four daughters of Philip prophesied (21:9); and the name of the church leader Aquila, who is mentioned several times in Acts, is always paired with the name of his wife, Priscilla. We are told that both Aquila and Priscilla together took a misinformed preacher (Apollos) aside and instructed him more fully in the truth (18:26). Given these examples, it seems appropriate to conclude that the early church women were making an important break from the past. No longer were they excluded from full participation in the life of God's people. The walls that divided the sexes were being dismantled.

When Paul turned to the subject of slavery, he did not endorse the practice. In fact, he encouraged slaves to get out of bondage if it could be done legally. One of his primary reasons for writing his letter to Philemon was to secure the release of the slave Onesimus. Given the conditions of society in his time, his positions on slavery would have been considered radical. Slavery was an accepted reality and an indispensable institution of the Roman empire. In a subtle and subversive way, Paul challenged slaves to understand that they were free in Christ even if they could not change their situation.

> Each man must remain in that condition in which he was called. Were you called while a slave? Do not worry about it; but if you are able also to become free, rather do that. For he who was called in the Lord while a slave, is the Lord's freedman; likewise he who was called while free, is Christ's slave. You were bought with a price; do not become slaves of men. Brethren, each one is to remain with God in that condition in which he was called. (1 Corinthians 7:20 – 24)

In Galatians 3, Paul speaks of the end of all these dividing distinctions, bringing them together in Christ and tying them to the promise given to Abraham. First, he reiterates that promise in verse 8: "In you [Abraham] all nations will be blessed"; then he shows how the fulfillment of God's promise to Abraham signaled the end to racial distinctions "in order that in Christ Jesus the blessing of Abraham might come to the Gentiles" (3:14). Paul is weaving the Gentiles — all non-Jewish races — into the covenant with Abraham. In Christ, God's kingdom is not just open to Abraham's physical descendants. It is now seen to be something bigger than a physical piece of geography; it is an eternal reality being offered to all people.

In Galatians 3:28 Paul goes on to address additional dimensions of this expanded kingdom. He moves beyond the racial divisions and shows that all classes of people within those nations now have access to the kingdom of God:

> There is neither Jew nor Greek, there is neither slave nor free man, there is neither male nor female; for you are all one in Christ Jesus. And if you belong to Christ, then you are Abraham's descendants, heirs according to promise. (Galatians 3:28–29)

The community that follows Jesus is no longer limited to a certain nation, a certain sex, or an elite class of people; it is open to everyone. From the top of society to the bottom, all are the same in Christ. There is no caste system in Christianity. When authentic Christianity spreads and real transformation occurs, it has the potential to affect everyone, at every level of society. That's the power of the gospel of the kingdom — it's unstoppable. It's the convergence of all distinctions into one dynamic, earth-moving force.

THE GREAT COMMISSION TODAY

Consider this question: If the gospel were to break loose in our world today, what are the divisions that would have to come down? I am convinced at least two major divisions would come down. The first division is a geographic and cultural division of the church into global compass points — east, west, north, and south. In recent years, Christianity has shifted from a primarily western and northern faith to a more eastern and even southern faith. Countries in South America, Africa, and East and South Asia are now leading the way in reaching people with the gospel and making disciples. Churches in the West often ignore these significant shifts, shutting their eyes to the big things that are happening in other parts of the globe, remaining narrowly focused on the diminishing Christian influence in our own society.

The church in the West has much to learn from these brothers and sisters in Christ. Before we can benefit from a global explosion of the gospel, we must break down the wall of arrogance that leads us to think that the Western church is the center of the world and the sole distributor of Christianity.

The second division we must overcome is the wall between religion and society. This wall is largely maintained by leaders on both sides of the aisle. But the religious and the secular were never meant to exist in constant opposition to one another. True disciples recognize that God is present in every area of life — not trapped behind cloistered walls and stained glass. As Christians we believe that God is present in every domain of life, and we are his witnesses — salt and light — as we live out our faith in society. Religious professionals, pastors, and marketplace disciples must come together to make this happen. The compartmentalization of the church is killing our potential for authentic witness in our culture.

It is only a matter of time before these barriers come down. It is already happening in many places. God is opening doors. Permission and freedom to go places in the world that have been restricted to believers are now being granted. We face two choices: to recognize the call, seize these new opportunities, and enter the flow, or to resist this new move of God, continue to compartmentalize and segment our thinking about religion and evangelism, and insulate our witness from the culture around us.

What if we took a lesson from Paul's approach? Instead of decrying other religions as false, what if we started with the ways we agree? When Paul went into a city, he began with Jews in a synagogue. Paul didn't begin his conversation with an attack on false, idolatrous beliefs; he began his discourse on points where he agreed with his listeners. He sought to be winsome and earn a hearing for the gospel message. We see this in his preaching among the pagan Greeks in the Areopagus. Despite the fact that the city of Athens was filled with idols and Paul was greatly distressed over their pagan idolatry, he did not begin by berating the Athenians for their ignorance. He introduced God as someone that they already knew, but only dimly recognized.

When Jesus spoke of false prophets, he was generally referring to errant teachers within his believing community, not the leaders of pagan religions. His harshest words were reserved for false prophets who were passing along bad theology and bad character and who were using God for personal gain to acquire money, sex, or power. To Jesus and Paul, people of other religions were simply lost, living "in darkness," and it was the calling of Christians to let the light shine so they could see Jesus.

This has direct implications for our witness among other religions today, most notably our witness in the Islamic world. Christianity began as a Jewish movement to the Messiah. But I'm convinced that for the Great Commission to be completed, it will need to speak to the Islamic community and move them from seeing Jesus as a great prophet to seeing him as the divine Son of God. We tend to ignore Islamic religious leaders except to denounce them. But what if we respected them and found ways to befriend them — serving them, loving them, and exposing them to the message of God's love living in us? This type of living witness is not restricted to religious professionals. It's something that every follower of Christ can do.

I no longer read many of the books written by Christians about Islam. Frankly, I don't detect a lot of love towards Muslims in those books. They seem to be texts for debate teams determined to win an argument. Christianity is far more than just an argument: it is also a way of life. Instead, I read the Koran to find out where we can have common ground with Muslims. And when I enter into dialogue with a Muslim, I approach him with respect, knowing that at some level he too is seeking God. It is the only effective way I know to break down barriers and get a hearing for the gospel message.

My goal is to get a hearing with everyone I can. The New Testament teaches me that the good news that inspired the Great Commission is for *all* people: Jews and Gentiles, men and women, slaves and free men, Hindus and Muslims. God loves each one of us equally and with passion. If we want to change the world, we must first recognize that God wants to use every single one of us to reach across these barriers. I hope I have convinced you that the Great Commission is not simply a call to pastors; it's a call to all of us, regardless of our occupation.

When Jesus told his followers to "make disciples," he was pointing them back to the example of Abraham in Genesis as the ultimate model for what a disciple should be. But with the focus on "all nations," Jesus was pointing them outward, setting their sights on the world beyond Jerusalem and indicating that the time had come for the fulfillment of God's promise to Abraham, that through him all nations — all peoples of the world — would be blessed. That promise is still being fulfilled today, as faithful disciples, ordinary men and women, live out faithful lives of witness in the places God has called them to serve.

Connection Steps

⊙ On a scale of 1 to 10 how serious am I about the Great Commission and why?

⊙ How has the gospel transformed me? Where am I on my journey of discipleship? How is the Gospel transforming my community?

⊙ If I really believed that God had called me to fulfill the Great Commission — immediately I would . . . .

MY STORY: HOW I TURNED _____ UPSIDE DOWN!

Pick a city anywhere in world that you dream of engaging. Assume you are right with God, filled with the Holy Spirit, and ready for action. List all your skills, talents, passions. Identify a specific domain to focus on. Daydream about how God would use you to see change in that city and how it would change you.

Hearing God's Call

*I therefore, the prisoner in the Lord, beg you to
walk worthily of the calling with which you were
called.* EPHESIANS 4:1

*To this end we also pray always for you, that
our God may count you worthy of your calling, and
fulfill every desire of goodness and work
of faith, with power; that the name of our Lord Jesus
may be glorified in you, and you in him,
according to the grace of our God and the Lord Jesus
Christ.* 2 THESSALONIANS 1:11 – 12

S ometimes we try to put God in a box. We anticipate his will for
us by assuming that what he has done in the past is precedent for
what he will do in the future. When he plants a seed in our hearts,
we often think we know what kind of tree will grow from it. But a
seed is a mysterious thing, a little nondescript pod that gives no hint
of the complex, towering, fruit-laden growth that can spring from
it. Sometimes when we see God's seeds sprouting and taking shape
with leaves, textures, and fruit that we don't recognize and didn't
anticipate, we are tempted to think God must have made a mistake.
He planted the wrong seed in the wrong heart. We've never seen a
plant like this, and it seems too big for the neat little garden we've
planned in our hearts.

But let me assure you, God makes no mistakes. He knows what
he's doing. I have found from my own experience that God delights
in using us in unexpected ways, giving us seeds to nourish, first into
saplings, and then into giant trees whose branches reach far beyond

our own comfortable territory. That's what he's doing in my life, and that's the story I want to tell in this chapter.

MY EARLY CALL

One of the biggest lessons I have learned has been understanding that God's call isn't just found in the big decisions and major changes we experience. Sometimes, answering his call is about taking one small step in the right direction. As we obey the call and follow him, taking that small step, more of his will unfolds for us. God never reveals the entire story all at once. Obedience matters far more than complete understanding. In fact, when following God's call, obedience is everything.

My call began when I was eight years old. I was attending a children's camp for the first time, and two events at that camp made a lasting impression on my life. The first happened when I was sitting on a plank bench in a big, outdoor, screened-in tabernacle, watching a missionary show his slides. I know such presentations have become so commonplace that they bore many people, but this was a first for me and I was fascinated. After the presentation, when the lights came up, I looked down, blinking in the sudden glare. There, just a step away from me, slithered a huge brown snake! I know now that it wasn't poisonous, but to an eight-year-old, a snake is a snake, and snakes (at least for me) are bad. So I did the natural thing. I screamed, "Snake!"

As you can probably imagine, my scream had the same effect as yelling fire in a crowded theater. The placid audience suddenly became a hotbed of pandemonium as everyone joined in a chorus of screams and jumped about to make space for the invading reptile. There was nothing Pentecostal about this camp, but you wouldn't have known that by the spontaneous dancing and sounds that erupted from that tent!

The next night, however, when the missionary spoke, I felt God move in my heart. How do I know that it was God and not just an effect of the excitement from the previous night? With my limited knowledge of God, I felt as if there was only one response I could give to the invitation from the missionary: if you love God, you are supposed to love others and care about the world. Naturally, God was calling me to be a missionary, just like the speaker. What else could it be? I went forward that night, and when I returned home to my church I did it again, becoming one of the countless children who "surrender" their lives to be a missionary.

A couple years after this incident, at age ten, I attended vacation Bible school at our church and learned about a doctor who served the poor in Africa. Listening to the missionary stories inspired me, and I came up with an idea for our church. What if I were to take a team of people from our church into a missionary field for two months to help in medical clinics, vacation Bible schools, and feeding programs? We could cap it off with a big revival meeting. People would come from miles around, and we could start a church from those who accepted Christ.

The more I thought about it, the more I felt that this just might work! I got out my pen and paper, and in my ten-year-old scrawl I wrote a letter to Baker James Cauthen, who was serving at that time as the executive director of the International Mission Board (IMB) of the Southern Baptist Convention. I explained my idea to him in my letter, knowing he would just love it, call me, and want me to go as soon as possible! But that wasn't quite what happened. Instead, I got a kind letter back from him, encouraging me to keep in touch, and in the meantime I should finish school, go to college, and consider attending seminary. After seminary, I could apply to be a missionary. Rejection! Although it was gentle and kindly written, I felt it deeply. Why was it so difficult to do what I felt God was asking me to do?

As a young child, I didn't really know what to do with all that I felt God was telling me to do. Three years later, I again heard God calling me, this time to preach. Once again, I wasn't sure what to do with this sense of calling. As a child, I stuttered so badly that I had been sent to a speech therapist. On top of that, I was still young, and I began to have some doubts. I had been mistaken before when I sensed God's calling to work in Africa. Was it possible that I was mistaken again? Was God really calling me to preach?

As I struggled to understand all of this, I happened to read Jeremiah 1:4 – 10 (NIV):

The word of the LORD came to me, saying,

"Before I formed you in the womb I knew you,
before you were born I set you apart;
I appointed you as a prophet to the nations."

"Ah, Sovereign LORD," I said, "I do not know how to speak;
I am only a child."

But the LORD said to me, "Do not say, 'I am only a child.'
You must go to everyone I send you to and say whatever I command you. Do not be afraid of them, for I am with you and will rescue you," declares the LORD.

Then the LORD reached out his hand and touched my mouth and said to me, "Now, I have put my words in your mouth. See, today I appoint you over nations and kingdoms to uproot and tear down, to destroy and overthrow, to build and to plant."

This Scripture shook me to the core. It was as if God was speaking directly to me, saying to me, a thirteen-year-old boy, "I have a plan for your life. You need not worry about making it happen; you need not worry about how I will bring it about. Just know that I will bring it about." I had read the story of how a Sunday school teacher had led D. L. Moody to faith in Christ, and I thought perhaps God had something like that in mind for me. I remember praying, "God, if I can't preach well enough to be a preacher, that's okay. But at least use me to raise up other people to preach." I had no way of knowing it at the time, but my impulse to pray this prayer was the start of a seed God was planting in my heart. Decades later, this seed — to raise up others to share the gospel — would yield a harvest of church plants all across the world.

MEETING AND MARRYING NIKKI

My little town of a thousand and my class of eighty-four students may have been small, but they happened to harbor the most beautiful girl I have ever laid eyes on! When I first saw her I was smitten! Her name was Nikki, and there was no hesitation on my part; we started dating. It wasn't long before we fell in love, and we dated regularly for the next several years.

In the years since that initial sense that God was calling me to preach, he provided opportunities for me to speak at several youth events. Whenever I preached at these youth events, Nikki always went with me, sometimes with several of my high school friends. In addition to these youth events, I also preached for a couple of years at a little Methodist church in Lindale, Texas, called Harris Chapel. The church consisted of a handful of old people, but I often boosted the attendance and lowered the average age of the congregation by bringing my football teammates and other friends. As a result, the little church slowly began to grow.

After graduating from high school, I enrolled in Baylor University, and soon Nikki and I began to talk of marriage. She knew of my desire to be an evangelist and supported it fully, but I warned her that it was also possible that we would wind up being missionaries. I gave her an ultimatum: if she couldn't handle that call, we could never be married. I was amazed and grateful to God for how quickly he spoke to her! She too felt the call of God and vowed to me that she would go wherever God called us. I asked her to marry me, and to my delight, she agreed. I graduated from Baylor on Friday night, May 16, 1980, and on the next afternoon Nikki and I were married.

THE SOUND OF SLAMMING DOORS

Nikki taught school while I continued my education at Southwestern Baptist Theological Seminary, Fort Worth, Texas, and pastored Garden Acres Baptist Church in Burleson, Texas. I had never wanted to be a pastor; remember, that wasn't my call. Besides, what could be more boring than being a pastor? Still, my preaching at youth events qualified me as a pastor in the eyes of many, and so a pastor I became.

Through my preaching at youth events I had seen many young people accept Christ. But it bothered me that among those who accepted Christ, many of the conversions didn't stick. I wondered why. I decided to study the people who accepted Christ in my church to monitor the aftermath of their conversion. Some of them slipped away quickly; some became nominal Christians, attending sporadically but never getting involved. Precious few exhibited any evidence of real transformation. The biggest problem we had in making disciples was that we weren't making them! How could I change that? Something wasn't right, but at the time, I didn't know what it was. As I searched for a solution, God planted another seed in my heart, a seed that would eventually lead me to a radically different understanding of conversion.

The church I pastored had grown, and there were many offers to pastor other churches. But I still wasn't all that excited about pastoring. As my graduation from seminary approached, Nikki and I once again began to pray about being missionaries. There were some potential roadblocks to following this calling, however. Nikki had some lingering health concerns stemming from two automobile accidents she was involved in as a child. The first wreck had cost her dearly, resulting in the loss of her mother and sister, and it had put her in ICU with a serious head injury. The second wreck had broken her hip and required several corrective surgeries. As a result, doctors had warned her that childbearing would likely be tenuous for her. But she insisted that we apply again, so we went through a long and involved missionary candidate process with our denominational mission board.

The application involved piles of forms, interviews, personality tests, leadership tests — it seemed like an endless process. There were about twenty-five couples going through it with us. In the risk-taking and adventure test, I ranked first of the fifty or so people in the group. Unfortunately, Nikki came in last. But when we took the domestication test, I ranked last and she was first! Everyone laughed at us. Nikki and I have always been opposites — extreme but highly complementary opposites.

Then came all the psychological interviews. The psychologist asked if I had ever been involved in any radical groups or behaviors. I started laughing, but he didn't crack a grin. I got immediately serious and thought about the question. Should I tell him how crazy I was growing up? In a town of a thousand a kid had to make his own entertainment. One thing we did was to turn an old car hood upside down, weld a chair to it, chain it to the bumper of a pickup, and hold on for dear life. We pulled that hood through fields with ramps and even on the interstate — screeching along with sparks flying like the wake from a speedboat!

I had a friend whose dad owned a local clothing store. We found a discarded female manikin in the storeroom, dressed her up, laid her on the shoulder of a country road, and hid in the bushes to watch. When passing motorists saw her they would slam on their brakes, and we'd pull the rope tied around her leg, making her disappear before the driver got around the car. Once we even threw her in front of a slow moving car. I'm not especially proud of all this and would have seriously disciplined my own kids had they done this — but at the time I didn't realize how dangerous it was. We were crazy. But I decided that even if these behaviors were dangerous and immature, they did not rise to the level of "radical." Needless to say, I passed that portion of the psychological review.

During the application process we learned that Nikki was pregnant, and her past injuries loomed large as a factor in our qualifying. Both of these were strikes against the possibility that we would qualify as missionaries. At the conclusion of the process the verdict was delivered: maybe later, but not at this time. Again, just like the letter I had received when I was ten, I felt the sting of rejection. Despite the many joys and blessings in my life, a sense of failure continued to dog me, and I questioned my calling to missions.

Since the mission field wasn't working out for us, I was quite open to the invitation to become the evangelism pastor of a church in Springdale, Arkansas. I would be preaching at revivals, heading up their evangelism program, and on occasion filling in for the preaching pastor. I couldn't wait. In many ways, evangelism is similar to missionary work, so I thought that maybe this was what God had been calling me to do all along. A year out of seminary, I headed north, expecting to find vocational heaven in Arkansas.

It wasn't heaven. At all! My dream job became a nightmare for me. The pastor was an exceptional and godly man, but I couldn't say the same for everyone in the church. A significant number of members were spreading destructive rumors about other people in the church — who said what to whom; who did what to whom, who was doing what with whom, and who didn't do what they should. Whether a rumor was true didn't matter; if it was juicy, it spread like an epidemic. There was continual turmoil and dissention in the church. For me it was a crash course in big time religion — the good, the bad, and the ugly. I quickly became disillusioned with my call to ministry.

The director of evangelism for the Baptist General Convention of Texas came to speak at the church, and I unloaded on him, telling him the ordeal I was going through. The man loved God greatly. He told me with his thick Texas drawl, "Bob, yo're a Texas boy, and Texas needs new churches. Y'all need to come back down to Texas and start a church!" He might as well have slapped me in the face. Church planting! I felt like his invitation was one of the greatest insults he could have laid on me! In Texas, pastors started churches only because the good churches wouldn't hire them. Church planting was a ministry of last resort — the place where those who couldn't make it in ministry went. Church planting, in my mind, was like an author printing his own book because he couldn't get a publisher, or a kid playing sandlot ball because he couldn't make the team.

Instead, I figured I'd try applying again to our denominational mission board. I called and was quickly informed that it was too soon for me to reapply. More time had to elapse between the first candidate process and the next one. I felt like I was in a downward spiral of rejection, and I didn't understand what God was doing with my life. I thought God had called me to be a missionary, hadn't he? Why were roadblocks appearing at every turn? In the midst of this challenging time, I consulted people I respected and turned to the Bible for answers. God rewarded me with several helpful passages, including this one suggested by a former professor, Dr. Roy Fish:

"Don't lift up your horn on high.
   Don't speak with a stiff neck."
For neither from the east, nor from the west,
   nor yet from the south, comes exaltation.
But God is the judge.
   He puts down one, and lifts up another. (Psalm 75:5 – 7)

Dr. Fish encouraged me not to feel like a failure and not to seek a prominent position in a church or a prominent role in the mission field. Instead, he challenged me to forget my ego, trust my future to God, and learn that he is in control and can do with me what he wants. At that time I also stumbled on another extremely helpful verse:

> For the eyes of Yahweh run back and forth throughout the whole earth, to show himself strong in the behalf of them whose heart is perfect toward him. (2 Chronicles 16:9)

Both of these verses were encouraging to me. I spent much of this time in prayer, and as I meditated on the Word and spent time with God in prayer, I began to learn an important lesson, one that I would carry with me for the rest of my life: *only God raises people up.* You can try to raise yourself up, but in the end, it's all in God's hand. Anything that doesn't come from him — even if it's a promotion to head pastor of a prominent church — is ultimately detrimental. We can try to run our own lives, but in the end we probably won't be happy with the result. But if you leave it to God, he will put you in places and connect you with whomever he needs you to be connected with to accomplish his will, be it a plumber or a president.

God gave me another verse that I didn't understand at the time, though I knew it was from him. I didn't know how it fit into anything, but I sensed that it had something to do with starting a church.

> Ask of me, and I will give the nations for your inheritance,
> the uttermost parts of the earth for your possession. (Psalm 2:8)

I was a bit confused by this verse. I figured it was the kind of verse that God would give to a missionary, not to a pastor. I guessed that maybe one day I would be a missionary, but for now it seemed that I was being called to forget my pride and move back to Texas to start a church. When I interviewed with the North Richland Hills Baptist Church and the Baptist General Convention of Texas to get approval for this endeavor, I told them that the only thing I would ever do beyond pastoring this start-up church was to be a missionary. I admitted that I had tried that several times, and it had never worked out.

So we moved to Keller, Texas, and started NorthWood Church. I went about my new responsibility all wrong. We did a door-to-door campaign and handed out a brochure, explaining our belief in the Bible and giving reasons why people should come to our church. Our approach did not even focus on reaching the lost. The first Sunday I preached the entire book of Nehemiah! You're probably wondering why people weren't beating down the door to get in. Admittedly, the preaching wasn't all that hot, but then neither was the music. Still, I laughed a lot in the pulpit and privately led a number of people to Jesus, so despite the preaching and the music, we actually grew! One positive thing about building a church from lost people is that they don't have any other preacher or church to compare you with, so most of the people in the church didn't really know that we were bad. To them, I was the best preaching they had ever heard!

In just a year we had over a hundred members, and that was pretty good growth for our church. So the denomination put me on a plane with ten other Baptist pastors from Texas and flew us to southern California. We had a chance to meet with several other pastors, one of whom was Rick Warren. This was in 1986, long before he had written his blockbuster books. I remember chiding him for not having Sunday night church services. If I didn't get to watch Disney, neither should he! We became good friends on that visit, and he has been a valuable mentor to me ever since.

As a result of Rick's influence, I began a "ministerial conversion" —a change in the way I thought about ministering to the culture I was in. I realized that a lot of the people we were reaching were from similar backgrounds and didn't necessarily reflect the general population in our area. I began to study the demographics of our area. What was the average age, economic background, church background, education? I studied all of the factors that made up our community, and then I challenged our church to consider the best way to communicate with them. I put particular emphasis on learning who were the unchurched in my area, how they thought, and how we could do church in such a way as to reach them. We transitioned our model of outreach, and again, we began to grow.

By 1989, NorthWood was solidly on her feet and I felt free to begin taking short mission trips here and there around the world. When Rick Warren asked me to replace him on a mission trip to Africa, I jumped at the chance. My heart was deeply touched by the great needs in Kenya and Tanzania. Here, at last, was my mission! I remember that on that trip I was ready to stay in Africa and send for Nikki to join me! I even called her and asked if she'd be willing to move to Africa. Wisely, she told me to come home and we'd talk about it. When I returned, I designed a complete plan for reaching Kenya and put it before our denominational mission board. Once again, I was told that my vision didn't fit their plans.

The Berlin Wall came down in 1989, and the former Soviet Union was quickly opened up to missionaries. I learned that our mission board needed someone to serve in Moscow, so — you guessed it — I applied! And — you guessed it — again, I was rejected. They wanted a veteran missionary for that post, not a novice who had never worked overseas.

Yet another opportunity for mission came up shortly afterward. I had been to Australia many times, and a few of the people I met wanted me to move there, plant a church, and then help other church planters. It felt like a dream come true. Nikki had been to Australia and loved it, and I would be working with the Australian Baptists — no U.S. denominational bureaucracy! We went to Australia to set things up, but I quickly ran into a wall. Several of the pastors in Australia were against the idea of importing an American church planter. We offered to shift our work to two other locations, but none of the Australia Baptist pastors would go for it. We returned home, rejected yet again. This time, after a series of rejections, I sensed that our dream of being missionaries was finally over, and it was time to quit pounding on a closed door.

Gradually, we began to reinvent NorthWood, and the church really began to grow. Rick Warren had a profound impact on the early days of my ministry there, and his insight on communicating with the local culture was a major factor in our growth.

We had built our first building on a donated piece of land. We were about to build there again when we found a fifty-acre tract in an incredible location. It was available for an incredible price, so we sold our building, bought the fifty acres, and moved into a shopping center to worship while we raised funds for a new building.

During this transition time, I concluded that I should remain with NorthWood long-term, and I made a public promise to the church. I still had a strong feeling that I was supposed to be doing mission work, but I had no idea what that might look like or how it could happen. Soon, I didn't have much time to think about it, as the church entered a particularly difficult period. Our growth slowed to a crawl, stopped, and then our numbers began to decline. As the church membership declined, so did the morale and the financial contributions. Our planned two years in the shopping center was stretched out to five. It was embarrassing and humiliating for me as a leader.

MY BREAKING POINT

Even though our church was in decline, we had a history of strong growth for several years before we sold our building, and other churches still saw me as a successful pastor. Two large churches offered me pastorates, and I was seriously tempted to quit and accept the positions. But I had given my word to NorthWood that I would stay, so I kept my word, even if I wasn't all that excited about staying on.

One Sunday, the pressure of declining attendance and my own sense of failure became too much for me to handle. The offering was meager. My attitude was abysmal. So I threw a little pity party for myself. I'd given seven years to this place, and everyone out there was passing me up. What was I doing wrong? Why hadn't God blessed me? I had never been more depressed.

I got up the next morning and walked to the top of a hill near my house. From that hill I could see the Fort Worth skyline, and many times I had stood on that hill and faced different parts of the world as I prayed for them. That morning I approached the hill with a strong feeling that God had let me down. I looked to the west and saw the steeple of a church with an attendance of several thousand whose pastor was in trouble because he'd had affairs with many women. I looked north toward the steeple of another church where the pastor was sentenced to prison for embezzling church funds. I'd turned down offers from big churches to stay on at NorthWood, but I was going nowhere fast.

In desperation and frustration I called out to God. "Those guys are scuzballs, and yet their churches have grown. I've kept my pants on and my hands out of the offering plate, and yet you couldn't give me just another hundred people yesterday? God, you've got a really good deal in me! Why aren't you blessing me?"

I know that none of my frustration was from the Holy Spirit. But in that moment, I know that God clearly spoke to me, asking me a simple question: "Bob, when will Jesus be enough for you?"

The old patterns started to kick in, and I began to assure myself that of course Jesus was enough, when suddenly the truth hit me: he wasn't. The root of all my unhappiness was really quite easy to see: *I was unhappy because I wanted Jesus and something else too.* I wanted to be prominent. I wanted to be on top of the heap. I wanted an empire. Every Sunday, in every personal encounter, I was promising people that Jesus was more than enough for them, and yet he wasn't enough for me!

I began feeling even more depressed. Why isn't he enough for me? What if what I have at NorthWood is as good as it ever gets? If God's promises are true, then it shouldn't matter whether I pastor a church of a few hundred or a few thousand. If my joy is in him and I'm where he wants me to be, I should be content. I have God's Word, the Holy Spirit, a wife and children who love me, a few hundred members who have stuck with me through thick and thin ... What's wrong with me, anyway? I began to sob.

I fell to my knees on that hill and prayed to the Lord, straight from my heart. "Father, from this point forward it's about your kingdom and not my empire." In the midst of my prayer, another thought suddenly invaded my brain, another question, but different than the first.

"What is the kingdom?"

What a strange question to think about at a time like this! As a seminary graduate, I knew how to define the kingdom. The kingdom is made up of God's people; we're all citizens of his kingdom. As I was thinking about all of this, I suddenly remembered something I'd heard a New Testament professor say at seminary: "If you want to know what a kingdom citizen looks like, you need to read the Sermon on the Mount." I had my Bible with me, so I sat down on that hill right then and there and read Matthew 5 through 7.

As I read these words of Jesus, it literally felt as if I was reading them for the first time. I didn't just read them; I absorbed them. When I finished I began sobbing again. I realized I was a great Old Testament believer and a solid Baptist, but I was a lousy follower of Jesus. I knew I had to change.

THINKING IN A NEW WAY

Shortly after this experience, God began to radically change my understanding of the kingdom and how we are called as disciples to engage the world. Leighton Ford, a brother-in-law and close associate of Billy Graham, selected twenty pastors to meet with him and glean from his wisdom and experience. I didn't personally know Dr. Ford, but someone had recommended me to be part of this group. When Dr. Ford came to Southwestern Seminary in Fort Worth to do a conference on evangelism, he called me and asked if I could help with some of the details for the conference.

To my surprise, the conference was on global evangelism and missions. *Great*, I thought. *All I need right now is yet another reminder of how I've failed to become a missionary.* It was like setting a drink in front of a thirsty alcoholic. It was torture. The speakers were talking about how they needed the best the church had to offer, the most educated and creative people engaged in missions. With a Doctorate of Ministry in church planting from Fuller Seminary and years of practical experience in the church, I figured that I surely qualified. Again, I felt some of that resentment begin to resurface; why hadn't God allowed me to be a missionary?

I went home that evening seething with pent-up frustration and anger. Nikki could sense that something was wrong, and I began spilling out my heart to her. "I just feel that God has let me down," I exploded. "I answered his call to be a missionary, and he knows how much I want to do it. But he slams every door in my face and then has me sit and hear all this stuff about how they need missionaries. Why would God put me through all that?"

Though I didn't know it at the time, God was preparing me to think in a new way about my life and my calling. The very next morning, I got up and headed to the seminary to help Leighton. As I was driving, I was still pretty upset, questioning God's work in my life. In the midst of my frustration and anger, God hit me with another one of those lightning bolt questions.

"What if the church were the missionary?"

What?

"What if the church were the missionary?"

Suddenly, it was as if the heavens opened up and everything about my life made sense. Why hadn't I seen it before? What if this wasn't just about me? What if God was not just calling me to be a missionary; what if *he was calling our whole church*? For my entire life, I had been trying to go it alone, looking for opportunities to be a professional pastor in a mission field. But the truth is that the Great Commission was given to the whole church — every disciple of Christ — and not just to vocational missionaries.

There was nothing preventing me from engaging in the work of a missionary. We are the ones who have vocationalized missions — not God! We, the church in the West, have taken disciple-making evangelism out of the hands of the ordinary people and turned it into a vocation for religious professionals. Does God ask nothing more from us than our money, prayers, and an occasional token mission trip? My mind exploded with fresh ideas and insights. What would it look like if the whole church were to be the missionary?

Over the next several weeks, I began to reconsider some of my assumptions about missions and the Great Commission. If the Great Commission was given to the whole church, then every Christian is called to be a missionary. Okay. But realistically, how could that work? I had never seen it done before. In my experience, pastoring a church and doing mission work were two entirely different things.

But did they have to be? Was there a different way of looking at missions in the local church?

With God's help, I began to reverse engineer the way we conceive of missions. Churches typically do evangelism in three ways. First, they support their denomination's mission board with a segment of their budget or contribute to the financial support of a vocational missionary in some foreign country. Second, they have sporadic campaigns in which they teach a few willing people a canned presentation on how to be saved and send them out to get conversions. Third, they encourage members on their jobs to be alert to their responsibility to witness and to be prepared for such opportunities by being "always [be] ready to give an answer to everyone who asks you a reason concerning the hope that is in you" (1 Peter 3:15).

I began to realize that we had the process reversed. If Jesus had given the Great Commission to all of his followers, there should be a way for every Christian — and not just religious professionals or those with specialized gifts — to engage non-Christians. There had to be more options than simply contributing money or awkwardly and artificially trying to find a way to slip religion into our conversations with coworkers.

As I looked around, I realized that there were many conscientious laypeople who were trying hard to find ways to use their jobs for God. Unfortunately, most of their efforts were focused on doing things for the church. An air conditioning expert might donate his time to install a system in his church, or a graphic designer might design church bulletins or presentation slides. Now finding ways to use one's vocation for the church is well and good, and the results are certainly a wonderful service to God. But serving in a ministry to the church is not quite the same as fulfilling the Great Commission.

What if we were to invert the process? Rather than encouraging people to use their vocations to serve the church, what if we made it the church's task to mobilize Christians to use their everyday vocations to serve people in need — both locally and globally? What would happen if Christians used their jobs, skills, and passions to directly answer Christ's call to minister to those in need? What if we started to feed the hungry, clothe the naked, minister to the oppressed, and shelter the homeless? Could this be God's plan for reaching the nations and fulfilling the Great Commission? The next step, to answer my question, was to put these insights into practice.

So, for the next few years I preached regularly on the kingdom of God and the Sermon on the Mount. In many ways, I was teaching myself even more than I was teaching the people at NorthWood. And I made a commitment that day, a commitment that redefined success for me. Instead of striving to be the biggest church in the area, we were going to *church* the area. From that time forward we began starting churches.

I didn't know at the time just how huge this change was. It was a seismic shift in thinking that completely inverted our approach to evangelism. Instead of focusing on building a church by bringing people into it, we focused on being missionaries to our area, making disciples who would fill churches.

As you can see from my story, I had felt, for most of my life, that God was calling me to be a missionary. But the truth is that God's vision for my life was about more than vocational ministry. He was calling me to participation in the kingdom. Stuck in the rut of my preconceptions and man-made definitions of success and failure, I wasn't able to see all that God had in mind. Through this experience, I've learned that when God calls me to a task, the shape of it is likely to be far different from what I expect.

When I heard God's call, I naturally visualized answering it in the context and culture I've been part of. But God's call is always to something different than we imagine — and always something bigger than we expect. Perhaps the disciples of Jesus thought he had called them to save Israel from the Romans. Only later did they learn the true scope of his vision, to save the world and bring people into eternal fellowship with God. The call of God is often what God uses to get us going, taking that first small step; but don't let your understanding of that call lock you into a preconceived path. With every step we must remain open and fluid to the work of the Holy Spirit.

When God called Abraham, he gave him a single command: "Get out of your country, and from your relatives, and from your father's house, to the land that I will show you" (Genesis 12:2). Most of us, when we hear God's call, want to tighten it down a bit and clarify the details. "Now where exactly is that land? What road do I take, God? Where's the map to show me the way?" The more we try to control our call, the more we limit God to our own abilities and fail to recognize the unique opportunities he brings our way.

OCCUPATION, PASSION, AND VOCATION

We grow up hearing many religious phrases that subconsciously shape our thinking, such as "born again," "decisions for Jesus," or "joining the church." One of these is "called into the ministry," a phrase which I now find highly misleading. As you will discover in this book, I am convinced that God has called the entire body of Christ to ministry, not just the few whose talents lead them to be pastors. Some followers of Christ are called to various specialized functions, but every one of us has a responsibility to engage with God's work in the world. There is within each of us a longing, a voice deep inside that calls us to something unknown. Throughout our lives, we may get glimpses of it, and it draws us forward to an undefined goal. C. S. Lewis attempted to describe this longing when he first experienced it as a child:

> It is difficult to find words strong enough for the sensation that came over me; Milton's "enormous bliss" of Eden ... comes somewhere near it. It was a sensation, of course, of desire; but desire for what?... Before I knew what I desired, the desire itself was gone, the whole glimpse withdrawn, the world turned commonplace again, or only stirred by a longing for the longing that had just ceased.[1]

For most of us, calling is something like this — a deep, private, personal longing that brings everything together in a single experience of great significance. God calls every one of us in many ways, often using these undefined longings we tend to ignore or pass over as mere feelings of the moment. Those who wish to follow God must learn to develop sensitivity to these moments, and when they come, to tune their ears to God for his call. Like my experience as a child, we may lack the ability to grasp fully what God is saying to us, but we will still recognize his presence and know that God is speaking. We can be sure that God is real, even if our understanding of his call takes time to emerge for us.

The French philosopher Maurice Merleau-Ponty once said, "Meaning is invisible, but the invisible is not contradictory of the visible: the visible itself has an invisible inner framework, and the invisible is the secret counterpart of the visible."[2] The meaning that is presently invisible to us is frequently the framework that God will build on to prepare us for future fulfillment of our calling.

Like most people, when you hear the term "God's call," you may be tempted to assume that it means a call to a religious occupation, such as being a pastor or a missionary. But I'm convinced that this is a misconception based our conditioning in the church. It's a mistake I frequently made when I assumed that God was calling me to become a "vocational" missionary. But I've learned that there is a distinct difference between our *call* and our *occupation*. Many of us may have an *occupation* — a trade or a profession — that is independent of our call. Typically, your occupation grows out of your interests, giftings, and skills. You follow those interests and gifts into a trade or profession, which gives you a job or a career by which you earn your living.

But our *call* is something altogether different. It involves our destiny before God, our relationship to him, and our openness and submission to his will, as well as our call to serve him in a particular way. Our call to be Christians and to serve God in a given capacity is not identical to our occupational skills, and its nature and direction will generally be revealed as an expression of our deepest passions or desires.

God calls each of us, in some way, to minister to others. So while there is a distinction between our occupation and our calling, God may use an occupation as the vehicle that carries us into our calling. When this happens, the merger of our occupational skills with our deep, inner passions, the result is our *vocation*.

The English term *vocation* is from the Latin word *voca*, which means "inner voice." Martin Luther took the idea even further with the concept of *Beruf,* a German word meaning "inner longing" or "a pull to something from God." Vocation is formed when passion and skills come together to fulfill what God has called you to do. Every follower of Christ has a deep longing that comes from God, a passion that we need to identify. When you identify that longing as a call from God, you will merge it with your skills and giftings, which will provide you with the means of meeting his call. At that point you have your vocation. Your vocation will put you into the domains of a society and enable you to engage and fulfill your call.

Let's illustrate all of this with the example of Dr. Albert Schweitzer. Dr. Schweitzer's skills and giftings led him to the occupation of medicine. Those skills led him to become a doctor. But his passion was to minister to people in deep need in Africa. That was his call. By merging his skill with his passion, he found his vocation — serving as a medical missionary to Africa.

In my own life, confusion resulted because I misunderstood the call I heard in that camp when I was eight years old. Neither my youth nor my misunderstanding meant the call was not real. What God speaks to us about is often what will emerge later. He places it firmly in our hearts when we are young so that as we mature we will recognize the continuity of his work in our past, in our present experience, and in our very being. As American painter Edward Hopper once said, "In every artist's development the germ of the later work is always found in the earlier. The nucleus around which the artist's intellect builds his work is himself ... and this changes little from birth."[3]

Already, deep within you is a voice you recognize is speaking. It speaks of a future that is bigger than you, a future not yet in existence that you can have a hand in shaping. What is it that is holding you back? Whatever it is, get rid of it so you can respond to God. Move your feet; do what you can today with what God has given you; be obedient in what you know to do, and God will be faithful to reveal what you need for the future. Don't sit around waiting for a master plan; look to the Master.

When you are seeking God's call, your skill, vocation, and passion are critical. But undergirding all of this are four things that are essential to hearing God's "full counsel" for your life.

1. The Importance of Prayer

Prayer is where it all starts. When our hearts are clean and our lives are an open book before God, he will often speak things in our heart that give us a sense of where he is leading us. You may recognize that when you are praying, there is an unusual amount of God's power or presence as a thought or a prayer is being directed toward God. You just can't escape it — you know God is speaking! You may not know all the details or understand where he is leading you, but there is a sense of personal revelation that God is giving to you.

Often, it takes time and additional prayer to fully understand what God has said. Struggling in prayer is critical as we listen. It develops qualities of perseverance and a commitment to move forward, even when circumstances are difficult. During times of hardship and doubt those who have persevered in prayer can always go back to the call and find renewed strength to push forward in faith.

2. The Guidance of God's Word

Scripture is indispensable. God called me to preach using Jeremiah 1. He called me to pastor NorthWood using Psalm 2:8. For most major decisions, God will often give me a verse or a particular passage of Scripture to meditate on. I journal with my Bible open for this very reason. God will say something as I'm reading or a verse will jump out as confirmation or rejection of an idea or opportunity. I've learned to listen to that. I read through the Bible every year and am continually amazed as I'm dealing with specific issues how God answers my prayers through a verse in my normal, daily Scripture reading and worship time.

3. The Counsel of Other People

Other people can be crucial in helping us determine our calling. Proverbs says that there is safety in the presence of many counselors (Proverbs 11:14; 24:6). I have a number of people who have spoken into my life. Family, peers, counselors, consultants, and intercessors are just some of those to whom I open my life up and tell what I'm thinking.

Sometimes, I don't even have to ask; they will see something I don't see and will challenge me to use it. Our church helps train young pastors to start churches, and we have a whole assessment process we take them through where we look at their gifts, skills, and abilities to be sure they have everything they need. This isn't to say that God won't call you to do something that goes against the counsel of other people. But a wise disciple of Christ will often seek counsel from people they know and love.

4. Divine Intersections

Finally, I frequently keep my eyes open for God's mysterious work—those divine intersections. Sometimes God has placed something on my heart, something I can't let go of, but I have no ability to do anything about it. The next thing I know there are people, resources, and situations emerging, beyond my ability to control, that are causing significant changes.

Even as I write this, I see it happening! There is a particular country that God laid on my heart long ago that is in the midst of a significant amount of strife. I've met some of the leaders of this country and have been following them in the news. Recently, churches here in the United States have begun to email me, asking me to assist them in developing ways to establish relationships with the government and the church in this country.

Even though I don't know anyone in this country, I've received a call from a man who wants to serve by helping to mobilize people interested in serving there. In a short period of time, many of the dots are being connected, and though I don't know where this will go, I've been around long enough to know that God is up to something in this country. He's still putting all the pieces together!

Connection Steps

- ⊙ Read Jeremiah 1:4–10; Ephesians 4:1–7; and Exodus 3–4, and reflect on these passages and put down your thoughts as you read them.

- ⊙ List your skills, passions, vocation, giftedness, Scriptures, words from others, and divine intersections on a sheet of paper. Is there a pattern?

- ⊙ Daily set aside a block of time to let God speak to you in personal worship. Look for God's voice in the normal activities of daily life.

CHAPTER 3

Your Job *Is* Your Ministry

*For I know the thoughts that I think toward you,
says Yahweh, thoughts of peace, and not of evil,
to give you hope and a future.*   JEREMIAH 29:11

Robert and Melinda Needs were in their early twenties when they came to NorthWood. Robert had a great position with American Airlines, and Melinda was a schoolteacher. They were faithful, active, and involved in church activities.

But then life threw them a curve. They had a little boy, Jacob, who was autistic. Suddenly many of their hopes and dreams came crashing down. But if you were to meet them today, you wouldn't know what a grueling challenge their life has been. Their disposition and outlook are sunny and positive.

Melinda's degree was in speech therapy, which was a God thing because it allowed her to diagnose Jacob's condition before the doctors could. They kept telling her nothing was wrong, perhaps because they were reluctant to make such a devastating diagnosis as autism at such a young age. But Melinda knew something was wrong. At eighteen months Jacob was often sick, and he began to lose what little language ability he had picked up. He wouldn't look people in the eyes. He didn't respond to the call of his own name. His lack of social interaction isolated him from the rest of the family. The dog would knock him over because he didn't know to get out of the way. He slept only two or three hours at night, often screaming the rest of the time. His health began to deteriorate in many ways.

Melinda had had an autistic student where she taught, and in order to help him she had thoroughly researched the subject. Now she saw similarities between that student and her own child, and she suspected autism.

Although autism is being studied now, its exact causes are still not known. It occurs more often in boys than in girls. It was virtually unheard of in the fifties, sixties, and seventies. Even in the eighties when Robert and Melinda were dealing with it, autism was merely a subchapter in medical textbooks. So Melinda didn't know where to turn until in a supermarket checkout line she met a woman who had a child with autism. This woman had studied everything known about the condition, and she took Melinda and Robert by the hand and showed them how to maneuver through the uncharted world of autism. It was like getting in on a deep, dark secret or being led into territory where the paths are not clear and the doors are not marked. To find helpful information, Melinda had to call many people and knock on many doors before answers and help began to emerge.

When Jacob was twenty-four months old, doctors confirmed Melinda's diagnosis. The projected cost of treatment was astronomical, both in terms of money and time. Doctors recommended forty hours of therapy each week at a cost of $3,000 per month. Insurance would pay nothing, so with the help of university consultants, the family set up a therapy room in their home. Caring for Jacob would be a 24/7 project. Robert was traveling three to four days every week, which put the brunt of the burden on Melinda. This meant she couldn't be there for her two older children, Michael and Alyssa. "I remember telling my daughter," Melinda said, "'I can't help you like I want to. You can take care of yourself, but Jacob can't.'"

The total effect of Jacob's autism on the family was devastating. Not only was Melinda continually fatigued, but expenses for Jacob's medical care and home therapy were fast destroying the family budget and depleting their savings. Yet God provided, though Robert and Melinda still can't explain how. On some days they would wonder just where the money necessary to keep going would come from, but somehow it was always there when needed — an unexpected refund, a gift from family, a check that arrived at just the right moment. God's hand was in the process from the beginning.

Many families do not survive the autism ordeal intact. It's awful. You become isolated and don't go out in public because your child screams, hollers, gets naked, or does unexpected things that are socially inappropriate. For example, Melinda was in San Antonio at a really nice hotel, and she took Jacob to the pool to swim. Autistic children like to be naked when they swim because of the sensory effect water has on their body. In the middle of the pool he took off his swimsuit, and it floated away. The pool was too crowded for her to get to him, so she had to ask a dad swimming with his three-year-old daughter, "I'm so sorry, could you hand my son his swimsuit." So, to avoid these and even worse incidents, families dealing with autism tend to draw inward and don't go out.

After two years of home-based therapy, a specialized behavioral school opened that agreed to take Jacob full time. After two years in the school, he made dramatic positive strides. His speech improved and he became potty trained, which made a huge difference in the lives of the family. With his new foothold in language, Melinda's school-teaching ability came into play and helped Jacob tremendously. She knew the hierarchy of language, which enabled her to build his communication abilities to a workable level. "God equipped me a long time ago to have Jacob," she told me. "When I see the other kids with severe handicaps, I can encourage the parents through my own experiences. I tell them, 'You can do this.'"

People often praised Melinda for what she was doing, but her typical response was, "I didn't choose to do this; it was handed to me. There is no such thing as being a martyr or hero. You just do what you have to do to get the job done. What you do for your child not only helps him, it helps the mom as well, and it makes life better for everyone in the family."

Perhaps the greatest blessing that has come from the Needs family ordeal is its positive effect on their relationship to God. As Melinda explained it, "God gave me an autistic child to keep me on my knees. Having to depend on God keeps me close to him. I never forget who my Maker is and what this is all about." When I asked if she would have had that closeness with God even without Jacob's autism, she replied, "No, I know I wouldn't have. Because Jacob keeps it real. He makes us remember what life is about. In our family we can have no pretense of having it all together. That keeps us humble and utterly dependent on God."

CONNECTING AUTISM AND VIETNAM

A few years ago I was in Hanoi visiting with the former mayor. He told me of a recently passed law mandating that all special needs children be mainstreamed into the public schools. But there was a problem. The schools had no teacher training or curriculum on how to work with special needs children. This often meant that a special needs child would no longer attend school at all but be kept at home, out of the way. If parents did send them to class, the schools could do nothing for them.

We had begun a special needs ministry at NorthWood when a twenty-seven-year-old special needs woman passed away. With that ministry and Melinda's experience, I knew we had considerable expertise in that area to share with the Vietnamese. When I mentioned the possibility to the mayor, he took me to the head of the Vietnam National University, where I met first with the rector and then with the head of the special needs program. I invited her to America to visit some of our universities and meet with our North-Wood special needs ministry. She accepted and came. As a result, several of our members who taught special needs children in public schools and universities wound up writing a curriculum and holding a conference on special needs education in Vietnam. For the past five years these people have returned to Vietnam annually to add to the curriculum.

Last year Melinda participated in the two-week conference in Vietnam. She was reluctant to leave Jacob, but she felt strongly that God was telling her to go. So she sent Jacob to camp for one week, and Robert took off work and stayed with him the next. Of all the people who have been to the conference, none has been better received than Melinda. Why? Because she not only studied special needs, she lived it. It has been her life. And this showed clearly in her work at the conference.

On Melinda's first day in Vietnam she was helping set up for the conference when a kitchen worker learned that Melinda had come to speak on autism. She cornered Melinda and explained that her sister's son had autism, and she desperately needed help to know how to deal with him. The woman brought her sister to the conference, and she took notes throughout Melinda's speech. Afterward she stopped Melinda in the hallway to ask all kinds of questions about how to handle her son in various situations. Through an interpreter Melinda was able to give her good answers and direct her to a Vietnamese university program and a local support group for parents of autistic children. Her ability to help the woman filled her with elation. She called Robert that night and told him, "Now I know why Jacob has autism. For the first time I feel that there's a positive in all of this."

Another woman who had attended every session of the conference came to Melinda on the last day and said in impeccable English, "You must come back and tell me how to deal with the guilt." The woman explained that while earning her doctorate, she had left her daughter in the care of others, and now the girl was autistic. The woman felt terribly guilty because she was convinced her daughter's autism was her fault. Melinda explained to her that autism doesn't come about that way and that she must not inflict guilt on herself. But the woman wouldn't listen even though she kept hugging Melinda, obviously grateful that she cared.

The next day when Melinda toured a pediatric hospital, she saw the woman and her autistic daughter. The poor woman was distraught, broken, and dejected. She had even told her husband to leave her because she was no good. Melinda spent considerable time with the woman and told her, "You are gifted in a way others aren't. Maybe there is a reason your daughter got you for a mother. It's because you're strong and smart, and she'll have a better life because of you. That's what you must hold on to."

After another conference session a man approached Melinda. He had an autistic son who would do nothing but watch television all day. From her experience, Melinda knew just what to tell him. "Turn off the TV and make him look at you before you will turn it back on. Make him join your world." She counseled him several more times during the conference, and as a result he made several positive decisions about the care of his son.

Melinda had always been willing to help other parents who dealt with autism, but her true focus had been her own family. Her experiences in Vietnam lit her passion to invest herself in helping others, both in that country and in her own community. In Vietnam she learned, "I have so much to give I didn't know I had. I always wanted to help people, but I didn't know I could make that big a difference. I can't wait to go back. I have so much more to tell them. These Vietnamese families go through the same kinds of difficulties I go through with my son, but the sad thing is that most of them don't have a Savior. I couldn't do it without him. Since I've come back from Vietnam I've met all kinds of people over here that I've been able to help. I did some of that before, but I didn't have the passion I have now."

Melinda has been as good as her word. This year she was an advocate for a Hispanic single mother. She persuaded the school to test the woman's son for autism, and when the results were positive she got a full range of benefits from the school to help the family. Melinda is also involved with autism seminars and programs with FEAT North Texas (Families for Effective Autism Treatment).

I tell you Melinda's story because it is a shining example of the primary point I'm making in this chapter, and indeed, in this book. Melinda is a person using her life's experiences, her education, and her job to minister to others and to show them the nature of Christ. This is the business of the church in the world, and Melinda's story is a prime example of how it is done.

EACH PERSON IS A MINISTER

Within every single one of us is something we aspire to and long for. We see it from a distance, and though it's vague and unclear, we recognize it as a noble call that draws us toward it. Often it's our experiences, our passions, and our jobs that prepare us and point us toward this undefined longing. Winston Churchill described this eloquently when he found himself leading a beleaguered nation in its darkest hour: "I felt as if I were walking with destiny, and that all my past life had been but a preparation for this hour and for this trial." [4] He accepted the challenge as the thing he had been prepared to do, consumed with a sense of providence and personal destiny.

Søren Kierkegaard spoke to the same need for a cause when he wrote in his journal, "The thing is to understand myself, to see what

God really wants me to do; the thing is to find a truth which is true for me, to find the idea for which I can live and die."[5] Os Guinness explains it more fully:

> As modern people we have too much to live with and too little to live for. Some feel they have time but not enough money; others feel they have money but not enough time. But for most of us, in the midst of material plenty, we have spiritual poverty … Calling is the truth that God calls us to himself so decisively that everything we are, everything we do, and everything we have is invested with special devotion and dynamism lived out as a response to his summons and service.[6]

God's fingerprint is all over you. He has put you together in a way that is like no one else. He created you for significance, to do things that no one but you can do. He has given you abilities and skills and desires that equip you for a particular task that is awaiting you. Those deep longings most of us feel to make a difference in the world are our dim recognition of God's call to us. In our heart of hearts, we want God to use us.

Many, when they respond to this longing, think the answer is to go into professional ministry as a vocation. I often see it happen. In our work locally and globally, it's not uncommon to have laypeople get caught up in a ministry and become so passionate about it that they want to go into church ministry. One of my biggest jobs is to keep these people from making this change. I help them to see that they are in the ministry already, and usually they are serving much more effectively than they could as a seminary-educated, church-supported pastor.

I was preaching at a significant church in another country on the domains of society and how every single member of the body of Christ should influence the culture through their job, right where they are. At the end of the service the pastor had people come forward who wanted to influence all the domains of society by going into full-time ministry as pastors. He missed the entire point of my message. His call, though well intentioned, could have ended up ruining many wonderful ministry opportunities.

I was once visiting with a pastor in another city who introduced me to one of his young associate pastors. He had been a brilliant, educated lawyer with a significant practice when a passion to serve God was ignited in his heart. He wanted to make a big difference, so he left the law firm and went to seminary. He is now a pastor in a church of two hundred people that is flat and stagnant, and he is frustrated.

Was there anything wrong with him making this move? Not necessarily. I know that he did it with the best of intentions. But he moved from influencing government, ethics, and business to shepherding two hundred people. Will he ever again influence those vital societal structures he left? Probably not. Is there another passionate Christian lawyer who will take his place? Probably not, and even worse, the loss of Christian influence in those domains is serious. I wish someone had sat down with him and helped him understand that being a lawyer is just as significant as being a pastor. He had a unique opportunity to bring Christian influence into areas where it is sorely needed and no pastor could reach.

God has given us varied talents and giftings so we can use them in the areas where they will bring about change that no one else can bring. I believe that the primary strategy for the transformation of communities and nations in our modern, global world is through the workplace.

Not long ago I met a nuclear engineer whose specialty is submarines. He had heard me speak, and he knew we encouraged our church members to engage society. But he had misgivings about applying such an idea to his own line of work. He told me, "Either North-Wood's system is so complex that there is no way other churches can do it, or it's so simple it's just stupid." I explained the concept in more detail, and at the conclusion of our conversation, he said, "It's so simple it's stupid — anyone can do it."

While I may not be too crazy about the term "stupid" being applied to our method, I think he is right: there is nothing complex or hard to grasp or unworkable about this idea. People are always looking for something complicated in what we do, and I sometimes suspect they're just looking for some reason to say, "There's no way we can do that," so they can walk away from making the effort. But it is not at all complicated. The vital resource for the church to engage the world is not standing in the pulpit; it is sitting in the pews. It is in the jobs and vocations of the ordinary members who come to church every Sunday. These are the people who must be called out into the community, the nation, and the world to make a difference. These are the people who have jobs that put them in daily contact with the people who need to be influenced. And their jobs give them the skills to move out and engage other parts of our society.

TAKE THIS JOB AND LOVE IT

One of the things I've taught my children and the youth of our church as well as the adults is to focus on doing what you absolutely love. As long as you can make a living, don't worry about how much money you make. Choose a job you can pour yourself into wholeheartedly. You will spend more time at your job than anything else in life, so you'd better be doing something you are passionate about and feel called to do. It is far more important to live by meaning and significance than to die leaving a huge investment portfolio to heirs you didn't have time to know because you were so busy making money for them to inherit.

If money has ever caused anyone to die at peace, I've never met that person. I've never stood beside the deathbed of anyone who gently held in his arms his checkbook, a stack of hundred-dollar bills, charge cards, and stock certificates and whispered, "So long, dear friends; you and I were so close." But I have seen people die in rooms that were cold, sterile, and lonely. They spent much time making money but built few relationships, and life was more about acquisition than about meaningful relationships. Better to die a poor man, with people nearby who love you and whom you love, than a rich man with loads of doctors to ease the last moments but no warmth of humanity or love of others. Each of us has a tremendous capacity to give, wealthy or not. The question is, what are you going to give?

In choosing your vocation, you must ask yourself what you are passionate about. What could you do all day that you would love so much it wouldn't feel like work? Make that activity your vocation and you'll be happy. If your vocation is not clear to you, it will be worth your time and money to consult a reputable vocational counselor. A good counselor will give you personality tests, leadership tests, gift tests, interest tests, and talent tests. Armed with the information gleaned from these tests, the counselor will guide you toward a vocation that matches both your passion and your abilities.

Here are some questions to ask yourself that will help you find that special vocation:

- ⊙ What am I passionate about?
- ⊙ What is my consistent life message wherever I am? What am I really about? What do I talk about? What do I live and breathe?
- ⊙ What am I unusually gifted at doing that does not seem like a drudgery?
- ⊙ What traits or abilities have others seen and affirmed in me?
- ⊙ What one trait or ability makes me unique?
- ⊙ What is the one thing of single focus that I could give my whole life to?

These are not questions to be glanced at and answered glibly. They require thought, introspection, and careful reviewing of your personal history. And it's essential to understand that answering them does not assure that you'll get your vocation right the first time. One of my greatest mentors is author and entrepreneur Bob Buford. I wanted my son Ben to be exposed to this man's wisdom and passion, so I arranged for the three of us to meet for lunch. Ben's degree is in international relations and economics, but he was selling cars at the time and wasn't happy about it. Bob told Ben, "Whatever you're doing, it won't be your last job." He explained that the important thing is to learn from every job skills that will help you in the next one. Ben liked that. He wanted to do more than sell cars. He realized that he could make even that job a positive experience by learning from it skills that would be useful when he found his true vocation.

Fulfillment in life is tied more to what we accomplish in the work we do than to anything else, other than our families. So here's the bottom-line question to ask yourself: If money were no object, if there were no restraints, and I could do anything in the world I wanted, I would _____ (fill in the blank). That's what you should probably be doing. It doesn't matter that you may not be the best in the world at that job; if it fills in this blank, you will find true joy in doing it. Life is too short not to be able to grin throughout the day.

TAKE THIS JOB AND DEVELOP IT

To find satisfaction in your job, you must look at its job description as the bare minimum you've been hired to do. Never view it as all you have to master; view it instead as where you begin — the starting point from which you expand and develop. Look at the job description as the basics, do the basics really well, then look for ways to improve, increase, and develop; then you'll be able to use your job in ways you never thought of.

This is the right way to achieve promotions. You don't have to climb over people to be successful; just do your job extremely well and you'll be promoted. Stepping on other people can come back to hurt you, whereas doing your job well gets the positive attention of management. People in human resource departments tell me that today it is harder than ever for employers to find good help. Doing your job well will make you a rare find in their eyes.

I was on a plane sitting next to a woman who was vice president of human resources in a big corporation. I said to her, "I get the impression from young people today that they are choosing to do what they love more than any generation before them. Is that true or false?"

"It's true," she replied, "There's no doubt about it. They are choosing work they like to do. But there's another side to the coin: they don't have the work ethic of previous generations, and that's a real problem for employers."

Earlier, I made the point that doing what does not seem like drudgery is a good indication of your passion. Nevertheless, I certainly did not mean you'd never have to work hard! Hard work is usually necessary in any endeavor, even those we're passionate about and love to do. The best of jobs or the highest of callings have tasks within them that no one really likes to do. People look at my life and see what they think is a glamour job — traveling, seeing the world, meeting with interesting people, expanding our global ministry. Often they tell me they want to be a part of all that. What they don't see are the many behind-the-scenes tasks that must be taken care of to keep things going — developing a schedule, making and changing travel arrangements, working on the plane, packing for a specific culture, keeping my shots up-to-date, encountering a thousand different opinions, getting little sleep, keeping my work on the home front going, and many other details, large and small.

Every job has its grunt work. Even in the most beautiful home someone must mop the floors, wash the dishes, clean the bathrooms, and carry out the trash. There is no perfect job.

When you work hard at your job, you will reap more rewards than just money. Omar Reyes, who is in charge of all our glocal ministries, is a prime example of this principle. He came to Texas from Central America, where he had been a successful businessman. When he joined our church, he volunteered to work in the inner city with us. Because he is Latino and speaks Spanish, he was ideal for that task. He never pushed his way forward, but he was faithful and diligent in everything he did. When asked for counsel, what he gave was always incredibly wise.

In time he was placed in charge of our Mexico work, and now he oversees all of our glocal (global and local) ministries and travels with me all over the world, giving me counsel and advice and putting things together at a level I never could have done. Simply by working quietly and diligently, Omar's good work got our attention and brought him to the top.

BUT *THIS* JOB — I WANT TO SHOVE IT!

Sometimes, even when you try to work hard and do your best, you may not like your job. All kinds of factors can enter into this, but usually it's because the job is not a true fit to your talents and passions. My first advice is get into something you like — even if it means a cut in pay — as fast as you can. But if that's not an option for you, you still have some ways to redeem your time.

Find the positive aspects of your job — and there are some even in the worst of environments. If nothing else, be grateful you can provide for your family. This is no small thing, and many people would be happy to have any honorable job just for that purpose. All honest work is noble in God's eyes.

Farming is one of the dirtiest occupations on the earth. My grandfather was a farmer who ploughed with a mule — not on one of those enclosed, air-conditioned tractors with cushioned seats and a CD player. I remember a time when my little brother and I were to spend the weekend at his farm. We did not want to go. What if we had to dig potatoes or pick peas, or hoe weeds or do some other kind of backbreaking, sweat-producing, blister-raising drudgery? He assured us, however, that we'd hunt and have fun in the big thicket of East Texas. So we went.

We got to his land, and as we pulled in you could see acres and acres of fields lined with neat rows of lush vegetables. As we got out of the truck, he looked over toward one field and said, "Oh no, wouldn't you know it; the butter beans are in. They can't wait. We're going to have to pick them." It was hot, sweaty, and dirty, and we hated it. After a few hours of filling bushel baskets and dumping them by the barn to wash and shell, I decided I'd had enough. So I crawled under the barn, which was on cinder blocks, too tired to worry about snakes and rats. I didn't care. I wasn't going to pick any more butter beans.

That is, until Granddad found me. He scolded me and shamed me with stories of the Great Depression when people worked their fingers to the bone sunup to sundown just to survive. His work ethic had been shaped by that experience, which kept him face-to-face with the bottom-line reality of why he worked. His greatest concern was to be sure that if there was another depression, we'd all be able to eat. He also lectured me on the joy of seeing things grow. I didn't feel the joy, but that didn't matter; I experienced a little woodshed therapy. Then he pitched me a burlap sack and sent me back out to work. I plodded back to the field, hating every step toward those insidious butter beans.

Had I been more mature at the time, here is what I should have thought: "I don't like this work, and it's not what I intend to do always. But here I am with no good option at the moment, so what can I learn?" That's the approach that can turn a bad job into a positive opportunity.

With my grandfather, everything of significance came together in farming. The work was necessary to survival; it enabled him to support his family, to give needed food to others. He was very good at it, he loved it, and seeing the miracle of growth connected him to God. Yes, it was hard, tiring, and dirty, but he hardly noticed that. It was completely swallowed up in his love and dedication to what he did. Farming never became my passion, but my grandfather's example instilled into me the need to work hard, work at something significant, and work to make a difference in the world.

As I mentioned earlier, my son graduated from New York University with a degree in international relations and economics. But the only job he could get was selling cars. It required long hours and it was frustrating work. He didn't like it, but he needed to work, so his back was against the wall. He made a living, but he was sometimes discouraged and joked ruefully about being the best-educated car salesman in Texas.

I tried encouraging him to look at his job as a training ground for better things to come. "You know, Ben," I said, "this job could be the best preparation you could get for going into any business. All businesses sell something, whether it's a product or a service. If you can sell cars, you can sell anything." He worked hard, and I was proud of him. Then the day came when he was invited into a company where he would do something he really wanted to do. He was soon recognized for his ability to market and sell. I asked him, "Ben, how much of that came from selling cars?" He replied, "A lot."

Sometimes God places you where you can learn a skill he plans for you to use later. Moses was educated in the best schools of the most powerful nation in the world in his time. Then God put him on the back side of nowhere in the wilderness of Midian, herding sheep for forty years. Why? God knew if he could learn to lead those stupid animals, he could lead his people, who had known nothing but slavery, to a land of their own.

David also had to herd sheep and defend them from lions before God placed him at the head of a nation where he would lead people and defend them from invaders. The disciples of Jesus fished on the Sea of Galilee before Jesus taught them to become fishers of men. If it's a job you want to shove, the key is faithful endurance and not giving up. Often, God has you in a season of preparation to learn something you may need to use later. Until that task comes along, focus on doing your present job well.

Another question to ask when you're on a job you hate is this: Who can you serve where you are? No matter what your environment, you can be sure it contains hurting people. The very ones who make your job miserable are probably hurting people. Who is near you whom you can encourage, motivate, challenge, help, and serve? God may have placed a certain coworker in your path because he knows you can help her. It may even be the person who gets on your nerves. Maybe God is allowing her to irritate you so she won't escape your notice. What if you saw that person through God's eyes and not through your own irritation? Remember, helping a person who bugs you brings an added bonus: change her and you improve your own environment.

BUT I DON'T HAVE A JOB TO LOVE OR SHOVE

You may be a student, a homemaker, or a retiree who is not employed by a company. That doesn't matter. The principles I've been presenting still apply; the only thing different is your environment. Students have association with other students in classrooms, organizations, activities, and friendships. They will experience some of the same kinds of contacts with hurting people as employees on a job. Homemakers with kids in school may have time (and a need) to get out of the house and engage in other activities. That's a perfect opportunity to serve others. The same applies to retirees. The question to ask is, what are you passionate about? Take some time to answer that question carefully and accurately, then look for a place to volunteer where that passion can meet a real need.

The greatest Christian servant I know is my mother. She never had a typical career — though when I was growing up she worked at a bakery during the holidays to buy Christmas presents for us kids. She reads, she thinks, she inspires, she encourages, she motivates, and she does Bible studies for women in prison. She was the best Sunday school teacher I ever had. She has a positive effect on everyone who knows her.

My mother is only one example of what a "jobless" person can do when they love God enough to let that love spill over into loving others. If God has not given you a paying job, you still have giftings and a vocation. Just like anyone else, you have to discover it, develop it, use it, and be ready for God to use you.

HOW TO USE YOUR JOB TO CHANGE THE WORLD

There is no uniform action plan for making a difference that fits everyone. Each of us is different, so each must find his or her own way. That's what makes this an adventure. As with any adventure, you will do better if you start with a map, and the following questions will help you draw that map. I recommend you answer them as an individual; if you're married have your spouse also answer them individually. Then sit down together and use your answers to come up with an action plan.

It's okay if you have one passion and your spouse has another. God made each of us unique. But it's critical that each supports and affirms the other in his or her passion. It is good, however, that you find at least one passion you share and can do together.

Finding Your Way

The thing I've been most passionate about that has stuck with me for a long time is _____.

The driving theme of my life has been _____.

What makes me truly unique is _____.

If I had a life verse (a biblical passage that defines my life or passion) it would be _____.

Something God revealed to me that I've never been able to let go of is

_____.

The most consistent thing I hear people say about me is

_____.

One thing I do well without thinking about it is

_____.

My personality allows me to _____.

I absolutely love _____.

The fruit I multiply in my life more than anything is

_____.

If there is anything I feel that God wants me to finish, it would be

_____.

If money and time were no object, I would

_____.

Once you've answered these questions about yourself, two others remain that will help define your objective. They deal with where and to whom you will direct your abilities and your passion if you intend to be glocal. And the questions are (may I have the envelope please?):

- ⊙ Who are those nearest you whom you can serve on a daily basis?
- ⊙ Who are the farthest from you whom you can serve at special times with your own unique talent?

Here's a clue to help you get the right answer. To determine where you should serve in the nearest need category, focus on the need that most breaks your heart. To determine where you should serve in the farthest need category, focus on the need you are most curious about that you would love to engage. These two questions will help you match your personality profile as determined in the first twelve questions with suitable points of need. This will go far toward ensuring that you will be effective in your service.

Finally, I suggest that after poring and praying over these questions, you put together a one-page action plan. This should involve your life mission and purpose; your vision, values, goals, and economic needs; and a timeline. Start with a skeleton plan at first and flesh it out from there. It can develop over time as new ideas and connections jell in your mind. Be flexible and willing to adjust. This is important to an adventurer, who must often encounter the unknown.

To fulfill one's calling involves courage and risk. It will not happen within the walls of the chapel but out in the fields under a hot sun. As Gandhi said, "We must be doing what we want the world to be." In order to bring about change, you must *be* the change.

This journey will require lifelong learning. What I saw at eight was different from what I saw at twenty-two, which was different from what I saw at thirty-eight, which was different from what I saw at forty-nine. And what I see now will be different from the way I see it at sixty, seventy, or beyond. If we are alive and alert, we learn continually. We change, grow, and gain wisdom, ability, and confidence. That is one of the best parts of the adventure.

I offer one more caution. It is all too easy to become self-focused on our call. It can easily become all about us and what makes us feel fulfilled. It's an easy trap to fall into because it's so subtle. We can fool ourselves into thinking we are doing God's work when at the bottom of our hearts we are simply trying to satisfy our own need for significance. You will not find God's call without true holiness, sacrifice, endurance, stewardship, and obedience. There is more than romanticism involved in fulfilling your call. It's all about self-sacrifice, and by that I mean sacrificing your own need to fulfill self. As Christ told us, those who lose their lives will find it. If we abandon ourselves totally to God and submit to his will for us, he will give us satisfaction, fulfillment, significance, and above all, true joy.

When all is said and done, we must find our joy in Jesus. It doesn't exist anywhere else. If we find our joy in Jesus, we will find joy wherever we are and in whatever circumstances we find ourselves, because he is with us at all times, overwhelming the effect of anything we have to endure with his love. This means engaging in an act of simple faith. It means taking the plunge, putting ourselves in his hands and placing ourselves at his disposal to accomplish whatever he wants. That is the key to fulfillment and joy.

I can think of no better way to end this chapter than with the words of the German martyr Dietrich Bonhoeffer. He was a famous theologian who was imprisoned during World War II, accused of assisting in an attempt to assassinate Hitler. After Bonhoeffer was executed, the following was found scrawled on the wall of his cell:

Who am I? They often tell me I would step from my cell's confinement calmly, cheerfully, firmly, like a squire from his country-house.

Who am I? They also tell me I would talk to my warders freely and friendly and clearly, as though it were mine to command.

Who am I? They also tell me I would bear the days of misfortune equably, smilingly, proudly, like one accustomed to win.

Am I then really all that which other men tell of? Or am I only what I myself know of myself, restless and longing and sick, like a bird in a cage, struggling for breath, as though hands were compressing my throat, yearning for colors, for flowers, for the voices of birds, thirsting for words of kindness, for neighborliness, trembling with anger at despotisms and petty humiliation, tossing in expectation of great events, powerlessly trembling for friends at an infinite distance, weary and empty at praying, at thinking, at making, faint, and ready to say farewell to it all?

Who am I? This or the other? Am I one person today, and tomorrow another? Am I both at once? A hypocrite before others, and before myself a contemptibly woebegone weakling? Or is something within me still like a beaten army, fleeing in disorder from victory already achieved?

Who am I? They mock me, these lonely questions of mine. Whoever I am, thou knowest, O God, I am thine.[7]

Connection Steps

⊙ Narrow your options of ministry by focusing on your call and job, filling in the forms given above.

⊙ If you had a single word focus for your entire life, what would it be? How does it relate to your job, skill, or passion?

⊙ If you don't have a job or this won't work for you, make a list of six things you can do right now to serve others. These could be things that don't require special skill, just love, time, and service.

CHAPTER 4

Linking to the World

Nothing has impacted our church quite like the exchange students we've hosted from Vietnam. We have had an incredible experience doing many different projects in Vietnam, but the single thing that has impacted our church the most are the children of Vietnamese leaders who have come and lived with our church members for their final year in high school. Most of these students go on to the university and do quite well. Their parents are diplomats, business leaders, and educators.

I remember when the first ones came to live with our church members — they weren't required to come to church, but they did and they still do. Some people were nervous having all these children of "communist atheists" in our church, but it has been a great experience for all of us. It has forced us to explain our faith in simple terms and often to distinguish between what the Bible says and who we are culturally as Christians. Vietnamese are not as "atheistic" as they have been portrayed. They worship their ancestors and are some of the most spiritual people on the face of the earth; we just disagree about who God is. Some of them sing in our choir or play instruments; some believe in God and some don't; some believe in a God different than the one we believe in. But we love them all the same.

Nikki and I had one such student come live with us. His name is Ti. Ti is a legend at NorthWood. I introduced him as our new "preacher's kid" the Sunday he came in the worship service, and he said real loud, "I pity the foo who mess with me." Ben and Jill no doubt had put him up to it. Everybody broke out in laughter. He's a nut to this day. He was here getting his degree in engineering after high school, so we have pretty well connected to him the past seven years. It was hard on all of us when he left. Someone can't stay in your home for that length of time and not be considered a part of your family.

A couple of months ago Nikki was going to Vietnam to teach health and hygiene. She was traveling alone at the time and unfortunately, once she was in the air I started getting calls from people in Vietnam telling me that the airport in Hanoi might close because they were having one of the worst floods in decades. I checked the status of the plane by calling and verified that the airport was closing. They told me that the flight would likely be diverted to Ho Chi Minh City. Not knowing where she'd end up, I called Ti, who now lives there. "Don't worry, Bob. I'll be there and pick her up." Ti then called his parents and put them on alert, just in case she landed in Hanoi.

Airport control, internet, phone systems, people placed throughout the country — I knew there were people at every spot ready to handle the situation. In the end, she was able to land in Hanoi and get to the hotel. But the entire experience was a powerful reminder to me that we live in a world of real-time connections between people, an invisible network of relationships that make global change possible in ways never before imagined.

WHAT IS THIS NEW WORLD LIKE?

If you were to ask me about my life focus, the answer would be simple: glocal transformation. To put it plainly, I want to see transformation take place locally and globally through Christians serving other people. People look at the accumulating problems in today's world, and fear grips them. In America we seem to have many reasons for fear, one piling on the other with no end in sight. Tonight as I write this, the headlines speak of the instability of the stock market, the skyrocketing price of oil, the collapse of the housing market, the war in Iraq, famines in Africa, nuclear weapons in Iran, the loss of American jobs to foreign outsourcing — the list goes on and on.

Thankfully, we do not have to fear these reports. God is in control, and we know the outcome of history. Things may be difficult, but that's often the nature of life in a fallen world. I always remember that God has placed each of us in our particular time and place for specific reasons. And he did it, not so we could cringe in terror or freeze with panic, but to be his agents of transformation in a troubled world. The difficulties of the world are not blights on our existence; they are opportunities for us to be what God intends us to be.

When we look at the magnitude of these problems and the massive size of the earth, it's easy to despair and say, "It's all too much for an ordinary person like me. There is no way I can make much of a difference in this huge world." But the reality is that through developments in technology, communication, and transportation, the world has become smaller and more accessible to the average person. For thousands of years, travel was slow, uncomfortable, expensive, and dangerous. People lived and died in their villages or cities, never venturing much more than walking distance away.

Even as recent as 150 years ago, missionaries moving to other countries recognized that because of the expenses and difficulties of overseas travel, their chances of returning home were slim. They would leave home fully prepared to be buried on foreign soil, using their coffins as packing cases. Christians wanting to change the world had few options but to be a vocational missionary, and that usually meant a one-way, no-return ticket to a foreign country.

But that's not true any longer. Today, the opportunities for travel and the reality of global communication make it possible for many people to go virtually anywhere, for any length of time. I was in one country where poor rice farmers would travel to other nations to farm rice and serve others and share the good news of Jesus! I've met maids and factory workers from other countries who with joy allowed themselves to be a part of a country's "labor market" and would share the gospel as they could. In many cases (and to our shame, with all of our money and resources), these poor followers of Jesus understand how to navigate these global systems much better than we in the West do!

THE THREE REALITIES OF ENGAGING THE WORLD

There are three realities in our global world today that actually foster and enhance our ability to make a difference and extend God's kingdom. These three concepts are not methods — we will discuss those later — but they are new ways of thinking about the world we live in, ways we must learn to embrace if we hope to be effective.

If we would change our world, we must first understand that there have been *changes in the way the world operates* and that there are significant *differences between cultures.* The following three realities are essential keys to understanding these global changes and cultural differences. To a large extent, your ability to understand and navigate these three realities will determine your effectiveness in fulfilling the call that God has given you. The three realities are decentralized connectedness, nodal networks, and post-Americanism.

Decentralized Connectedness

Not long ago I was flying somewhere and got bored with my books. So I pulled the airline magazine from the pouch in front of me and thumbed idly through its pages. I came across a two-page ad for UPS. On the left-hand page was a drawing similar to this:

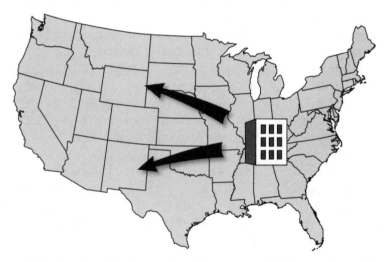

This drawing illustrates the old concept of doing business. In the past when transportation modes were limited, most businesses thought of their market as the U.S. only. It occurred to me as I looked at this page that many people live their lives under the influence of this kind of limited thinking. Just like those people of the past who knew no world beyond their own villages, many Americans today see life in terms of their own nation only and are generally disconnected from the world at large. People outside the U.S. sometimes describe people in the United States as isolationist. Perhaps it's because we are boxed in on every side by two huge oceans and two countries with roughly similar religious and moral beliefs.

I then looked at the right-hand page of the UPS ad and saw a drawing similar to this:

This drawing illustrates America's concept of doing business today. In the post – World War II economic boom, U.S. businesses connected nationally like never before. Then during and after the Vietnam War these businesses began to connect globally. And when these connections began to stimulate the global economy, other nations got the picture and began to participate in international trade. But the U.S. remained the central hub of the global economy. This picture accurately depicts how most Americans view globalization.

But something still bothered me about this picture. It didn't seem quite right. Then it hit me. This is not true globalization; it is essentially just an expanded nationalism. As long as the hub remains in one dominant country, that country is effectively in control, and global prosperity is dependent on that economic center. True globalization would mean equal participation and instigation from points all over the globe. What would that kind of globalization look like?

I went to the back of the magazine where I found a map of the world showing the flight paths of the airline routes. I took out my pencil and began to connect the cities all over the world. The result looked more like a grid or net, like this:

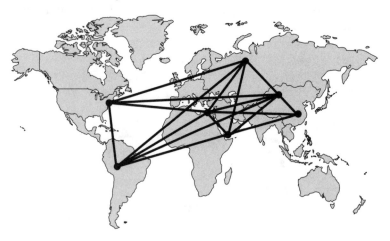

Here I had a picture of true globalization — a grid with everything connected to everything else. There is no center; its form is a net spread out with all points connected to all other points. A spiderweb has a center, and if you follow any strand from the outside you'll arrive at the spider at the central point. A net has no center. Think of a tennis net or a fishing net: it has many strands, all connecting to many others, but none originates in a center or leads to a center. This is how the world is becoming connected today. No arrows — just many lines connecting at many points.

This means that we no longer live in a top-down world, but a bottom-up, side-by-side, in-and-out world. The world is becoming a decentralized and interconnected grid in which everything is attached to everything else.

I was speaking at a meeting of U.S. pastors, trying to explain globalization and how we should organize and relate to the rest of the world. I sensed that they were not getting the picture, so I pulled out my drawings. The Canadian in the room immediately got it. "This is it, Bob," he said, enthusiasm bubbling in his voice. "I've heard you speak many times, and nothing you've ever said communicates it better than this picture." Maybe a picture really is worth a thousand words. For this man, the picture helped him to grasp the concept, and it was as if a light had been turned on for him. It enabled him to realize the possibility of a different world order. The Americans, by contrast, looked at the picture and thought, "Hmmm ... that's interesting." The lights didn't go on for many of them. Why? Because they were still immersed in an American-centered view of the world.

The response to this drawing has been much more positive with pastors and Christians outside the U.S. In the spring of 2008 I was in Kenya, meeting with a small but influential and strategic group of men from all over the world. We were studying how we could work together to engage the world globally. For a while our conversation was all over the board, with various ideas bouncing in all directions without focus. I decided it was time to pull out the drawing. It had an immediate and profound impact, giving us a focal point of common understanding. A few days later I met in a room with another group of global pastors, and as we spoke about globalization I pulled out the drawing again. It had the same impact.

In both cases, we were wrestling with a persistent dilemma: If God is saying the same thing to several pastors all over the globe, how do we follow his leading and put the concept to work? How do we connect and engage the worldwide church to carry out the Great Commission? Enthusiasm in the group was high; our commitment to the Lord was unquestioned. But we lacked a format, a template, a grid on which to base a plan of action. The drawing on the airline map provided the grid for us. It made a new concept of connectivity clear to all of us, and our thinking took flight from there. I call this concept *decentralized connectedness*.

When you have centralized connectedness, as in the UPS hub plan of global shipping, you are dependent on the hub for everything. When applied to global evangelism, this limits creativity, allows little organic flexibility, and makes little room for interchange of ideas.

Everything flows from the hub, and those on the receiving end are passive participants.

But with decentralized connectedness, you get the best of all worlds. Each connection in the net is a point of origin. Each area in the grid is capable of generating its own ideas and responses. Each is capable of contributing to the whole on its own initiative. When things connect and converge in a net instead of a web, each area has the potential of improving other areas, just as the convergence of technology and biology results in the creative area of biotechnology.

Jesus called his disciples to be fishers of men. The net of decentralized connectedness has the potential for catching more fish than we ever dreamed of. As American Christians, we need to recognize that the Great Commission will be fulfilled, not simply by "us" going and doing it all alone, but by "us" connecting with what God is already doing around the world. There needs to be a natural flow back and forth, us to them and them to us! Perhaps the greatest hope of the church in the West today is the church in the East. Who knows? Maybe we are on the edge of experiencing a reversal of flow in the direction of missions. Personally, I think it would be hilarious and marvelous if God chose to work in that way.

Nodal Networks

In the Gospels, Jesus tells us that the kingdom of God is like a net. So how does a net work? As I mentioned in an earlier chapter, Omar Reyes is the pastor for glocal impact at NorthWood Church. He's in charge of everything we do that is related to engaging the society and community, locally and globally. Omar is part Palestinian, Mayan, Spanish, Brazilian, American, and God knows what else he hasn't told us. So coming at things from a highly global perspective is in his genes (literally). Omar made a discovery recently that added a necessary dimension to my grid. He pointed out that what makes the grid work are the knots that tie the net together. I'd like to suggest that those knots represent cities all over the world, cities that contain believers and churches. The key to engaging the world is recognizing the importance of the knots.

As Omar and I were studying this concept, we discovered that there is something of a connection between the word *knot* and the word *node*. He went to Wikipedia, a highly connected online encyclopedia, and pulled off the following article:

> A NODE (Latin *nodus*, "knot") is a critical element of any computer network. It can be defined as a point in a network at which lines intersect or branch, a device attached to a network, or a terminal or other point in a computer network where messages can be transmitted, received or forwarded. A node can be any device connected to a computer network. Nodes can be computers, personal digital assistants (PDAs), cell phones, switches, routers or various other networked devices.
>
> Role of nodes in networking: A node is a connection point, either a redistribution point or an end point, for data transmission. In general, a node has programmed or engineered capability to recognize and process or forward transmissions to other nodes.[8]

What's the implication? In addition to recognizing the role of cities on a global scale, each one of us is also a "knot" in a net. Our lives, as individuals, exist at a point where multiple lines of relationship and influence intersect, lines that connect with hundreds of other nodes, or knots, each of which connects with hundreds of others. As nodes, each of us, in this sense, is a redistribution point capable of delivering to other distribution points. This network of relational nodes is vastly different from the method of the past, which was to store and distribute from a centralized point. This kind of centralization, where a single distribution center would serve vast numbers of receiving points, was limited in many ways. The sheer volume served by the single centralized authority forced it to be selective as to who received what.

For most of history, the centralized model has been the method used by the church, as we have connected to the world through centralized denominations and religious infrastructures. But the future of the church will be found in nodal connections between individual followers of Christ. Instead of the Great Commission being dependent on centralized authority, such as a pastor or vocational missionary, it will be released into the hands of committed individuals connecting naturally to other committed individuals and transmitting works of service and the gospel through a myriad of nodes. This method is already resulting in true globalization.

This is how pastors and churches were originally intended to function. As we saw earlier in chapter 1, there were several unidentified individuals in Acts 11 who struck out on their own and planted the good news in Antioch. Later, Barnabas was sent from Jerusalem to Antioch, and after he saw the potential there, he went to fetch Paul to help him, apparently on his own initiative. He didn't run it by anyone or check with the Jerusalem elders. What we see are simply two nodes working in the net, independent of central authority (Acts 11:22–26).

Barnabas's example illustrates that nodal networks require great openness and creativity. In the past, people related to centralized authority in command-and-control–like structures. In fact, it's important to recognize that Barnabas himself was sent out by the central authority of the Jerusalem church. Nodal networks are not intended to entirely replace central authority. But they have the potential to accomplish what centralized authority cannot. Barnabas remained open, on his mission, to whatever opportunities he encountered and was able to exercise his own initiative.

So don't misunderstand me. I'm not saying that we should eliminate all forms of centralized authority and remove the key organization centers from the net. Indeed, there will always be centralized authorities, and there should be. But they will not be like the rigid, highly structured and authoritative organizations of the past. Jesus taught his disciples that they should not lord their authority over others, but rather be eager to serve them (see Matthew 20:25–26). In the kingdom of God, everybody gets to play a role. When everyone finds their place at the table, the party can finally get started! Together, united in Christ, we can do more than we could ever do alone.

In their groundbreaking book *Wikinomics*, Don Tapscott and Anthony Williams have written: "Twenty years from now we will look back at this period of the early twenty-first century as a critical turning point in economic and social history. We will understand that we entered a new age, one based on new principles, worldviews, and business models where the nature of the game was changed." The authors go on to say, "The new art of wikinomics is based on four powerful new ideas: openness, peering, sharing, and acting globally." They list the basic characteristics of wikinomics as:

Openness — candor, transparency, freedom, flexibility, expansiveness, engagement, and access.

Peering — new models of organizing based more on horizontal leadership than hierarchal.

Sharing — collaboration and customer driven innovation.

Acting globally — it's not enough to think globally; in today's world one must act globally as well.[9]

We see increased evidence of the wikinomic model on websites today. There is still plenty of the old model — websites that are essentially brochures designed like static advertisements in printed media. They may have stepped up to a new platform, but they still use an old form of communication. But we see other websites that are alive, active, and serving as a nodal point in community. When our church discovered this principle, we began to put interactive features on our website. These included daily Bible readings, blogging, forums, downloads of resources, and so on. Immediately our hits increased dramatically. We had instituted the nodal principle. These interactive devices on our website were little knots in the net that connected outsiders to our ministry.

Tapscott and Williams identify three keys to surviving and embracing open-source culture and strategy:

First, play to your weaknesses. Look for where you have blundered and how collaboration can help you. Second, take a balanced approach. Can you do it alone, or what would happen if you joined existing movements? Third, adapt to community norms and clock speeds. Do not try to lead until you have built credibility in the community. And do not criticize ...

Critiquing the community is a right reserved for those who have proved themselves by making valuable contributions. Finally ... perceived risk can be higher than it really is.[10]

To be nodal is to be *organic* — not centralized or categorized in the Greek fashion, but flowing, adaptable, and holistic. This means returning to an understanding of the church as a "grass roots" movement. Each one of us has the ability to do something truly significant with what God has given us if we will just step out and do it. The nodal mode gives us the grid on which that can happen. Anyone, at any knot in the net, can impact everything else in the net. What's more, anyone with a creative idea can become his or her own network center to share with others whatever interest, skills, or assistance God has given. That's what we mean by organic. You can either join someone else's net or you can create your own. Nodes can be started or activated by other nodes.

So what would it be like to be a part of a church like this? That's the vision we are trying to pursue at NorthWood. We may not always be successful, but one thing is sure, we're not going to win the world for Christ alone. It's only when we come together and work together with other ministries and churches, holding each another accountable to the mission that Jesus gave us, that we can really get traction.

Post-Americanism

Newsweek editor Fareed Zakaria recently wrote a book titled *The Post-American World*. It's an incredible book. I love the title, and I think the term is descriptive of today's global reality. I'll be honest with you — I get a little irritated when I hear people in the West talk about the "postmodern world." If they are living in the "postmodern" world, then their definition of world is small. It may be proper to call certain parts of the Western world "postmodern," but it's simply a mistake to use that term when referring to the entire world.

Most of the people who talk about postmodernism as a global reality are U.S. citizens who have traveled to Europe or visited Buenos Aires or dropped into a coffee shop in Jakarta. They've gotten the tourist's view of the world, and that view looks highly Americanized. But that's not the real picture you see when you peer behind the tourist façade. Before the world can be postmodern, many parts of the globe need to make the transition to the modern world! The truth is, most of the world is premodern, longing to be modern. Postmodernism is the philosophical construct of an affluent, disillusioned society. To be postmodern you've got to have it all and then come to the realization that "all ain't where it's at."

Even though the term "postmodern" doesn't really apply to the new, global reality we live in, I do think Zakaria is right in labeling the world "post-American." For a while, especially after World War II, American influence grew to where it became the driving force in the world, both economically and culturally. Those arrows really did fan out from the U.S. like the strands of a spiderweb. It's still not clear exactly what the driving force of the world is today, but most people agree that it's not what it once was. At this point in history, the beginning of the twenty-first century, America is the only true superpower. And while America may retain that status for the next few decades, being a superpower does not mean that American leadership will go unchallenged or that the United States is the lone defender of Western civilization. The days are over when a single superpower can rule uncontested and force its will on the rest of the world.

Zakaria has written not just about the fall of the West, but about the rise of the rest and what it will mean in the future.

> The tallest building in the world is now in Taipei ... soon to be overtaken by the one being built in Dubai. The world's richest man is Mexican, and its largest publicly traded corporation is Chinese. The world's biggest plane is built in Russia and Ukraine, and its leading refinery is under construction in India, and its largest factories are all in China. By many measures, London is becoming the leading financial center, and the U.A.E. is home to the most richly endowed investment fund ... The number one casino is not in Las Vegas but in Macao ... The biggest movie industry ... is Bollywood, not Hollywood ... Of the top ten malls in the world, only one is in the United States, the world's biggest is in Beijing.[11]

You can see the power and the initiative shifting from America to points all over the globe. This also means a shift in global attitudes toward America. We cannot deny the anti-Western mood we see in the world today. Just because other cultures like some of our clothes, some of our music, and some of our stuff doesn't mean they necessarily like us or want to be like us. When travelers from the U.S. get off planes around the world and see an abundance of McDonald's restaurants, Coca-Cola, or Wi-Fi areas, they think American culture has prevailed. But I believe this is a mistake. Yes, America has influenced the world and impacted its cultures, but American culture has not even begun to replace cultures that existed hundreds and thousands of years before McDonald ever made his first burger.

We have had dozens of kids from Hanoi come and live in our community here in Texas. They dress like American kids, listen to American music, and some even have iPods and Play Stations. Yet there are some deep cultural differences. These aren't American kids. They have a sense of pride that Vietnam is an emerging economy gaining in global influence. I won't deny that people from all over the world want to live in America. But in many cases these immigrants, once they arrive, are not mainstreaming into the culture. Instead, they are creating enclaves of their own culture within the broader culture, much like the Irish and Italians did when they first immigrated to America. The cultures arriving today, however, are not Western or European, and they are not primarily Christian. This means the church in America, with a Western European history, will have to work harder at understanding the differences and reaching out to their neighbors.

The center of Protestant Christianity is also shifting. We know that there are far more Christians in the global South and East than there are in America, and on the whole these foreign churches exhibit a zeal and fervor largely unknown here. Yet in many places in America, we still act as if all roads lead to Colorado Springs.[12] This simply is not the case. Increasingly, the global church is pushing back when the Western church shows up with her well-oiled missionary machine churning out theological formulas to save the rest of the world. They sense that Americans now need saving more than they do. Some Eastern churches are now even sending missionaries to America!

Unless we recognize and come to terms with these global shifts, we are deluding ourselves about reality, and our attempts at fulfilling the Great Commission will remain ineffective. Things have changed, even within the last twenty years. Here is how Zakaria describes it:

> U.S. Secretary of State James Baker suggested in 1991 that the world was moving toward a hub-and-spoke system, with every country going through the United States to get to its destination. The twenty-first century world might be better described as one of point-to-point routes, with new flight patterns being mapped every day. Today, they bypass the U.S. and go direct to one another.[13]

Do you see how the nodal system is replacing the centralized spiderweb in international relations? It's not even true to say that other countries are necessarily rebelling against America's dominance. More and more of these shifts are being driven by changes in modern communication and transportation, shifts that allow countries that were dependent on the United States to bypass the hub and disentangle from the American web. As Zakaria puts it, "The world is moving from anger to indifference, from anti-Americanism to post-Americanism."[14] The world is globalizing but not necessarily Westernizing. The world may speak English like Americans, but it doesn't necessarily want to do things the American way.

As Americans, we have enormous oceans on each side of our continent, which tend to isolate us from the rest of the world and hamper our ability to understand other cultures. Truth be told, we have enough trouble even understanding Mexico, our southern neighbor. Our strained relationship with Mexico is not just about securing the border. Rather, it's about a larger problem: a failure to understand the people outside our own world. We are simply out of touch with the world that is changing around us. As a Texan involved in significant relationships with government leaders all over the world, I cringe when I watch the news and see how we respond to illegal aliens and Mexico. Again, Zakaria expresses the situation eloquently: "The

United States succeeded in its great historic mission — it globalized the world. But along the way it forgot to globalize itself."[15]

One example of how the world is changing from an American web to a decentralized net is the practice of outsourcing. American manufacturers have found that they can get many goods and services and much labor from sources outside the U.S. Outsourcing means the direction of many of the arrows have reversed. Instead of America being the supplier to the world, many countries are becoming suppliers to America. Outsourcing is occurring at the nodal level. Individual businessmen are setting up their own networks of worldwide suppliers. It's not anything the government can control, so it's not something any presidential candidate can promise to fix.

Is there anything we can do? One thing is certain: we can no longer bend the world to our will. That day is over. From my perspective, either we can whine and pout about these changing realities or we can innovate. The winners in the new world order will be those who understand the global environment and are able to effectively communicate within it.

On a recent trip to Africa, I came across an example that illustrates the influence of the global network. I had read in Zakaria's book about how China wants the kind of stability that leads to peace and prosperity. Their campaign to accomplish this has led to many slogans to inspire the Chinese people. One of these is "Peace and Prosperity." India wants the same kind of stability, and it has also bought into the use of motivating slogans. I was driving through Africa's Rift Valley in June 2008 when I saw a campaign poster featuring a picture of Kenya's incumbent president, Mwai Kibaki. What was the motto printed beneath his picture? Peace and Prosperity! If that seemed suspiciously Chinese, it's because it was. In a nodal network word gets around, and America is no longer the primary source.

WHAT DOES ALL THIS MEAN TO YOU?

With the decentralization of global networking, the world has never been more connected than it is today. With these connections come more ways of accomplishing goals than we've ever had before.

If your church gets this new reality, thank God and rock and roll! Sadly, I meet people all the time who are waiting hopelessly for their churches to get it. Stop waiting. Get up and get busy — do something. In light of these new realities, it is no longer necessary to find the hub of activity, qualify yourself to the central authority, and move out from there. In today's world you, as a disciple of Jesus Christ, are the hub, wherever you are! You don't necessarily need to convince a church to see the light and send you out. As a follower of Christ, *you* are the church, and when God calls, you have a responsibility to listen, follow, and obey.

When Paul said, "You are the temple of God," he was making a nodal statement (1 Corinthians 3:16; cf. 6:19). Each of us has Christ alive in us, and it's up to each of us to respond to the prodding of the Spirit to get up and answer God's call. But this does *not* mean you have to go it alone. When God moves, others will sense the call, and you will find opportunities to connect as you respond in faith. Find others who share the vision. Connect to others in the net. Don't wait to answer God's call — step out today!

Connection Steps

- ⊙ Create a people map of your own social network. Involve your family, friends, work associates, and peers.

- ⊙ Build your own global map from where you are to where you touch the world from the clothes you wear, to products you buy, to services you experience overseas, whatever ...

- ⊙ Describe your perceptions of how people saw Americans twenty years ago and how they see them today. What is the difference and why? How does this help or hinder global engagement?

Living as a Disciple

About three weeks after the tsunami in Indonesia in December 2004, some of my Indonesian friends asked me to come over and help. So I went. There I met for the first time Eddie Leo from Abba Love Church in Jakarta. His church of almost 30,000 members was already engaged in serving the Indonesians in this disaster. When he told me the story of his church and ministry, I was highly impressed. His membership had exploded, and his people were engaged in ministry all over the world.

So I asked Eddie the natural question: What was his philosophy and model of ministry? I was interested in ministry models because I had just finished the manuscript for my book *Transformation*, which focused on how to make disciples. The book explained the discipleship model we use at NorthWood, which we call T-Life. It is essentially a Hebraic approach. Western civilization has been built largely on Greek philosophy, which tends to be analytical, dividing and subdividing subjects into classifications and categories for study. The Hebraic model is more holistic and integrated. It depends less on abstract study and more on hands-on, interactive experience. We learn how to live right by doing life together.

Our model consists of three integrated components. The first is an "interactive relationship" with God, which consists of personal and corporate worship. This is critical because it enables us to learn to hear God's voice in a regular daily way, seeing God in even the small moments as opposed to seeking God's will just when there is a big decision or a crisis. The second is "transparent connections," which consists of our small group ministry that leads to accountability and community. In our teams we pray, study God's Word, and serve together. The third is what we call "glocal[16] impact," where we use our jobs as the platform from which we serve together in our community and the world. That T-Life model also underlies this book.

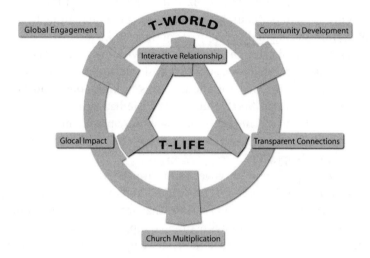

All three elements must be present and operative for a disciple to emerge. If you have only one or two, or if you try to implement them sequentially instead of simultaneously, you will not get a transformative disciple. And unless you have transformative disciples, they cannot be ambassadors of reconciliation.

Our church members and our staff had worked together to develop this model from our own experience. I thought it was new and unique, and therefore I was not prepared for Eddie Leo's answer to my question about how he and his church did ministry. He outlined a model that — apart from the terminology — was exactly like ours!

How was that possible? My book hadn't even been published yet! I quickly realized that God had given him a similar vision for ministry. A few months later Eddie and I were together talking with a pastor from Central Asia about our models for discipleship. As it turned out, the Asian pastor also shared a similar model for discipleship in his church. As if my head were not already spinning, one of our interns brought me a book by Alan Hirsch called *The Shaping of Things to Come*, which contains a chapter describing discipleship in the same way, even using some of the same geometric diagrams I had used in my book. I quickly realized that this was bigger than me; it was bigger than our church. God was saying the same thing to each of us, ministering in different parts of the world.

Later I was sharing these experiences with my friend Dave Bellis, who has directed publications for Josh McDowell for over thirty years. He told me that the model I was talking about had been described by Justin Martyr in AD 120. He had called it "believe, belong, and behave." In reality, our "new" discipleship model wasn't really all that new. We had simply rediscovered an ancient, biblical model for discipleship.

Many of the "new" discoveries in ministry that we have made have been like this. As I travel the world, I find that God is reminding his church of certain spiritual realities that need to be present for him to work. New understandings of discipleship, a renewed understanding of the kingdom of God, and greater emphasis on personal brokenness, prayer, involvement in society, and reconciliation are just a few of the things we have seen rediscovered in places where God is at work. I am convinced that God is preparing us all for the next great movement of his Spirit, a movement that will have global impact.

When the Great Awakenings came to the American continent in the eighteenth and nineteenth centuries, the people shared a common language and the gospel spread like wildfire. Today, though we may speak different languages, God is doing a new work. Our common language is now the internet, and it seems that this time God is setting the stage not merely for a continental awakening, but for a global revival.

Sometimes it seems that the pastors and religious leaders are the last to catch on. Recently, I had lunch with a young man in the marketing business who was excited about Jesus and had come to understand the true nature of discipleship. He was eager to engage in serious, sacrificial ministry anywhere in the world, but he was disillusioned with his church. He candidly admitted that his church was not central to what God was doing in his life. He understood the necessity of belonging to a local church, but didn't feel as if his involvement in the church was really making much of a difference in the world.

As we spoke, I encouraged this young man to rethink the way he thought about the church. "If you're a part of the body of Christ," I told him, "*you are the church.*" Local churches should be focused on ministry, but if they are not, the individual must still follow Christ in obedience. In the past, religious institutions could regulate what, where, when, and even how their members were to engage in ministry. But today, an individual can find many ways to function in transforming ministry, even if his or her church offers no help or encouragement. You'll learn about some of the ways you can get involved in this book.

Engaging every disciple in ministry — pastors, ministry professionals, and laypeople — is important because I believe it will prepare us for the next big movement of God. We are facing a new world, a world that is ripe for transformation. Not since the discipleship explosion in the book of Acts have ordinary believers had the opportunity to engage the world as we can today. Recently I spoke to an investment banker who was captured by this vision at age sixty-five, and now he's involved in starting churches all over the world. There are thousands of stories just like his.

So what does this vision mean for us, practically? The apostle Paul summarized our task by calling us Christ's ambassadors.

But all things are of God, who reconciled us to himself through Jesus Christ, and gave to us the ministry of reconciliation; namely, that God was in Christ reconciling the world to himself, not reckoning to them their trespasses, and having committed to us the word of reconciliation. We are therefore ambassadors on behalf of Christ, as though God were entreating by us: we beg you on behalf of Christ, be reconciled to God. For him who knew no sin he made to be sin on our behalf; so that in him we might become the righteousness of God. (2 Corinthians 5:18 – 20)

In this chapter I will show you what it means to be an ambassador of reconciliation and describe the kind of person needed to take this commission to the world. The answer may surprise you! Let me begin by telling you the story of Andy.

ANDY'S STORY

Andy came into my office, a man at the end of his rope. I've seen hundreds of people like him. He sat across the desk from me, looking down at his feet in dejection. "I know my marriage is over," he said, "and it's the hardest thing I've ever faced." I knew what was coming next. I'd heard it hundreds of times — some kind of bargain with God. If God would give him back his wife, he would give his life to God forever. I wanted to be sympathetic with Andy, but I was ready to do what I always do — try to get him to the point where he will follow God even if things don't work out the way he wants. When a person bargains with God, his underlying motive is not really God but his need.

But I was wrong about Andy. The next words out of his mouth were, "But I'm ready to follow Jesus anyway. No bargains, no promises. I'm coming as I am, warts and all, and if he'll have me, I'm ready."

"Of course he'll have you, Andy," I replied. "God is ready and willing to accept you if you'll just accept him."

Andy's story is actually remarkable. His father died when Andy was ten, and at fourteen Andy got out on his own because, as he put it, "I didn't like the man my mom was going to marry." He stayed in the house where he grew up, while his mom moved into her new husband's house three blocks away. He attended school during the day and stocked shelves for Safeway at night. He bought his first car at age fifteen, getting a hardship license in order to drive it.

Andy quit Safeway when he found he could make better money roofing houses, and before he turned seventeen he had his own roofing company. The following year he married a fifteen-year-old girl (and no, she wasn't pregnant). It lasted two and a half years — not too bad by today's standards — but it ended like a steamy episode on *Days of Our Lives.*

Andy isn't a dummy; he graduated sixth in his class of 450 at a Dallas metroplex high school and scored an incredible ninety-eight on a civil service exam. He immediately enrolled in the Mike Monroony Aeronautical Center in Oklahoma City and graduated first in his class at age eighteen — the youngest ever to go through the school. He immediately became an air traffic controller at a large airport in Louisiana, but in 1981 he was fired along with 12,500 other controllers for going on strike.

After trying several odd jobs Andy was back in Texas working as a bartender in Arlington. He married again and went from bartending to managing nightclubs. His all-night hours were not conducive to married life, so he took a PACT test at the police department of North Richland Hills, a Fort Worth suburb. He aced the test, and after Police Academy served twenty years as a policeman, both as an undercover narcotics and vice officer and on the SWAT team. After ten years on the police force he began to build houses on the side to supplement his retirement nest egg. Along the way he fathered a daughter, Ashley.

One day, Andy's wife asked him to meet her at a local Mexican restaurant. After two margaritas she took a napkin, drew a line down the middle, and on one side wrote "mine" and on the other "yours." "I want a divorce," she said as she began to list on her side of the napkin all the stuff she wanted from the settlement. She put Ashley on Andy's side.

Andy was stunned. As far as he had known everything was wonderful between them. But his wife gave her reasons — the marriage and their daughter, Ashley, were hampering her career goals. At Andy's pleading she agreed to go to counseling, but it was ineffective. After numerous attempts at making things work, Andy gave her an ultimatum: "You can have the divorce, but you're going to be the one to tell Ashley."

His wife went home, sat Ashley on the kitchen counter, and told her she was leaving. Ashley burst into tears and promised to be a better girl if her mother would stay. But his wife had made up her mind. She left, and for seven nights in a row the devastated little girl cried herself to sleep.

That was Andy's life before he came into my office that day. His wife had left him alone with a seven-year-old daughter to raise, and now he wanted to follow God.

What initially brought Andy to God was his daughter. "We didn't go to church," he told me. "My daughter had never been inside a church. But for some reason on the seventh night of crying herself to sleep after learning of the divorce, she looked up at me with tears streaming from her reddened eyes and said, 'Daddy, can we go to church?' That's when I reached brokenness," Andy said. He called a friend who was a member at NorthWood and asked, "Can I go to church with you?" He came to church the following Sunday and was warmly welcomed. That afternoon he met me in my office and came back to God.

From that day on Andy brought Ashley to church regularly. He quickly became involved in the kids ministry and in worship. Eventually, I invited him to accompany me on a trip to Vietnam. On that first trip Andy saw that he could serve and help people with skills he had learned. Andy couldn't use his police background or his FAA background in Vietnam, but he put his construction and home-building background to good use in building showers. Soon he was bringing teams of plumbers to Vietnam to set up water purification systems. As a result of his hard work and service to the Vietnamese, Andy became one of the chief promoters of our work in Vietnam. That was eighteen trips ago. Andy now regularly leads groups to Vietnam to minister to the needs of people.

When Andy found that he needed some additional funding for the work in Vietnam, he contacted John Barfield, a Dallas/Fort Worth builder who had been his primary client when he had been in the construction business. John is a craggy, cantankerous old Texan, but he has a big heart to help others. But instead of jumping on board with Andy's projects in Vietnam, John shared with Andy the story of Tracy Goens, a medical doctor who worked with the Fulani people in Nigeria. The Fulanis respected Goens so highly that they had made him a king.

It just so happened that Tracy Goens had recently made a moving presentation on the Nigerian mission to John's church. John was so impressed with Goens's work that he turned the tables on Andy and asked if NorthWood would consider helping with the work in Nigeria. Since NorthWood's policy is to stay focused on one location to deepen our impact, Andy declined the invitation. But John Barfield is not the type of man to take no for an answer, so he pressed Andy into arranging a meeting with me.

When Andy and I met John for lunch, he put on the full-court press and challenged us to at least consider making a visit to Nigeria with Tracy Goens. He even offered to pay all of our travel expenses. With a deal like that, how could we refuse? What followed was one of the wildest trips of my life. We saw the work that was being done in Nigeria, and it was similar to much of what we have been doing in Vietnam. The ministry there has built orphanages and schools and set up water systems. They also operate a hospital and are currently looking at a potential project that involves cattle ranching — a natural fit for us Texans!

Why am I sharing the details of this story with you? Do you recognize the nodal system at work here? We didn't have a grand plan to develop ministry partnerships in Nigeria. There was nothing centralized about the way our ministry in Nigeria came about. Our church did not take over the Nigerian project or begin directing it. It all started with Andy, an ordinary disciple of Jesus, who saw the need and responded. Without any help from our church, Andy carried the vision forward, securing help from other churches for the project.

I asked Andy why he does all of this. He said to me, "It's because God calls us to every tribe, tongue, and nation. When I was married to my ex, we wanted to travel the world as tourists. Now I'm doing exactly what I wanted to do, but I'm doing it serving God."

As we talked, Andy paused a moment to reflect on his past and how God had miraculously transformed his life. "You know, God never gives up on you, and he's always there for you. So many times you have to reach the point of brokenness before he can put you back together."

THE POWER OF THE DISCIPLE

Andy's story is typical of those who get involved in glocal ministry. God doesn't just rely on preachers and pastors to bring change to this world; he uses people in every domain of society, with the skills and the conviction needed to advance the Great Commission. The disciple is the key component in the nodal network. Disciples are the nodes, the knots in the net where things happen — where connections are made to other nodes.

The disciple is the carrier of the virus, the connector on the grid of society created by the nations. I have mentioned before that lay disciples have two advantages over pastors and religious professionals. First, they can get into many foreign countries that traditional religious workers can't. Second, they bring varied professional and vocational skills that are useful in all societies. When we focus on discipleship as a model for ministry, we are getting everyone on the field playing the game, not just the coach.

But aren't our churches already full of disciples? Isn't every Christian a disciple, in some sense? If this is what discipleship is supposed to look like, then maybe what we really need is a *different kind* of disciple. Part of the problem is that pastors, church leaders, and denominational workers in the West are largely focused on reinventing the church because it has lost its impact on society. Frankly, I think this is a waste of time. Theologically, it's inaccurate to talk about reinventing the church. Historically, it has not been proven to work. Practically, we see little sign of success. In spite of all the innovative programs we've developed to reach society, the church in America is losing its influence.

We need to remember that the kingdom of God expands, not by institutions, programs, or new and improved churches, but by something much simpler and organic: the activity of committed disciples. If we want a different church, we need to change the way we make disciples. Focusing on church growth is *not* the answer. The focus needs to be on the growth of our people in true discipleship. The health of a church is largely determined by the growth of people as disciples of Christ. Disciples set the DNA of a church, forming the core of its identity and shaping the way the church grows and reproduces.

I frequently hear from denominational leaders that the key to denominational revitalization is found in planting more churches. I believe this is a myth. In the end, any apparent success will be short-lived. Denominations would have a far better chance of survival if they looked outside their walls to the hurting in their communities and served those people in love. A brochure and a big service may attract a crowd — but if that's all there is, it won't last. There has to be something more.

The two questions every church needs to ask today are: "How are we producing disciples?" and "What kind of disciples are we producing?" Most of the disciples produced in churches today are nicer, even more moral and biblically educated than their neighbors. But they are not necessarily living a transformed life, and seldom do their lives bring real transformation to the community. The problem is actually easy to recognize: *disciples cannot pass on what they do not have.* If you look at the disciples in the book of Acts, you'll see that in addition to being moral, biblically educated, and prayerful they were transformational. They didn't just grow in morality and education; their lives made an impact on those around them.

WHAT IS A DISCIPLE?

He said to all, "If anyone desires to come after me, let him deny himself, take up his cross, and follow me. For whoever desires to save his life will lose it, but whoever will lose his life for my sake, the same will save it. For what does it profit a man if he gains the whole world, and loses or forfeits his own self? For whoever will be ashamed of me and of my words, of him will the Son of Man be ashamed, when he comes in his glory, and the glory of the Father, and of the holy angels. (Luke 9:23 – 26)

Recently I read the book of Luke and Acts twice over a three-day period. How is it, I wondered, that they were able to produce so many disciples in such an incredibly short period of time? How were they able to "turn the world upside down"? I think there are at least two reasons. First, consider what was being asked of them. When Jesus called people to follow him, it was a decision that required complete commitment. It was a call to abandonment: a disciple must "deny himself, take up his cross," and be ready to lose his life!

In most churches today, we do the exact opposite. We try to ease people into the church. We encourage them to "try God." But that's not what Jesus did. His call was hard to follow. It demanded something of his followers. In the passage I just cited, Jesus says that you have to be willing to die to follow him. This was a serious decision that could literally cost you your life.

Second, however, I think there was a different understanding of what it meant to be a disciple. In our churches today, we try to gather a few people together, pour our lives into them with lots of teaching and study and conversation, and then repeat the process again and again. In sixteen years or so we figure we'll have enough people to win the world for Christ. But it hasn't happened that way. Underlying all of this is a belief that if we just educate, teach, and encourage people to be good and moral, such people will naturally grow.

While Jesus did teach and talk with his disciples, there wasn't a set curriculum to follow. The earliest disciples didn't have seminaries where they went to study. They lacked many of the study resources that we have today. People learned whatever they could from other disciples who were living the life that Jesus had taught them to live. When issues and questions arose, Paul and other leaders in the church addressed them in the books and letters they wrote. But the growth of the kingdom of God was not dependent on education programs or attaining a certain level of theological knowledge. The only real barrier to kingdom growth was a lack of obedience.

In the Scripture passage cited earlier in this chapter, the apostle Paul describes a disciple as an ambassador for God. This is a helpful way to think of discipleship, particularly in today's global context. *Ambassador* is a governmental term. An ambassador travels to a foreign country to represent the interests of his own nation to another nation. Ambassadors don't speak their own message or set their own agendas. They can make recommendations and relate information relative to their government's policies, but the ultimate authority and decision-making power resides with the president, king, or leader they represent.

The term *ambassador* fits disciples of Jesus perfectly. As his disciples, we are sent out to serve on behalf of the King. As his ambassadors, we engage the world by engaging nations within the world, societies within nations, and domains within societies.

How is this done? Ambassadorship is not accomplished king to king, but through the subjects of the king, person to person. As Christ's ambassadors, disciples are the viral agents of engagement that bring the gospel down to every single individual. Disciples are the ones designated to bring Christ's reconciliation to people and structures. This is what we mean by *face-to-face diplomacy*. It involves personal relationships between individuals.

As the world changes, so does our understanding of diplomacy. President Dwight Eisenhower introduced into government the concept of people-to-people diplomacy. His contention was that if people of nations knew one another and their cultures better, it would promote understanding between countries and allow problems to be discussed before they got out of control. It was diplomacy based on relationships, or what some call *relational diplomacy*. This is the concept that Jesus, our King, has given us for engaging the world. As his ambassadors, he wants us to engage others relationally. This means person-to-person engagement, or relational diplomacy applied at ground level.

Ambassadors, of course, must know their king or president, his policies, his intentions, his aims, and his will. This means one must have certain qualifications and training to become an ambassador. At NorthWood we learned a long time ago that we cannot judge the effectiveness of a disciple by how many verses he has memorized or how often she has attended church or taught Bible school. There has to be a new standard for discipleship. A disciple should be living in line with God's Word. A disciple should care deeply about people and have a deep desire to minister to them. This means he or she should be deeply engaged in transformative ministry glocally. It's a question of producing fruit. Knowledge is important, but knowledge is only the seed. Once it is planted, it should bear fruit.

The responsibility of the ambassador disciple is to fulfill the Great Commission of the King, Jesus Christ, which means bringing about reconciliation of people of all nations to him. When a disciple is fruitful in fulfilling this responsibility, we should see people accepting Christ as their Savior. Their efforts should be leading to reconciliation within the community and exemplifying a consistent lifestyle of servanthood. If disciples are created through disciples sharing Christ's message of reconciliation, person to person, this process raises a question that you need to think about: Who discipled you? Many of us who follow Christ have never actually been discipled by another person. Does our lack of personal discipleship disqualify us from being disciples? I don't think so.

You see, person-to-person discipling is the ideal. It's the primary way Christ set things up and the most effective. But discipleship can occur in many different contexts using various methods. Many of us end up learning a little bit at a time from a variety of different sources — various people in our lives, books, and sermons. At some point, in our process of learning, we feel a conviction, make a decision to follow Christ, and are brought into God's kingdom. Many people come to know Christ in this way and become his disciples.

CHARACTERISTICS OF A DISCIPLE

The kind of disciples I'm talking about — transformational disciples — will have certain unique traits in common that set them apart from other people. As I have noted, disciples may be moral, churchgoing people, but they will also have characteristics that go beyond a surface-level, cultural Christianity. Let's look at seven of the most prominent characteristics of an authentic, transformational disciple.

1. A True Disciple Is Broken

John the Baptist was known for preaching a message of repentance. When Jesus arrived on the scene, his message was virtually the same: "Repent, for the Kingdom of God is at hand." All true discipleship starts with repentance. The process of discipleship begins when we experience brokenness over our sin and our waywardness from God. God seems to enjoy using broken people to accomplish his purposes. These are individuals who have encountered crises, dealt with failures, faced major disappointments, and experienced crushing blows that drove them to their knees and forced them to admit they were at the end of their rope.

A few years ago I was invited to attend a special meeting in Atlanta with fifteen other church leaders. We all had several things in common. We had all started our own churches, we were all starting other churches out of our existing churches, and we were all involved in working globally and in our own inner cities. But when we spent some time digging beneath the surface, we discovered that every single one of us had been broken, and we were all obsessed with the kingdom of God. During that time, we learned that it was our brokenness that enabled us to be open to whatever God might call us to do. Our effectiveness in missions and church planting was rooted in our common experience of brokenness.

Brokenness is necessary for a disciple because it teaches us to get ourselves out of the way of what God wants to do. Before we are broken, we tend to be focused on our own agendas, which we follow in our own strength, and our self-sufficiency leaves little room for God's power to work in us. But when our plans collapse and we find that our strength won't put things back together again, we are in a position to open our lives to the power of God and trust him to accomplish great things through us.

The biggest obstacle to God's working in our lives and using us in powerful ways is typically not our circumstances. It's often not some person or problem standing in the way, and it may not even be the devil (though he is easy to blame). It is often our own self-centeredness, plain and simple.

If you're old enough to remember cartoonist Walt Kelly's Pogo comic strip, you may remember Pogo's famous line: "We have met the enemy — and he is us." God wants to use us in more ways than we can imagine, and he can certainly do it, if we will just get out of the way. God is waiting for each of us to release control, open up our lives, and give him unrestricted access to our heart. That's not easy. It means we have to lay down our dreams, our plans, our goals, our agenda, and learn what it means to live out Luke 9:23 (NASB): "If anyone wishes to come after Me, he must deny himself, and take up his cross daily and follow Me."

Notice the word "daily" in that passage. Many Christians become disillusioned when they make a commitment to Christ and later find themselves slipping back into self-sufficient mode. Why does that happen? Some disciples have a misguided understanding of discipleship, where they think all the lights on the road should turn green and life becomes an easy, smooth drive. But that's not the way it works. Committed transformation isn't a once-and-for-all thing; it's a continuing process.

I remember hearing that some people were upset when they learned that Mother Teresa was occasionally tormented by doubts about God. But why should that surprise us? Don't we all have moments of doubt — moments when our faith falters? Mother Teresa was simply honest about her struggles, aware of her weaknesses, and wise enough to know that she needed to rely on God for help. Her doubts were an expression of her brokenness, leading her to greater reliance upon God.

Continually working with hurting, suffering, broken people can sometimes make us question the power of God. We know we can't do it all, we can't fix every problem, and we struggle to understand why there's so much pain and poverty in the world around us. But transformed disciples keep moving forward because they ignore the negative voices and learn to follow the voice of their leader, Jesus Christ. Our greatest value in serving Jesus is not found in self-sufficient reliance on our own strengths and gifts, but in our broken dependence upon God.

Brokenness also defines the difference between how the world gives and how a Christian gives. A person of the world will first take care of their own needs, agendas, and retirement account, and then they give to others from whatever is left over. We hear of billionaires who give billions of dollars to noble causes. But is that kind of giving really hard for them? Does it involve personal sacrifice on their part? Don't misunderstand my point. I think it's a good thing that they give so abundantly. But according to the standard of Jesus, when we compare his giving to that of the widow in the New Testament who gave two mites, such giving is rather paltry. The widow gave *everything* she owned. Hers was a radically different way of giving. Though she was desperately poor, she gave everything she had, not merely a portion out of massive abundance, but out of poverty and brokenness. She didn't even leave enough to care for herself, but trusted God for her needs.

I believe that people learn this kind of humble dependence from loss, not from acquisition. Having more does not necessarily make someone a more generous person. In fact, if a person builds his life around a passion for acquiring things, he or she will eventually become a disciple of wealth. Money will be the master.

True disciples of Jesus do what they do, not because they have it all together, but because they have been broken by their sin, and they know that they have nothing. When the pieces of their lives were too shattered for anyone to put them back together, Jesus stepped in and picked up the pieces. Repentance has taught them that if they give themselves to God, God can do something with what they give. Sacrifice and self-denial becomes a way of life.

2. A True Disciple "Obeys"

When Jesus speaks, the disciple's response is *obedience.* Jesus tells his followers to "take up your cross daily, and follow me!" When Jesus says "Go!" the disciple moves out. A disciple is defined by his or her willingness to follow the master. They move forward, trusting their master, even if all the parts are not in place. Disciples have an expectation that God will supply *what* they need *when* they need it. Their task is simply to obey.

Going where their master sends them implies that disciples have the ability to hear the master when he speaks to them. This means that a disciple must have an intimate relationship with Jesus so that in worship, prayer, Scripture, and life situations he or she can recognize God at work and respond accordingly.

This does not mean that when a disciple is asked to move forward, every step is outlined in advance. One of the biggest myths in the church today is that when God calls disciples to action, he also tells them right then and there everything they need to know so they can assemble the right resources and move out. Individuals and churches can be paralyzed, waiting for God to reveal all the details. If we keep waiting for a huge master plan, complete with a budgeting process and eager donors, it's likely that we'll just keep waiting … and waiting … and waiting. That's why faith is such a vital component to being a disciple. A disciple trusts his or her master, and when the master says go, the disciple must be willing to trust and obey, believing that the resources will come when they are needed. We move forward with what we know, and as we move, God provides.

I think God has good reasons for not giving us his whole plan at once. Like a good Mexican meal, the whole enchilada may just be too big for us to digest at one sitting! Sometimes God's vision can be so big that we never even get started because the sheer magnitude of the undertaking intimidates us. The project must be scalable, something we can visualize and understand, but also something that can grow with each accomplishment. Credibility as a disciple is not simply gained by creative vision and God-sized aspirations, but by what is actually accomplished when a person obeys God and does the work in faithfulness to what God has said.

Going where we are sent implies hearing from God, and hearing from God implies participation in spiritual disciplines. If disciples expect to hear from God on a daily basis and not just an occasional mail drop or email from heaven's headquarters, they must also know what it means to worship daily, to pray daily, to be in God's presence daily, and to recognize God in the people and circumstances that surround them. I'm convinced that this is why Paul said, "Pray without ceasing."

I think of Tevye in the movie *Fiddler on the Roof*. As this Jewish milkman made his deliveries, he was continually in conversation with God, as if God were his closest companion, walking along right there beside him on his milk route. As a result of his intimate companionship with God, Tevye was sensitive to God's leading when situations with his daughters called for radically different ways of thinking.

God's movements, his call, and his will for us will become obvious when we focus on developing a closeness with him. He opens our eyes and ears to the nuances of his activity in the world. A disciple doesn't just sit down, read the book, fill in the blanks, and then wait for everything to line up. When a disciple hears the call from God, he or she gets up and gets moving. And when they move, they find God stepping in beside them, guiding them, and providing for them.

3. A True Disciple Is a Learner

How did Jesus teach his disciples? He took them with him wherever he went. The Great Commission is a command to teach others to observe all that Jesus taught his first disciples. As the early disciples traveled, Jesus was their constant companion. He not only taught them and illustrated great truths with illuminating parables, but they had the opportunity to watch him minister to people and live his life right in front of them. I find that most people today have a notion that discipleship takes place in a classroom, or it involves the use of a workbook where you fill in the blanks. Transformational discipleship is not learned through passive and sterile processes. It is *absorbed* in the context of doing life together.

At one of our staff prayer meetings we began to talk about discipleship. Randy Miller, our discipleship pastor, made an insightful point about our biblical role as shepherds of our congregation. A shepherd's job is to take the sheep to a pasture and let them graze. The shepherd finds the food and places the sheep in a position to feed on it. The sheep do not need to "baaaaaa" continually at the shepherd, nagging him until he puts the food into their mouths. The sheep just graze on what is placed in front of them. Randy said that he has never read of a case where Jesus grabbed a sheep, tucked it under his arm, and crammed the grass down its throat!

A disciple's job is to learn from the shepherd, which means actively feeding on what Jesus places in front of them. It requires remaining in constant companionship with the one who provides the meal. The kind of disciple who can change the world certainly studies the Bible to hear the voice of God, but he or she also listens for the master's voice in other ways. They listen to the voice of other people and will often hear God speaking through them. By this I don't mean to suggest that disciples can *only* listen to other Christians. It's fascinating to see how we can hear from God in the most unexpected places. Remember that God once spoke to a prophet through a burning bush and even through the mouth of a donkey! A sensitive disciple in tune with God can sometimes discern God's voice speaking through the culture.

I appreciate Karl Barth's statement that you should read the Bible with one hand and the newspaper with the other. I sometimes wince when I hear people say that they don't watch the news or read the paper; they read only God's Word. That may sound pure and holy on the surface, but it wouldn't square with the thinking of Paul, Peter, or other disciples. The earliest followers of Jesus did not remain aloof from what was going on around them. They knew and understood the context in which they worked and proclaimed the gospel message. Parents and spouses must know what's going on in the lives of their family members in order to communicate and serve them effectively. The same is true of the world. God created each and every culture, and I am convinced that we must understand the unique characteristics of each culture if we are to serve that culture effectively.

When I begin working in a foreign culture (or even in another state), I find someone who understands the people and ask for the most informative two or three books on that culture. I want to understand who these people are — their needs, the unique things about them, and areas where I should be particularly sensitive. I read up on the culture's history because its history is its story. I also read books on how the people think. Another way of learning about the people I plan to reach is to plunge into their culture. Eat their food. Listen to their music. Watch their movies. (My daughter Jill and I love to watch Bollywood movies from India!)

4. A True Disciple Engages

A transformed disciple engages God in prayer, and he engages men and women in servanthood. Make no mistake about it, every true disciple prays. But having prayed, they get up off their knees and get to work.

Their work doesn't start with the project or task, however; it starts with building relationships. Before disciples engage the gears, they engage people. Disciples don't barge into a culture as the omnipotent expert ready to show off their superior knowledge. They don't try to impose their will on a culture, show up the supposed ignorance or inferiority of those they serve, or challenge their beliefs in a bull-dozer attempt to "save" them. Instead, true disciples stand beside those they serve, become working partners with them, and together begin to impact the culture.

Engagement always begins with people. Disciples use their skill and training in their vocations to become involved in the lives of the people they serve. This kind of engagement involves a disciple in what they are most gifted and called to do, and it benefits the culture by using that asset to meet a need. By engaging the culture in an area of gifting and passion, disciples can begin touching the society as a whole in a way that has transformational impact.

5. A True Disciple Discerns

Transformed disciples also have the ability to read people and situations and respond accordingly. This gift is more than a personality trait or natural skill; it grows out of their spiritual disciplines — their active prayer life, their sensitivity to God's voice, and their openness to him.

Discernment works in two important ways. First, it is spiritually sensitive to the inner life of other people and is able to see beneath the surface to the real need. Second, discernment demonstrates cultural sensitivity through the way we engage with people, by taking the time to understand the cultural or personal barriers they may have that could hinder effective service. When facing cultural or personal barriers in their work, disciples must be able to hold on to truth firmly but also have the patience and sensitivity to present it and live it in a way that inspires and challenges people — instead of condemning and shaming them. Discernment is an essential attribute of a godly person in both the Old and New Testaments:

> Then you will understand [discern] righteousness and
> justice,
> equity and every good path. (Proverbs 2:9)

This I pray, that your love may abound yet more and more in knowledge and all discernment; so that you may approve the things that are excellent. (Philippians 1:9)

Sadly, discernment is often one of the missing elements in ministry today. When Jesus ministered during his earthly ministry, he could simply look at people and read them — discerning their hearts, motives, and intentions. His discernment was more than mere opinion. Biblical discernment is the ability to accurately perceive where people are and where they're headed, and then gracefully show them a different way to move forward.

6. A True Disciple Has Faith

I know that *faith* is a noun, but I keep looking for a way to define it as a verb. Faith is not merely a passive belief in a set of propositional truths; it is an active and dynamic embrace of those truths. Anyone can believe that God exists and still do nothing about it. Some can believe that and even work against him, as James reminds us when he speaks of the demons and their belief in the existence of God (James 2:19). But that type of belief is not *faith*. Faith involves personal trust, and when you trust someone, you *act* as if their word is true. If you believe in God and God tells you to "go," you go.

You believe that what God has told you is *trustworthy*. You act on your belief even if it costs you something. In this sense, faith is not just a belief; it's also an action that flows from our beliefs. That's why I keep wanting to use it as a verb. Faith is not simply something that every transformational disciple must possess; faith is something he must do. Faith is your response to the call of God on your life.

Faith is not easy. It requires believing what God says to the point that you willingly put your life on the line. Faith is getting out so far on the limb that when the wind starts blowing, you feel it swaying and hear it creaking; and if God doesn't come through, you're going to come crashing down. In those moments when things do not go well — and every disciple has them — it's easy to let the mood of the moment take over. You may, at times, feel like chucking the whole thing; "if God is really with me, he wouldn't let this sort of thing happen." In these moments we must remember that circumstances and moods shape and color our perspective. They come and go. But God *always* remains true to us, and faith means that we remain true to him and his Word to us. C. S. Lewis said that one important element in faith is holding on to what you know is true in spite of your changing moods.[17]

My friend Omar and I were speaking at one of Bishop Kitonga's churches in Kenya. It was the longest worship service I've ever attended in my entire life — over three hours long with lots of singing, much prayer, and three preachers! At the end of the service they asked Omar to give a final word. He was greatly inspired by the enthusiastic worship, and he received a strong impression from God that he should address the question Jesus asked in Luke 18:8: "When the Son of Man comes, will he find faith on the earth?" Omar saw the joy in the eyes of the people in spite of their massive poverty and suffering. And he told them, "Yes, there is faith on the earth, and it is present in Africa." When people trust God and his Word and exercise their faith, the fruit of the Spirit — love, joy, and peace — will be evident in their lives.

7. A True Disciple Loves

A transformational disciple loves others, but even more than he loves other people, this sort of disciple loves Jesus. Other people will always let you down — but not Jesus. In the end, it doesn't matter what we do in serving others; if we don't do it out of a genuine love for Jesus, it's all for nothing.

> If I speak with the languages of men and of angels, but don't have love, I have become sounding brass, or a clanging cymbal. If I have the gift of prophecy, and know all mysteries and all knowledge; and if I have all faith, so as to remove mountains, but don't have love, I am nothing. If I dole out all my goods to feed the poor, and if I give my body to be burned, but don't have love, it profits me nothing. (1 Corinthians 13:1 – 3)

But there is still a strong connection between our love for Jesus and our love for others. In fact, one of the primary ways that we really show our love for Jesus is through our love for other people. The apostle John reminded the church of this truth: "If a man says, 'I love God,' and hates his brother, he is a liar; for he who doesn't love his brother whom he has seen, how can he love God whom he has not seen?" (1 John 4:19 – 20).

So how is our love for Jesus shown? It's not through Scripture memorization, or through church attendance, or through moral behavior, or through merely believing in the right doctrines. Jesus gives us the answer: our love for him is primarily seen through the way that we serve others (see Matthew 25:34 – 40).

These are the seven characteristics of a transformed disciple — one whose life will truly make a difference for the Great Commission and who has the potential to change the lives of other people. If these seven attributes of a disciple are not present in some way, we do not have a truly transformed disciple.

As you can see, these attributes add up to produce a radically different kind of disciple than the disciples we find in most churches today. That is why I believe it is vitally important for churches to concentrate their efforts on discipling and training, not on expanding their programs or increasing their institutional position. For churches to have any hope of changing their communities, they must first concentrate on transforming each individual member of their congregation. I believe that the only way to really grow churches is to grow transformed disciples of Christ. Transformed disciples make up a vital and world-changing church. There aren't any shortcuts in this process.

If it helps, think of following God as an adventure, a journey where you only have enough supplies to get by for three or four days. The journey will require the very best that you have to give. It will require continual dependence and trust. It will challenge you and change you like nothing else in life. It's not for the faint of heart!

I believe that if we presented discipleship to people in this light, people would really start to get excited about it. Most people want to do something significant with their lives. They don't want to waste time in rote church services and rituals that pump them up for the moment but have little meaning in real life. I believe that people are looking for churches that offer more than just a nerve-stimulating Sunday event. If we present a God-sized challenge, people will rise to face it, even when it demands total commitment and constant sacrifice.

Connection Steps

◉ If there were one thing I couldn't abandon to follow God it would be . . .

◉ Write out your story of brokenness.

◉ On a scale of 1 to 10 rate your personal worship, small group experience, and glocal impact.

◉ What one country have you followed in the news recently? If you were the ambassador, what would you do for that country?

CHAPTER 6

Engaging Society

But this is the covenant that I will make with the
house of Israel after those days, says Yahweh: I will
put my law in their inward parts, and in their heart
will I write it; and I will be their God, and they shall
be my people. JEREMIAH 31:33

I had never really gotten into art that much — that is, until I saw the paintings displayed in the galleries of Hanoi, Vietnam. Some of the greatest impressionist painters in the world are emerging there. The influence of the French during the colonial years exposed Vietnamese painters to artists such as Monet, Van Gogh, Degas, and Renoir and has had a profound impact on their artistic style. When people from the United States visit Vietnamese galleries, they are often taken aback, amazed at the quality of art they find. In an interesting twist, it was my exposure to the fine art of Vietnam that led to me study up on Van Gogh, Cézanne, Pizarro, and other European painters.

Hanoi now has scores of art galleries where you can buy excellent original art at a fraction of the price you would pay in America. A lot of copy shops, or "knockoff" shops, have also emerged, where you can buy amazingly accurate copies of famous classical paintings. My kids came to dread going with me to these Hanoi galleries. I would show off my new "expertise" in art techniques, comparing the work of contemporary Vietnamese artists such as Minh Song, Mach Son, Phong, and others to the great artists of the past.

On one of my trips, I bought a number of these knockoff paintings and even a few originals to hang in our church and our home. For fifty to a hundred bucks you can get some really good knockoffs that most people cannot tell from the real thing. It's not that I'm trying to fool anyone into thinking we have original Rembrandts and Van Goghs in our home; we simply enjoy the paintings for their innate beauty.

One day the owner of a Hanoi gallery arranged a lunch for me to meet with many of the local painters. It was incredible. I was able to ask questions about who influenced their art, the types of painting they had done, and where they got their inspiration from. Their answers fascinated me. Then they began to ask *me* questions — who was I and what did I do? I explained that I was a pastor leading an American church to do development in Vietnam.

Over the next several years, I became friends with many of these artists. On every trip to Vietnam I made time to visit their galleries and frequently accepted invitations into their homes for meals. We generally would sip green tea together and chat about Renoir, Monet, or Jesus — though I never pushed Jesus on them. But whenever they asked, as they often did, I was ready to talk.

I quickly developed a close relationship with one artist in particular — an impressionist named Minh Song. He told me that when he painted, he felt a sense of "divine inspiration." Following up on this potentially spiritual point of contact, I commissioned him to paint a picture of a church that we could hang in the new worship center we were building back home. He had grown up near a Christian church, and he had seen the few Catholic churches in Hanoi. So drawing from those references, he composed a painting. It featured a beautiful countryside at dusk, complete with a clear lake around which people lived a simple country life. Beside the lake was the church building, glowing from the lights inside. The painting was rendered in Minh Song's typical impressionistic style with brushes and palette knives. It was incredible. I hung it in a prominent place in our church.

Every time I returned to Vietnam, I would take people along with me to the art galleries and to Minh Song's studio. Among these visitors were some NorthWood members who are into art. Without exception, they were blown away by what they saw. These North-Wood art types arranged for Minh Song to visit America to display his art. It would be his first trip to the U.S., and Minh Song was beside himself with excitement. To be honest, so was I! We shipped thirty of his paintings in advance of his visit, and when he arrived he began to sell them. He charged a fourth of what he should have, but he didn't care. He wanted his paintings to sell so that word would spread and create some demand. During his two-week visit, he sold all but four of the paintings! He was ecstatic. It was his most successful sales venture ever.

On Minh Song's first Sunday in the U.S. we displayed his paintings in the church hallways, and I asked him to come up during the worship service to be interviewed. He told the story of how he began painting and talked about the painters who had influenced him. NorthWood received him warmly. In his interview, he told me that he felt something of God, something that inspired him and was within him. I wasn't sure what this Buddhist meant when he referred to God, but I noticed that it was the second time he had mentioned this divine inspiration.

That day I began a sermon series called "Eraser." The topic of the message was forgiveness and how God erases our sins. The first week centered on God's forgiveness, the second week on forgiving ourselves, and the third on forgiving others. That first Sunday I focused on what Jesus did on the cross and how no one has to live with guilt and shame because Christ can forgive any sin in our hearts. I knew that although Jesus forgives readily, people often have trouble accepting his forgiveness — of feeling it and experiencing it in their lives.

Consequently, we had devised an activity to make the concept more concrete for people. We had wooden crosses spread throughout the worship center, and in each bulletin worshipers could find a small piece of paper. I told our church that if there was a sin in their life for which they just could not seem to experience God's forgiveness, they were invited to write that sin on the piece of paper and place it at the foot of one of the crosses. Though God's forgiveness is real, I have found that a physical act can often confirm an inner reality.

There was another cross near me at the front of the stage. I said to the people gathered, "If you want to give your heart to Christ today, you can declare that decision by coming to stand by this cross." Throughout the worship center people began to move to the different crosses, where they prayed for forgiveness and asked others to forgive them. It was very moving, and Minh Song was deeply touched by it. He told me, "I always wanted to know how to find forgiveness." We spent the afternoon talking about forgiveness and what it meant. It was an incredible conversation, and toward the end of it I asked him what he wanted to do with his life. He answered that God had given him the ability to paint, and he wanted to keep on painting in order to have money to give to others. Later that day, acting on what he said was a strong inspiration, he went outside and painted a picture for Nikki, my wife, and me. He called it sunset, and it now hangs in my study at home. It reminds me of our time together and to pray for him every day.

I don't know how many times I've shared Minh Song's story, but the wonderful truth is that his story is typical of many, many others we have seen throughout the world. Sometimes the people we befriend decide to follow Jesus and sometimes they don't, but in every instance they have an opportunity to hear and see the love of God. I share the story of Minh Song to show you how glocal ministry — world-changing, cross-cultural ministry — can mushroom from just a tiny beginning. It doesn't take a rocket scientist to engage the Great Commission. Any Christian can do it!

After Minh Song's visit, our Vietnam ministry exploded. Several doors of opportunity were soon available to us. One example, as I related in chapter 3, was that of some of our members bringing several Vietnamese educators to the U.S., taking them to the appropriate universities, and working with them to write the curriculum that would be taught to the professors who would teach the Vietnamese public school teachers. We are now in our fifth year of that program.

We have one member who is a plumber. He spent his two-week vacation in Vietnam, where he dug water wells and set up a water purification system. We have several doctors who have paid their own expenses and donated their time to go to Vietnam and set up clinics. As I write this we have mechanics, carpenters, heating/AC specialists, and teachers who are now in the process of developing a vocational school for tribal people in the northern Vietnam provinces. They are donating their vacation time, and they provided their own funding for their trips. The list goes on and on. These aren't church programs or even "official" ministries — this is glocal ministry that utilizes the gifts and skills of people with a heart to follow Christ wherever he opens the door for ministry.

GLOCAL MINISTRY: WHERE EVERYONE IS A VOCATIONAL MINISTER!

Now I will admit that NorthWood Church *does* have those church-sponsored projects — like an orphanage in Vietnam — that everyone can get involved in. But that's just the tip of the iceberg. We have many projects in Vietnam and other places around the world that are initiated and carried out by individuals acting *independent of church leadership*. These are the projects we get most excited about. We love it when people take the job they have and begin to use it to make a difference. The engagement of every Christian in ministry is so important to us that a key focus of our new members class is to help people identify their domains (gifts, skills, and passions) and learn how to use their job and their skill set to engage society for Jesus.

One of the important things we teach new members is that when they engage in ministry, they are not engaging in "religious" work. I find that many churches teach or model a distinction between "secular" work and the work of ministry. But we are convinced that if you really understand the scope of God's kingdom, all the work that a disciple does is "religious" work. The distinction between religious and secular is artificial and unbiblical. As I will soon explain, religion is not just a category of life; it is the relating of all of life to God.

As we noted in a previous chapter, Paul tells us that the scope of God's plan of redemption is cosmic: God intends to redeem not only individuals, but everything he created. That's why our ministry must be to the nations, the cultures, and the societies of the world, not simply to individuals. Everything has been corrupted by the fall, and God cares about *all* of it. Redemption on this scale is going to involve more than preachers and pastors. Every disciple of Christ should be able to verbally share what Christ has done for them and how he can make a difference in the lives of others. Each of us should recognize that God wants to use our work, our gifts, and our skills to bring reconciliation to this world.

I find that one of the biggest reasons why church "members" don't get involved in missions is because they see it primarily as something that involves preaching — an activity they are willing to fund, but not something they feel called or gifted to do. Disciples must come to understand that God has called them to use their jobs, their gifts, and their skills to fulfill the Great Commission — just as a pastor uses his gift of preaching to share with others the message of God's love.

The real key to fulfilling the Great Commission will come when the church learns to focus on the disciple as the agent for mission, setting him or her loose on the society. Much of the focus in missions and evangelism is on finding preachers and getting them to start churches. While this model will see some success, unless we shift our orientation for engagement with the world, we will never see transformation of society. If we shift our focus toward producing a different kind of disciple, embracing a vision of discipleship that involves the whole of life and the integration of everything Jesus taught, we will not only see and increase in the number of people accepting Christ and the number of churches planted, but communities will be healed and transformed.

The endgame of the Great Commission was never Israel or even the church; it is the reconciliation of all peoples and all nations to God. This global vision of reconciliation includes all levels of society, every domain of work, and is open to all individuals. When churches work globally, they often don't see the big picture, a vision that involves reconciliation of both people *and* the structures of society. The goal of the church in fulfilling the Great Commission is to help each person use his or her job and calling to bless others with the love of Jesus, both locally and globally. The natural basis for their connection is not primarily through a volunteer ministry at the church but in the area of their domain — their area of expertise in the society and the world. Churches need to equip and train disciples to serve the world in the area of their calling.

All societies, rich and poor, advanced and primitive, are made up of the same basic core elements. To be successful in evangelism, we must learn to identify these core elements and address them directly. Churches are failing to engage people in mission today because they fail to engage these basic elements of society. Instead, churches get caught up in largely irrelevant, internal conversations about what Christians can or cannot do on Sunday and what their moral and political stances should be. Worshiping biblically and voting your conscience are fine things, but they are not really the primary way to engage the disciple in society. God has called us to be more than just a church attender or a religious voting block. He has called us to be salt and light in the world — agents of change and transformation throughout society.

At NorthWood we use the chart below to help members understand how they can use their jobs locally and globally (glocally) to serve others. The chart is actually a human resource map of domains, or jobs. Often, when churches use the term *marketplace ministry*, they have a limited understanding that involves sharing your faith with unbelievers in the workplace through Bible studies or informal conversation. While faith sharing is certainly a good thing (and should certainly be done), there is far more that a person can do with their vocation than have a Bible study at work. Why can't they use their job skills and expertise to serve others for Jesus?

The circle in the center of this chart shows the deep core of society

— the elements most important to people who work together to make

a harmonious and fulfilled life. These core elements work outward from the center, beginning with the individual and working upward through one's relationships at expanded levels, and downward through the activities and values that define one's life. Around this center circle you see the domains of society — the broad categories of vocational activity that feed the core and keep it functioning. Then around the domains you see smaller circles that give examples of the kind of trades or professions that feed the various domains.

Notice that religion is not listed as one of the domains of society in this chart. Faith is represented on the chart by the crosses adjacent to every trade, profession, and domain. This reminds us that our faith should permeate every domain as disciples are living out the gospel of the kingdom. This model illustrates that instead of starting churches that try to draw individuals out of society and into the church, a more effective model is for disciples to go out and engage the society within its domains. This will lead to transformation that spreads virally throughout the nation in every segment of society.

That's the big picture, the grid of engagement. But we still need to get down to the details. What does it mean to "engage" society? How does the disciple actually make it happen? What are some of the rules of engagement that will increase the likelihood of success in this endeavor? I want to offer five tried-and-true ideas for disciples as they relate their faith to the culture they are hoping to reach.

FIVE TRIED-AND-TRUE IDEAS FOR DISCIPLES

1. A Faith That Is Public, Not Private

Christian writer and thinker Os Guinness eloquently summarizes the modern attitude toward religion held by many people today:

> Three attitudes are widely prevalent in educated circles in the West: that religion in the modern world is irrational, archaic, retrograde, and on the way out; that what remains of religion is the leading source of evil and conflict today; and that a central task of politics is to curb the illiberal power of religion, above all in the public square. In short, the idea that religion is a wild

card in human affairs is admissible, but the idea that it could play a central and constructive role is absurd.[18]

As people grew more educated and societies became more technologically advanced, many people expected that God would just vanish from the scene. They believed that a time was coming when people would be embarrassed to admit they believed in the old fables of the Bible.

While this is true in some circles, in reality, the opposite has happened. During the past few decades Christianity has exploded throughout the world. Excellent, scholarly work has been done that supports the veracity of the Bible, the existence of Christ, and the likelihood of miracles. In some places, prominent scientists are now admitting that it's unlikely that the cosmos just happened without an intelligent cause. Followers of Jesus Christ today have no reason to be "embarrassed" about believing the Word of God or keeping their faith a private matter. Jesus makes it clear that his followers should be bold and confident in expressing faith: "I tell you, everyone who confesses me before men, him will the Son of Man also confess before the angels of God; but he who denies me in the presence of men will be denied in the presence of the angels of God" (Luke 12:8 – 9).

Keep in mind that this isn't an invitation to make arrogant pronouncements of our faith or judgmental indictments of others. It means that our faith should be such a natural part of our lives that denying Jesus would be like denying ourselves. While we are called to be open and public with our faith, we must remember to be tactful, understanding, gentle, caring, and civil in the way we express it. It pains me deeply that this kind of understanding and civility is often missing when Christians talk about Islam and try to engage the Muslim world. In many cases Christians have isolated themselves from Islamic people by ignoring what they say and denouncing what they think. According to Os Guinness, this is the opposite of what a Christian should do:

Name-calling, insult, ridicule, guilt by association, caricature, innuendo, accusation, denunciation, negative ads, and deceptive and manipulative videos have replaced deliberation and debate. Neither side talks to the other side, only about them; and there is no repentance or democratic engagement, let alone a serious effort at persuasion.[19]

Proud, arrogant debate drives people apart, polarizes them, and entrenches them in their own positions, making conversion and discipleship much more difficult, if not impossible. Because of the "bull-in-a-china-shop" approach of many Western Christians, their faith comes across to others as a political agenda or a power play, not a healing message of God's goodness and an invitation to peace. In some cases, I can hardly blame people for being turned off to the message of the gospel. Being right and having the truth is not enough for an effective witness. Christians must be consummate diplomats in all their dealings with other cultures.

Many diplomats engaging in international affairs have been unprepared to negotiate with followers of Islam. Now governments are trying to catch up, but they still have a long way to go toward cultivating genuine understanding of the Islamic world. As disciples of Christ, our interpersonal and relational engagement with global societies should make us the experts that professional diplomats turn to when they need insight into a culture. Unfortunately, that's not the case. Because of the dismal track record of Christians in dealing with Muslims, few diplomats ever think of seeking help from us.

When diplomats do turn to Christians, they often turn to liberal Christians, who have a universalistic attitude toward all religions and little conviction in their own faith. You might be surprised to hear that this kind of Christian rarely gets any farther with Muslims than the confrontational, judgmental approach. In my dealings with Muslims, I have found that they are people of conviction, and because of that they respect those with convictions. They would actually prefer dealing with people who openly and honestly hold strong convictions about God.

When you travel to other cultures, it's natural for people to ask you about your faith. They are usually genuinely curious and simply wanting to dialogue about differing views. To be candid, I find that people outside the United States are frequently more open to discussing issues of religion than many American Christians. Because we don't usually talk about our faith in public settings, we don't know how to discuss our faith in a natural way. When other people express even a slight interest in Christianity, it's like a light starts blinking and a voice starts repeating in our heads: "Convert — convert — convert!" Immediately we go into "preacher overdrive" and deliver a canned presentation on how to be saved.

It doesn't have to be this way! Non-Christians may truly be interested in your faith, but they first want to see what a real Christian looks like. They will be watching the way you act and listening to the things you say. The way you live your life is your best evangelism tool. This means your first step is usually to build a relationship and engage in an extended dialogue that promotes mutual understanding. Putting the full-court press on anyone to change religions is generally not the best way to build a friendship. In other words, be civil in all your dealings. As Os Guinness says, civility can make a world of difference:

> The Christian faith is not only the world's most numerous faith but the world's first truly global faith, so its present stand for civility today, along with its struggle for justice and freedom, is of world historic significance.[20]

So don't be afraid to be unabashedly open about your faith. Don't water down your convictions or try to hide what you believe. Yet at the same time, don't use your faith as a weapon for hitting others over the head, and don't treat people as an opportunity to cut a new notch in your conversion belt. The point is not to demonstrate the superiority of your faith. You don't have to water down your faith in order to minimize the differences with other religions. Take the high road. Show that you genuinely care about those you are with by serving them and finding ways to solve their difficulties and improve their lives. Above all, be gentle, understanding, and civil in all your dealings.

2. An Integrated Faith, Not an Isolated Sect

Christianity is an integrated faith. It permeates every area of life — family, work, government, play, and relationships. This is why at NorthWood we encourage our members to use their God-given jobs, skills, and passions to serve others. When committed disciples integrate their lives into their domains, the truth and life of the Christian faith is injected into society, and this engagement can actually strengthen the community by creating a culture of care and understanding. Author Jonathan Sacks explains:

> Civil society is therefore a grand and continuing exercise in balancing government and society on the one hand, and unity and diversity on the other, thus cultivating a healthy freedom that keeps the balance ... Thus ... all voluntary acts of giving, caring, engagement, and participation that they encourage, have two important functions. They create the lifeblood of civil society and are the surest way to accumulate social capital, and they are also the best way to keep the government at bay and so to sustain the vitality of freedom.[21]

Many Christians shun the public square for various reasons. Some may be intimidated by the current push for "separation of church and state," while others may believe that Christianity is a purely "spiritual" religion with no business mixing in mundane human affairs. But the book of Acts shows that Christianity was all over the public square — in public forums (17:22) and in trade guilds (19:23 – 40), affecting government officials (8:26 – 39), military commanders (10:1 – 48), merchants (16:14), and even entire towns (9:35). Taking our cue from the apostles, Christians today should see public schools, public companies, or public *anything* as ideal vehicles for spreading the gospel.

When we work in our domains, we are engaging the public square. As Os Guinness puts it, the public square should not be naked or sacred, but civic. Its purpose is to integrate all domains and elements in a culture in order to hold the society together and enable it to prosper. Faith plays an important role by giving the culture a solid bond of commonality based on godly principles.

This won't work if Christians pull their wagons together in a circle and try to keep their faith private, insulated, and isolated from the rest of the world. When a religious group sets itself apart and does not participate in the general society, we call it a sect. Sects are known for their separateness, their isolation, and their withdrawal from the activities of society. They do not affect society and they fail to answer the call of the Great Commission to make disciples that change the nations.

There is, of course, a sense in which the Christian must not be part of the world. We must not adopt society's ungodly values or participate in any immoral behavior or act even if it's fully accepted by the culture. But we must be careful not to isolate ourselves from society's vital functions — its domains and the elements that hold it together as a cohesive unit.

The philosopher Hegel once observed that "for modern man reading the papers has taken the place of morning prayers." Jonathan Sacks explains the positive side of this change: "The daily press meant that large numbers of people followed the same news, told in the same words, in the same language at the same time. Newspapers helped create a sense of national community."[22] Of course, keeping current with the news should not dilute one's spiritual focus, but Christians should work to stay current with what's going on in the world they live in. Staying informed helps us to understand the culture so we can relate to it and engage it more effectively.

Many Christians fail to engage society and live in isolation caused by fear of impending doom aggravated by questionable theology. They see the world going to hell in a handbasket and develop a bunker attitude that huddles together and waits for the end to come. Brian McLaren calls these attitudes "fatalistic eschatologies of abandonment." Guinness quotes one leader who in the midst of the recent "Left Behind" craze observed, "For God so loved the world that he gave us WWIII."[23] What kind of gospel is that? Where is the hope? Where is the salvation? This is far from the hope and expectation and wonder of God and the mystery of reconciliation he offers. Why have we exchanged doomsday eschatological charts for God's true theology of hope?

Our hope for the future is found in the message of Jesus that transforms all nations. This must be the message that we, his followers, lift up and spread to the farthest corners of this globe. We must live out our identity as the Easter people, the people defined by the resurrection of Jesus, a people characterized by hopeful anticipation of the future. Closing up shop and sitting on the sidelines while we wait for the end is not a choice that is consistent with the message of Jesus. The message of Jesus is that nations and people can be transformed.

When Christians bring godly values into a society, they help to keep the society cohesive and stable, even if there is not a large-scale conversion to the Christian faith. This is one reason why we should not be working against Jews and Muslims when we enter their cultures. We share a common ethical norm with these cultures, even if our worldviews have significant differences. Whenever we perform our service in the name of Jesus, our common ethical ground with these other religions must not be undermined. When a society loses its common agreement on basic standards of right and wrong, there's trouble ahead. Patrick Devlin explains:

> Society means a community of ideas; without shared ideas on politics, morals, and ethics no society can exist ... If men and women try to create a society in which there is no fundamental agreement about good and evil they will fail; if, having based it on common agreement, the agreement goes, the society will disintegrate. For society is not something that is kept together physically; it is held by the invisible bonds of common thought.[24]

I have learned through firsthand experience that what Devlin says is true. Even if people I meet in other cultures don't accept Christ, if I integrate my life with theirs, get to know them and serve them, it goes a long way toward building peace and stability in their world. And it often does much more. I've learned that seeming failures can sometimes open additional doors in unanticipated places, enabling others to accept Christ further down the road. As Christians, we must live in light of eternity and not simply judge our effectiveness by the seeming failure of the moment. We must recognize that God can use even our failures to plant seeds of growth for his kingdom.

Societal integration with Christianity is critical to the long-term success of the Great Commission. Christians cannot withdraw into a defensive posture of isolation that promotes separateness and creates a sectlike religion. Sacks writes:

> The inward turn is good news for Jews, Christians, Muslims, Hindus, Sikhs and everyone else who cares for the continuity of traditional identities. But it is not good news for all of us together. For what it means is that we have ceased to see ourselves as all-of-us-together.[25]

When we integrate with others, it doesn't necessarily mean complete assimilation. As followers of Jesus, we do not let the world swallow us into its value system and give up our convictions, beliefs, and values. Integration simply means that we live in community and have genuine relationships with our neighbors no matter what their cultural or religious background. As Sacks points out, this is exactly what God calls us to do:

> Twenty-six centuries ago, the prophet Jeremiah sent a letter to the Jewish exiles in Babylon: "Seek the peace of the city to which you are exiled and pray to God on its behalf, for in its peace and prosperity you will have peace and prosperity." This is probably the wisest advice ever given to a religious minority. Jeremiah was telling the exiles to work for the common good … the principle of integration without assimilation.[26]

3. A Bottom-Up Faith, Not a Top-Down Faith

In my travels I have often been privileged to meet with high officials and top leaders in many countries. People often ask me how I manage to meet people like that. The answer is simple: I don't try to meet them. Why would I want to meet them? Rubbing shoulders with bigwigs is not my purpose in going to these countries. But I've found that when you enter a society and start serving the common people at the bottom, your work eventually leads you into contact with the country's gatekeepers and leaders.

We go into a country following the model of service Christ outlined in Matthew 25. He taught his followers to meet the needs of people who need food, water, clothing, healing, hospitality, and care while in prison. We serve where we are needed, doing whatever menial things are required. Matthew 25 doesn't teach us to focus on the gatekeepers or those with money or power; it says that we should touch those who are suffering.

When we serve those on the bottom of the social ladder, we reach the masses, those who make up the majority in every society. At the same time, we are building credibility in that culture. Credibility is not gained through your vision for the future or by what you aspire to do or be; it is gained by what you are doing — right where you are. Building credibility takes time, and it develops out of those small, faithful first steps.

4. A Serving Faith, Not a Coercive Faith

Christ has called us to a life of servanthood. Ideologues tend to think and write, while servants tend to sweat and serve. I learned many years ago that most people don't want to listen to our message because they don't believe that we really care about them all that much. It is certainly true that serving others often opens the door for you to share your faith, but the truth is that we should serve someone whether or not they are interested in our Savior. I serve others, not to convert, but *because* I've been converted. Do I want everyone to know Jesus? You bet I do! But who, when, how, and where — I have to leave that in God's hand. He does the saving; I do the serving and the sharing.

A serving faith is always respectful and never arrogant. We should guard against coming across as condescending or superior because we have something that others need. And we must never pressure anyone to become a Christian or tire them out with endless attempts to convince them that we are right. That kind of coercion develops resistance to the message, not acceptance. We begin with faith in our hearts, a faith that gives us the desire to serve humanity. Through the example of our service and our love, God opens the door for faith to take root in others. Serving others is the best way of applying our faith in such a way that it leads to real transformation and change.

Servanthood means that we do what we do *voluntarily*, out of love, not using our service as leverage for coercion or to put others under obligation to us. We do it simply because we love. And why do we love? Because God first loved us. God's love instills in us a desire to show his love to others through our service. As Christ himself said, "Even so, let your light shine before men; that they may see your good works, and glorify your Father who is in heaven" (Matthew 5:16). I delight in telling people that I come to them in the name of Jesus to love and serve him because he first loved me.

5. A Social Covenant, Not a Social Contract

Serving others in this way requires that we abandon the prevalent American concept of entitlement and rights. A focus on rights and privileges is a focus on self. Those who focus on their rights are saying, "I am due certain things and I expect to get them." To serve effectively and fulfill the Great Commission, we must first shed that way of thinking and replace it with an attitude of responsibility, particularly our responsibility to God, but also to the society we live in, to our neighbors and to our community. Our attitude must be, "I see a need and I will do all I can to fulfill it."

Rights are not necessarily bad things. They develop out of what we call a social contract, which is upheld by the state. The social contract is an agreement between all people within a given society; it says, in effect, that we all agree to common rules of conduct in order to ensure that everyone is treated equitably and fairly, enabling all to pursue their individual goals and needs with relative freedom. Rights are typically codified into laws, enforceable moral standards that allow for a stable social order.

While rights are necessary in every society, it is equally important for us to remember our *responsibilities*. In his book *The Home We Build Together*, Jonathan Sacks says, "Rights are enshrined in law, responsibilities are born in the moral imagination."[27] Today, our greatest need is not a contract that says, "I'll stay on my side of the fence if you'll stay on yours," but a *covenant* that emphasizes our moral responsibility to one another and says, "Each of us is committed to looking out for the other's needs."

Social contracts alone are never enough. They emphasize individual rights and serve to warn other individuals that they should not overstep their bounds. A social *covenant* emphasizes moral responsibility, in which the individual chooses to shift his focus from his own rights to the needs of others.

We see the dominance of rights throughout American culture. Among the most obvious examples of this is the growing culture of victimhood. When rights ascend and responsibility declines, people begin to deny responsibility for their own actions and start claiming their right to indulge in destructive behaviors with impunity. We've seen people suing restaurants for burns they received when they spilled hot coffee on themselves, or overweight people suing fast-food chains for selling them hamburgers, or smokers suing tobacco companies for the harm caused by their own indulgence. Again, Sacks observes:

> The culture of victimhood negates the moral basis of the Judaeo-Christian tradition. What makes that tradition distinctive is its emphasis on personal moral responsibility, the beliefs that we are free to choose, that we are made by our choices, and that we are morally accountable for the way we act.[28]

This emphasis on individual rights has also poisoned our churches. "Worship wars" (as they're commonly called) frequently involve groups in a church demanding their own preferences in styles of worship. One group wants traditional songs; the other wants contemporary. One wants a full band with drums, guitars, and horns; the other wants only an organ or piano. Churches split over these demands, fighting for the right to "worship" God in a way that fits their own individual desire and preference. What a tragic picture of God we show the world!

As Christians, we need to recover the biblical concept of covenant and shift from an emphasis on our rights and privileges to our responsibilities to God and to one another. I believe that this type of shift would lead to an end to the worship wars as well as a move away from the culture of victimhood that we see in American society. In place of a mentality that emphasizes selfish desires, we would begin to see a growing, love-inspired desire in every disciple to minister to the needs of others. Joseph Allen elaborates:

> To be in covenant with other people involves believing that we and they belong to the same moral community; that in this community each person matters in his or her own right and not merely as something useful to the society; that we all participate in the moral community by entrusting ourselves to others and in turn accepting their entrusting; and that in the moral community each of us has enduring responsibility to all the others.[29]

The social contract, with its emphasis on protecting the rights of the individual, has led to a fracturing in our society as individual rights come into conflict with one another. In place of this contract, we need a covenant, an integrating act generated from the ground up by people acting freely and responsibly. Again we turn to Sacks, who explains it well:

> Social contract creates a state; social covenant creates a society. Social contract is about power and how it is to be handled within a political framework. Social covenant is about how people live together despite framework. Social covenant is about how people live together despite their differences. Social contract is about government. Social covenant is about coexistence. Social contract is about laws and their enforcement. Social covenant is about the values we share. Social contract is about the use of potentially coercive force. Social covenant is about moral commitments, the values we have, and the ideals that inspire us to work together for the sake of the common good.[30]

Sacks's explanation reminds us that social covenants are only effective when they grow out of the internal moral character of the people who adopt them. This understanding of covenant aligns closely with the prophecy of Jeremiah, defining the kind of covenant God would one day establish with his people:

> But this is the covenant that I will make with the house of Israel after those days, says Yahweh: I will put my law in their inward parts, and in their heart will I write it; and I will be their God, and they shall be my people. (Jeremiah 31:33)

God's covenant with his people is a covenant of the heart — a covenant of free people sharing God's love with others as they willingly embrace the responsibility to love God and love others. The love of Jesus, alive in the heart of his disciples, is the key to moving a society from a rights-oriented contract to a loving covenant. Jesus didn't come to enforce the moral law and protect individual rights; he emphasized our responsibility to love others, even if it meant giving up our personal rights and privileges!

Jesus taught that if someone takes your shirt, you should give up your coat as well; if someone forces you to go a mile, you should go two miles; if someone hits you on the right cheek, turn the other to him as well. In effect, Jesus was saying: "Don't stand on your rights; develop a heart of love that wants to serve others instead of looking out for number one." Jesus himself modeled this way of living, giving up his divine rights and privileges to serve others, even through the painful ordeal of the cross.

Contrary to what many Christians think, most people are not turned off by Jesus, his teachings, or his example. Even unbelievers find his way of life attractive. If we, as his followers, focus on emulating him in this way, giving up our rights and opening our eyes to the opportunities to engage in responsible care for the welfare of others, I am convinced the gospel will explode. My goal is to love and serve someone in such a way that if they decide not to follow Christ, it's because they genuinely reject what he did or what he taught, not because of my poor example as his follower.

Connection Steps

- ⊙ What domain(s) are you already involved in?

- ⊙ What could you do with your job to serve others?

- ⊙ How integrated is your faith, your life, and your work? Why?

- ⊙ Are you treating your faith-walk like a contract or a covenant?

CHAPTER 7

Serving Together

Often when people talk about their church, they will tell you about the great praise band, the contemporary songs, the wonderful preaching, the excellent classes with great teachers, the superb programs for youth and kids, and the excellent child care facilities. They mention these things because they are important to them, and they assume they will be important to you as well.

In this chapter I want to tell you about our church. My purpose is not to set NorthWood up as the perfect church or the Edenic ideal that all churches should aspire to emulate. It would be presumptuous for any church to set itself up as the model for all others. God is creative, and he never does the same thing, in exactly the same way, twice! In your church, the specifics of ministry and the details of implementing these ideas will no doubt look altogether different from ours. My hope for this chapter is not to replicate what God has done at NorthWood, but to help you see the central importance of ministry to others, so that your church can truly be all that God intends it to be.

I hope that telling you about NorthWood will do two things: show you what we value as a church, and illustrate some of the principles I have already set out for you in this book. To this point, we have discussed the importance of recognizing your call and of using your job and passions to serve God, and we've looked at the significance of understanding the world, the disciple, and the society we live in. In this chapter we will present the last factor that must come into play if we are to fulfill the Great Commission: glocal ministry through the local church.

NORTHWOOD CHURCH — "MADE IN VIETNAM"

Early on Sunday morning a week before the grand opening of our new worship center, about fifty NorthWood members gathered at the church building to pray. We had waited a long time for this day—twenty-three years! In my experience, one of the first goals of many new churches is to build a big auditorium for their worship services. It's what they live for and dream about, and in the early days of my ministry I was no exception. But over the years, my vision for growth had changed. I now believe that a big auditorium is one of the *last* big ticket dreams a new church should have. As carriers of the Great Commission, the church should be focused on becoming a kingdom people who first learn to engage in service to the community and the world, not building an empire of our own congregation.

This way of thinking had changed everything at NorthWood as we began to engage our local community here in America and serve globally in places like Vietnam. This shift in our focus had diverted our resources, both human and financial, and delayed the completion of our worship center by more than a decade. But we didn't have any regrets—it was a decision that has made NorthWood what she is today. We are not a building or a location, not even preachers or the staff, but a people on a mission.

So there we were that morning, fifty of us praying and sensing God's presence. We were kneeling, walking, sitting, talking, praying individually, and praying in groups. I went up into the highest section to pray over the seats, which would soon be filled with people. As I looked down, I noticed a sticker on the back of a chair that read "Made in Vietnam." As I stood there reading that sticker, it suddenly hit me just how true that statement really was for our church. In a real sense, our church was "Made in Vietnam" as we learned to serve people with God's love. My emotions welled up at that moment and I began to pray out my gratitude, thanking God for what he had done in our church as the result of our work in Vietnam.

As churches with a heart for mission, we go to places all over the world thinking that we will change them. But for NorthWood the opposite has happened: we have been changed through our involvement with people outside the walls of our church. Communists, atheists, Buddhists, and animists have taught me more about loving God and serving others than any book save the Bible or any speaker save Jesus. The experience of engaging a culture so completely opposite mine in philosophy, values, and cultural practice has deepened my understanding of God and his mission like nothing else I've done. Working in Vietnam has taught me to treat all people as people of value and worth, cherished by God and included in his love. This was a lesson I desperately needed to learn, and as I stood there that morning, praying with our church family, I felt a deep surge of gratitude to God.

On those first visits to Vietnam, I was surprised to find that the Vietnamese were more willing to be my friends than I was to be theirs. They treated me with respect and listened to me — not that they always agreed with me, or I with them. They even accepted me as I was — a Christian. I had to ask myself: *Was I willing to return the favor and accept them as atheists, Buddhists, animists?* Ultimately, I was able to accept this, but to be honest, it was their acceptance and respect that drew me out of my small, narrow box of relationships, where I could only relate well with people who were just like me.

Working in Vietnam has helped me understand that I am not called to set up a predetermined standard of who I'm supposed to love. God calls me to love the people whom he brings into my life, regardless of whether they accept my view of God or come to know my Savior, Jesus. Some of the people I first met in Vietnam are now among my closest friends. I consider their country my second home. These friendships have changed how I read the words of Jesus and have shaped my understanding of what he expects of me.

You see, I had always accepted the foundational truths of my faith, but I had substituted orthodoxy (right belief) for orthopraxy (right practice). Even though I believed the right things, I had not learned that the truth was more than something we believe and accept; rather, it's meant to be lived and practiced — and not by following a standard pattern that fits with American Christian culture, but by living out the truth within the context of each unique culture. All of this was a hard lesson for an East Texas boy to learn, but God was gracious to me — I think I'm finally starting to understand!

The Vietnamese let me serve in their country and partner with them to help their poor. The experience of working with them opened my eyes to the reality of poverty and the pain of human suffering. I felt a deep conviction that I, as an American and as a Christian, could not just choose to ignore people who needed help. Ignoring their needs would be a denial of my Savior, Jesus Christ. These experiences in Vietnam helped me to understand that the kingdom of God is about more than just getting people to pray the sinner's prayer. God's kingdom is about the reconciliation of all things — individuals, society, and cultures — to God. It's about more than just individual salvation; it's about transformation. Working for transformation in the lives of the people I served required more from me than a revival meeting and a prayer. It required effort, commitment, time, and love. To pray "Just send a revival, God," was always much easier for me than sweating and serving, and it absolved me from any responsibility to the people.

When we began to engage the Vietnamese through the jobs and callings of our members in the domains of education, art, communication, health, agriculture, and governance, I quickly learned to redefine my role as a pastor. My responsibilities grew from a focus on Sunday preaching to mobilizing our people to engage society. In one sense, I moved from the concept of a "seeker" church to a "seeker" *world*. I'm still not sure what to call it! But I could see the change all around me. Our church was changing from a Sunday audience of pew-warmers to a dynamic organism.

I believe that there are many pastors who can contemporize a worship service but have not yet learned how to contemporize their church. They can learn to communicate with unchurched Americans, yet still be dropouts when it comes to defining an understanding of the church that goes beyond the Sunday morning experience of their members. Through our experience in Vietnam I came to recognize that my job as a pastor was not to focus on doing "religious" work, but to make disciples who would engage society through their jobs, skills, and passions.

Working with the Vietnamese gave a whole new meaning to the idea of people-to-people diplomacy. I found that they value friendship much more than we do in the West, and they had a much more global perspective on things. Not only did they teach me many things, they showed me genuine love, which was something I wasn't expecting.

After some time, we reached a sufficient level of trust and our Vietnamese friends became interested in sending us their children as exchange students. At the time of this writing, about fifty of these students have visited our church, lived with our church members, and become part of our families. As I stated in an earlier chapter, our own family took in a Vietnamese boy, Ti, and we love him deeply. He is now a part of our family. Through having Ti in our home I have learned many new things. For example, I have learned that Vietnamese kids don't like to be hugged or told they are loved as much as American kids do. While they like the love, they aren't as comfortable with overt demonstrations of affection. The best way to say "I love you" to a Vietnamese kid is to set a big bowl of Pho in front of him!

"Made in Vietnam." That phrase defined us to a T. As I stood in our new worship center that morning, I was also very aware that the lessons we had learned in Vietnam did not come without a cost — in our time, money, and labor. The cost had meant delaying our new building and doing without other typical church "needs" for many years. But as I considered the amazing work God had done, I was deeply grateful. Today, we are what we are, a church with a strong, biblical DNA and a far-reaching, global perspective. We are engaging cultures around the world and shaping churches all across America. Buildings are not what define our church. The character of our church has been shaped by our involvement with God's gracious work in Vietnam.

As I prayed for our building, I took a moment to honor my dear friends. I prayed for the Vietnamese whom I had never met, yet who had made many of our friendships possible. "Mr. General Secretary, Mr. President, Mr. Prime Minister, Mr. Ambassador, businessmen, educators, tradesmen, farmers, and laborers: Thank you for all you have done for our church and what you have taught us. We would not be who we are today were it not for you. We are the ones who came to serve you, but you are now shaping this American church! The practice of our church has been forged in Vietnam. I pray that when this life is over, all of you will be with us in heaven, and that God will allow me live in the Vietnamese section. We'll sit by the streets early in the mornings drinking green tea and talking about the love of God and our marvelous Savior Jesus."

Global ministry and cross-cultural friendships continue to shape the DNA of our church. Our opportunities in Vietnam are still growing and expanding. I've had opportunities to meet with many different people in Vietnam — from farm workers to leaders of corporations and government ministers. The road we're traveling stretches out far ahead of us, and we are eager to continue on this global journey.

MAKING A DIFFERENCE IN THE LOCAL COMMUNITY

Our global ministry has given us an equally active local ministry. As people began to serve in Vietnam, we started looking at our own community, asking, "How can we make that happen here?" I once heard a question that I then posed to NorthWood Church in order to get our members to think more intentionally about our impact on the community: "If this church were absent from our community would anyone miss it but your members?" We wanted NorthWood to be a church that would be missed, so we committed to having members involved in community projects all over the area.

I had learned that in Little Rock, Lewis and his church adopted a disadvantaged school and engaged in an amazing ministry to the students and teachers. Several NorthWood members used this project as their model and did the same thing in our community. They adopted one of the poorest schools in Tarrant County, a Title I school for children from low-income families who are disadvantaged economically and speak only limited English.

Our primary contact at the school was Olga Hernandez-Coar, a longtime volunteer bilingual reading specialist. Olga was herself raised in poverty and was able to identify with the needs of the children. Olga's father had worked for the railroad, and during the school months the family had lived in a house next to the tracks. At night they would lie in bed and watch the trains roar by. In the summer months, the children would travel with their dad, living in a boxcar. Olga now has a husband who also works for the railroad and a grown son who is a banker. She lives next door to her widowed mother, who does all the cooking for the family.

Olga has volunteered at the school for over ten years. What's the payback? Why does she keep doing it? "Because I love it," she says. "Those kids need me. I feel a joy when I can see the growth in the kids. They care about me; I care about them. Parents do things for me, and they sometimes pay me with a taco or burrito or tortillas to take to my family."

Olga is a devout believer in Christ, but her own church limits its charity ministries to evangelism or overseas missionary work. She had never heard of a church interested in simply helping people by meeting their practical needs with no strings attached. When North-Wood began its ministry in her school, she said, "With your church you've opened up my eyes to lots of ways to be there for people and serve — be it filling out forms, or whatever. I didn't realize what I was doing was mission work. I just truly loved the community and believed I needed to help. I didn't know what mission work was until you came, and your work opened my eyes."

The first thing our church did for the school was to help them paint their classrooms. It was a small, simple thing for us, but it had great value because it allowed us to engage with the school workers — to get to know each other as real people. Other opportunities began to present themselves, and soon NorthWood people were engaged in several ministries and special projects at the school. Here are several examples of ongoing ministries that we are involved with at the school.

1. ESL Classes

We have conducted ongoing ESL (English as a Second Language) classes for the parents of the schoolchildren for four years. The classes are held twice weekly. NorthWood member Gus Astorga teaches one day and I teach the other. Gus Astorga came to NorthWood from Chile almost ten years ago. He accepted Christ at NorthWood and has been involved in serving in Mexico and this local school ever since.

Gus loves the parents he teaches, and the parents love him. He's generous with his time and extremely patient. He treats each parent as an individual, staying after class as long as necessary to listen to their problems and help find a solution. When Gus's father passed away, the sympathy and care of the class were so great you would have thought they had lost their own dad.

Gus has brought more parents from the community into the English class because he was a second-language learner himself, and he can relate to the frustrations they experience. Having gone through that difficult journey himself makes him an effective leader of others. Gus is able to use his skills, life experience, and passion to teach in order to link with God's work right in his own community!

2. Café for Kids

Café for Kids is a feeding program for kids from poverty-stricken families. Many of the children at the Title I school live in motels or trailers, and most of the time the gas and electricity are turned off, making it impossible for families to cook even if they do happen to have food. Children who come to the school are fed their supper in a cafélike setting where they are treated with dignity and respect. They would go hungry if it were not for this café. Volunteers from North-Wood feed and mentor fifty to sixty kids at the Fort Worth Christian Center and a local volunteer center.

One of the volunteers is Rusty Mayeux. Rusty came to North-Wood several years ago, just a Sunday-go-to-church person who recommitted his life to Christ. He has been a positive force ever since. He often works with us in places throughout the world and assists in other nonprofits and ministries, even mentoring and tutoring at the Title I school. Rusty told me not long ago, his voice choking, "The greatest thing I did was help a couple of third graders pass to the fourth grade." But his real passion is his regular commitment to Café for Kids. He loves those kids. No challenge is too big, whatever the need. If one needs a coat, she gets a coat. If one needs shoes, he gets shoes. The kids love Rusty; they know he's there for them.

3. School Supplies

Most of the children at the school cannot afford their basic school supplies, nor can the school budget handle everything they need. Before our church was involved with the school, teachers would often dig into their own pockets to buy supplies. NorthWood took over the supply problem, lifting the financial burden from the teachers. Olga Hernandez-Coar explains the sensitivity with which the supplies are distributed: "We bag them up for Meet-the-Teacher Night when the parents come to the school's open house. We put the students' names on the bags, and the supplies are there at the students' desks when the parents arrive. This way no one is made to feel poor — all children get a bag."

Olga explains the difference NorthWood is making at the school. "It all shows up in our achievement scores. This year we came very close to being a higher-rated school, and I'm convinced it's because of NorthWood — the food program, the medical clinic, the volunteers, the supplies; they build our children's self-esteem. They are totally different creatures than when I came ten years ago. Now they believe there's nothing they can't do or achieve. These people are working side by side with our kids and helping them achieve their goals. Every volunteer works with the child until they get it. Now all the kids think, 'Somebody cares about me.' That has had a big impact on the school."

4. Medical Clinic

After these ministries to the school were successfully underway, Rusty Mayeux asked Olga what the school needed next. Without hesitation she responded: "A medical clinic." Before I knew what was happening, the school had its own medical clinic. Normally, cutting through miles and miles of governmental red tape would have daunted our Christian volunteers. But as it happened, Rusty had been in the business of buying and selling hospitals most of his career, so setting up a medical clinic was a piece of cake for him. Not only did he vanquish the red tape, he also involved the community, the county hospital, and the school district in the project. Rusty was able to successfully connect his skill and life experience with the work that God wanted to do through this medical clinic — engaging his particular domain (health care) as a disciple of Jesus Christ.

When it came time to build the clinic, another NorthWood member, Peter Paulsen, came to the rescue. Peter is a builder, and not long after he became a Christian he helped an inner-city family refurbish their house. The experience moved him so deeply that he began to devote much of his time to working on inner-city homes. When Rusty was ready to put his plans into action, he called Peter. They found an old dilapidated building in the right location, and Peter went to work. He called in lots of favors to get subcontractors and financing, and — voila! — we have a clinic! Together, these two members were able to link their expertise and job skills with God's work in a way that served the school and allowed us to broaden our ministry to the community.

The medical clinic not only helps the disadvantaged children in the school; it also helps their families. These are people who have neither insurance nor the means to pay even for basic medical care. For a token fee of five dollars they can get well-checked or treated for minor injuries and illnesses. At the dedication of the clinic, I stood beside Peter and his wife, Stacey, and their boys. No pastor could have been more proud of his church members than I was of these dedicated and caring Christians.

5. The Carnival

Every fall members of NorthWood, working independent of any official church plan or program, provide a carnival for the school-children and their families. These people can't afford Six Flags or even many of the lesser amusement parks. But at our carnival they don't have to pay anything — free food, rides, games, and candy for everyone, parents and children alike.

The carnival was the idea of NorthWood member Omar Reyes, and it is completely created and run by our church members. Intern church planters set up a full spread of food and serve it. The youth provide the midway games, which include a bean bag toss, pitching a hockey puck through a hole, bobbing for apples, fishing with a magnet, a basketball shot, face painting, and many other games. In addition there is a wide variety of other activities, including bounce houses, slides, and obstacle courses. The carnival fills an elementary school field in a Fort Worth suburb.

These Christians have hosted the carnival now for four years, and plans are well under way for the next one. Unlike the supplies, the clinic, and the kids' café, the carnival is not strictly a necessity. It's simply a fun thing. But we think recreation is important and adds dimension to the hard life these families endure. And it gives us one more way of engaging society.

6. Home Makeovers

Last year about seven hundred NorthWood members converged on four different homes of low-income families and totally restored them. The houses were chosen from the families of children who attend the Title I school. It was one of the most significant things our church members have ever done as a group, because it involved so many people. The families in the homes were so deeply touched that they could not stop talking about how beautiful their made-over homes now are. This year we are scheduled to do four more of these makeovers, and NorthWood volunteers are already coming out of the woodwork.

This project grew out of an idea NorthWood member Chris Shabay had while watching the TV show *Extreme Home Makeover*. Chris assembled four volunteer teams, which took on the four houses, simply copying the format of the show. We can now say thank you to Ty Pennington for helping us learn to be better Christians!

7. School Volunteers

Several NorthWood members volunteer to help at the school on a daily basis. Title I schools get virtually no parental volunteers or teacher assistants, so many NorthWood members fill these gaps. They assist the teachers in various ways — reading, organizing materials, grading papers, helping kids with questions, working with them one-on-one, and taking many other burdens off of already overworked teachers. Right now these volunteers are helping in twenty-five classrooms. It pays off in many ways, not only easing the load from teachers, but improving classroom efficiency and even improving behavior and self-confidence on the part of the kids.

WHAT HAPPENS WHEN THE CHURCH ENGAGES SOCIETY

When the church engages society with no agenda, no strings attached, and no motivation other than love, it makes a huge difference, not only in the lives of the people they touch, but also in the hearts of those who witness their work. Olga Hernandez-Coar, who is not a member of our church, expressed the effect the NorthWood ministry to her school had on her: "NorthWood has made me a better Christian. Maybe I thought I was a Christian, but you've taught me what it really means to be a Christian. I now have a totally different concept of what it means to love God, what his work is, and how you treat people. All of that has happened since you came to the school. I've always read the Bible, but just coming to the NorthWood church and listening to people that come from there, I've become better acquainted with the Bible and understood verses in a new way because I see the action and the work of God. Now I open my Bible and read a Scripture and say, 'That's what NorthWood is doing; that's how they're sharing.'"

THIS IS THE CHURCH!

I tell you these stories not to lift up our church or promote our ministry as a model for every church. I share them because I believe that they demonstrate what *any* church can look like when its leaders shift their focus to making disciples instead of mere converts who fill the pews. Our church members, involved in these ministries, are not merely converts to a belief system. They have not come to serve as a way of achieving personal salvation. They are disciples: followers of Christ, imitators of his life — dedicated to his call upon their lives.

The NorthWood building where we meet for worship is not the church. The pastors, staff, and teachers are not the church. Our new worship center is not the church. The church is not simply a place where we gather for worship; it's a network of interconnected disciples who serve in the community and in the world. Our building is simply one division of the operational headquarters; our staff and pastors serve as motivators and enablers. But our church itself is really made up of the people who fan out from the building and link their jobs and skills with the work that God is doing all over the world. This is the church in action, engaged in kingdom ministry.

Nowadays, everyone seems so focused on reinventing the church, and these efforts are sucking up much of our time and energy. Studies, definitions, new ways of organizing our members, creative ways of attracting new members, new ways of worship — what does all of this really accomplish? The church will never be what it's meant to be if we spend all of our time focused on theories, charts, worship styles, or methods for attracting new people. What we need is not a new definition of "church," but a recovery of the definition that Jesus gave us. The church is simply his followers living out their faith: disciples engaged in society. This is the church; it is Christ's followers engaged in ministry, both locally and globally — the "glocal" body of Christ engaging society.

In his book *The Call*, Os Guinness writes, "The call of Jesus is personal but not purely individual; Jesus summons his followers not only to an individual calling but also to a corporate calling."[31] Too much of a focus on our individual callings tends to put the emphasis on ourselves and our own salvation. A corporate calling reminds us that we are disciples who live in community with one another and the world around us, and it gives us a better sense of our responsibility to serve the world that doesn't know Christ. I believe that the church is missing out on fulfilling the mandate of the Great Commission because we have grown deaf to this corporate calling from God.

One practical benefit of recognizing the corporate call of God is that it enlarges the resource pool. At NorthWood, as we have shifted our focus to our corporate call as a church, we have seen God raise up people from within the body with all kinds of skills and passions to fit the domains of the community where we work. We've even seen how God can draw on the skills of members in *other* congregations to enlarge the scope of our effectiveness as we work together to fulfill this corporate call.

Let me explain how that works. First, we start by taking the call of Jesus seriously. He told his disciples that they should "be witnesses to me in Jerusalem, in all Judea and Samaria, and to the uttermost parts of the earth" (Acts 1:8). As a single congregation, we know that we cannot literally go into all the world to reach every culture and people by ourselves. With that in mind, we deliberately limit our own mission to what we know we can handle. As a church, we have decided to focus on Haltom City (our contextual equivalent of Jerusalem), northeast Tarrant County (our Judea), Puebla, Mexico (our Samaria), and Hanoi, Vietnam (the uttermost parts of the earth).

If we weren't focused and instead tried to go out in a dozen different directions, believing the success of Jesus' call rested entirely on us, our efforts would be so diffused they would be largely ineffective, and we would be increasingly frustrated by the lack of fruitfulness. But if we shift our thinking and learn to think of ourselves not simply as one church among many but as one small outpost of the universal church, the picture changes. We become free to lend our skills, resources, and talents to other groups to help them be more effective in domains of society where they are linking with God's work, without taking ownership of the entire project.

For example, my wife has just returned from Romania, where she engaged in a health and hygiene service with Living Water International. I just returned from Kenya, where I met with pastors from around the world. My friend Andy Wallace is working in Nigeria with a group of thirty people from several other U.S. churches. None of these are "NorthWood" projects, but our church members are participating in them as part of God's corporate call. They are laying aside their denominational identities and working alongside other disciples of Jesus as part of the church universal. Os Guinness sums up the concept:

> In the New Testament, it is not so much that there are different churches in different places as there is one church in many places. Each local church embodies and represents the whole

church, so the church is both local and universal, visible and invisible, militant and triumphant.[32]

When Christians partner with other Christians around the world, the partnerships and friendships that form broaden the perspective and understanding of all those who are involved. Each culture sees things in a slightly different way because of its own history, outlook, and environment. These varying insights can enlarge the vision of the whole. Oscar Muiriu, pastor of Nairobi Chapel, told me of how one culture, on hearing the Genesis account of Joseph, came away with the conviction that Christians should always care for their families. I've never heard that in the American reading of this story. Typically, we see the moral as a reminder to always hang tough in adversity and by trusting God you will succeed in life. Maybe our success-oriented culture can learn something from Christians in more family-oriented cultures!

Pastor Muiriu also shared with me his own adapted translation of 1 Corinthians 12, which addresses the mutual need that global churches have for each other. It's too good not to share with you.

If the American church would say, because I am not of Africa I do not belong to the body, it would not cease to be the body. If the whole body were European, where would the sense of joy be? And if the whole body were African, where would the sense of order be? But in fact, God has arranged the parts of the body, every one of them, just as he wanted them to be. If they were all one part, where would the body be? As it is there are many parts, but there is only one body. The Canadian church cannot say to the Asian church, "I have no need of you." The Asian church cannot say to the European church, "I don't need you." On the contrary, the parts that seem to be weaker, like the Japanese church, are indispensable to the body. African parts less honorable should be treated with special honor. And the Latin American parts that seem unpresentable should be treated with modesty. The presentable parts like the big American church need no special treatment. [Except for TEXAS!] But God has combined the members of the body and has given greater honor to the parts that lacked it, so that there should be no division in the body, but that the parts should have equal concern for each other. If one part suffers, every part suffers. If one part is honored, every part is valued. Now you are the body of Christ and each one of you is a part of it.

All churches around the world are part of one body, the body of Christ, and we all contribute to the health and function of the entire body. Churches in different cultures will naturally differ from each other in many ways, but that should be seen as a benefit to the overall body, not a problem that we need to fix or cover up. In today's shrinking world of instant communication and real-time connections, it is essential that churches learn how to work together in partnership. We will all be enriched by the experience of serving together as one body.

In his book *Halftime*, entrepreneur Bob Buford writes about what he calls "fifty-fifty" churches.[33] Fifty-fifty churches spend half their money on themselves and half outside themselves, helping the poor, assisting other churches, or engaging the world. I like that concept. I fully endorse the idea, even as I admit that our church isn't quite there yet. But we are working toward that goal.

At this point, our church dedicates about 25 to 35 percent of our total annual receipts to ministries outside of NorthWood. While I realize we've got a bit farther to go in our selfless giving, I also think it is important to remember that giving and servanthood is about much more than just the amount of money we give. It's also about giving time, energy, and effort. It's about the work we do, serving others and caring for the lost and the least. Personally, I would love for us to be a "ninety-ten" church. I've actually met a few ninety-ten individuals. They give away 90 percent of their income and live on just 10 percent. Not everyone can do that, of course, but I'm convinced that when people are transformed into true disciples, their budget will also be transformed and their giving proportion will increase dramatically.

I love the meaning behind the Greek word *ekklesia*, which is the word for "church" used in the New Testament. *Ekklesia* literally means "the called-out ones." It's essentially a diplomatic or political term that captures the idea of people gathering together and then going out. I find that most Christians today think of the church as a static group called out from the world. That image conveys isolation, insulation, and perhaps even a defensive posture in relation to society. But the true meaning of the word does not stop with the idea of just being a gathered community; it indicates a scattered community — a community called not just *from* the world but *to* it. It is a community charged to live the life of Christ and engage others.

The way we've traditionally thought of church makes it more of an *agora* than an *ekklesia*. An *agora* was a place in ancient Greek cities where people assembled together. We've made the church into more of an *agora*, a place where the gathering is everything. We've lost the second part of the definition of *ekklesia*, the part that reminds us that we are scattered into the community. The purpose of our gathering is to receive our marching orders, get equipped, and engage with others who participate in the call. The church is where our calling moves from *me* to *us*. Church reminds us that it's not just about me and what I feel called to do; it's about what we are called to do *together*. It's about what we are called to do together for *others*.

When we first began to receive exchange students from Vietnam, some members found it a bit disconcerting to have several high school students from Hanoi invade our youth Sunday school. "Here come all these foreigners bringing their Buddhist, atheist, animist, and God knows what other false religions into our church!" But what better place than in the church environment for our kids to be exposed to the world and learn to respect and love people of other cultures? And what better place for Vietnamese to be exposed to Christians than in the context of the gathered church?

Os Guinness quotes American economist Arthur Burns, who prayed with a group of Christians at the White House: "Lord, I pray that you would bring Jews to know Jesus Christ. I pray that would bring Muslims to know Jesus Christ. Finally, Lord, I pray that you would bring Christians to know Jesus Christ."[34] Christians come to truly know Christ when they serve others. As Jesus told his disciples, service to others is counted as service to him: "Inasmuch as you did it to one of the least of these my brothers, you did it to me." (Matthew 25:40).

In other words, Christians also come to know Christ through *being the church* — the church that God intended us to be. As the church, we are his body — his hands, his feet, his heart of compassion that ministers his love and service to those in need. Christ lives in his body, acting through us to take his love to the world. You cannot get any closer to him than that!

Connection Steps

⊙ How has the world defined your church?

⊙ If your church were to focus on one spot globally and one spot locally, how would that change the outreach ministry of your church.

⊙ If I got serious about fulfilling the Great Commission my church would . . .

CHAPTER 8

Sweating the Work

We have spent much of our time talking about ideas and concepts, but now it's time to get practical, down to the nitty-gritty of being a disciple … where the rubber meets the road. What does it really mean to link your job, your skills, and your passions —your call—with the work that God is doing in your community and around the world? I can't think of a better way to dive into all of this than by sharing the story of Mark, a man who saw the need to get his hands "dirty" doing the work of the kingdom.

MARK'S STORY

Mark was raised in a mainline Christian denomination. Religion in his church was dead and dry, and there was nothing inspiring about it. In fact, the youth pastor would go out and drink with the sixteen-year-olds in his group. "It keeps the kids out of trouble," he said. Mark's father never really got involved in the church because he thought it was all about money. He believed that churches taught damnation in order to put fear into members' hearts so they would give money. When the family moved to another state, they stopped attending church — and Mark didn't miss it.

Mark married when he was twenty and divorced at age twenty-five. Sometime later, friends introduced Mark to Bette, who had also gone through a traumatic divorce. She had a baby and he had a dog. Neither Mark nor Bette was looking for a relationship, but things clicked between them. Two or three weeks after meeting her, Mark got a job in a northern suburb of Fort Worth, and he invited Bette to come to Texas with him. When their divorces were finalized they got married, and their union was blessed with two children.

The couple never went to church. Bette's spiritual beliefs did not mesh well with Mark's high-church background, and it was easier for them not to go at all than to deal with their differences. They drank too much, even to the point of being "weekend alcoholics." But when Mark's mother died of alcoholism they quit drinking altogether. Mark and Bette became friends with Krisanne and Brian Stewart, who invited them to attend worship with them at the NorthWood Church. They declined the invitation, but they did send their daughter, Kayla. Kayla loved the church, and because of that the couple began to attend occasionally, especially on Christmas and Easter. Then 9 – 11 hit, and Mark realized that his life was not as secure as he had presumed. He had always felt that God had blessed America, but now he feared that those blessings might be withdrawn. Anything could happen. So they began attending church regularly.

Mark's thinking slowly began to change. He became more sensitive to the possibility that God wanted something more from him. As he put it, "When we walked out of church after Bob preached on discipleship and serving others, I would look at Bette and say, 'Wow! It's as if that guy on the stage was talking directly to me, like he knew right where I was and just what I was struggling with.' God was practically blasting things into us, but I kept hearing the skepticism of my father. My business was off and running full bore, we had money in the bank, a nice house, and a BMW 535 in the driveway. My goals were met, and my wall of self-sufficiency kept me from committing to join the church. But week by week, Bob was breaking down that wall."

Throughout this time, Mark Kimmel, a NorthWood pastor, stayed connected to Mark and Bette, calling on them every month. His persistence eventually paid off. Mark began to get involved in church activities, and soon he made a firm commitment to the Lord and was baptized. Bette resisted conversion for a while, but eventually her own study convinced her that her former beliefs were in error. She made her own commitment to Christ, and the results were dynamic. She and Mark began to teach in children's Sunday school. Today, Mark is involved in teaching the youth, and according to reports from the kids, he is "awesome."

One night Mark's small group studied Matthew 25, where the Lord separates the goats from the sheep. Mark was struck by the acts for which Jesus commended the sheep. They had ministered to the hungry, the thirsty, the naked, the sick, and those in prison. That was just what Mark was looking for. "There I had a list," he said, "Jesus' own catalog of things disciples can do to show their love for him." Shortly after this study, a member of his small group challenged him to attend a weekend event with a Youth Prison Ministry. He accepted the challenge, and at the event discovered a passion for jail ministry.

Mark's faith continued stretching and reaching outward. Mark's son, Blake, and Blake's Sunday school teacher learned of a need for people willing to work with disadvantaged minorities in downtown Dallas. They were making plans to travel to the city, but Mark convinced them that it would make more sense to address a local need than to spend hours driving back and forth to Dallas. He and several others from NorthWood visited a local apartment complex filled with disadvantaged minorities, and they found that an outreach program to the apartments was about to be dismantled, including a much-needed tutoring program for the kids. That was all Mark needed to hear. He took the program under his wing and organized a new tutoring program using NorthWood volunteers.

On the very day Mark assumed leadership for this tutoring program, he received news of a mentally unstable mother of three who tried to burn her oldest daughter to death. While the mother was being placed in a public mental institution and the youngest children were being placed in foster homes, the oldest daughter, who was eighteen, was left out in the cold. She wanted to attend beauty school, but she lacked the funds and the needed supplies. So I made an appeal to the church for help. Enough members came through with funds to enable Mark to furnish and pay for the apartment, purchase the young woman's beauty supplies, get her certified by the State of Texas as a beautician, and raise her younger brothers and sisters.

Shortly after this, Mark learned of a local facility that served as a rehabilitation unit for the Texas youth justice system, a part of the Texas Youth Commission (TYC). Since Mark was already involved in NorthWood's youth ministry, it was natural for him to volunteer with the youth at the rehab unit. After several weeks of ministry, he found that the needs were much greater than he could meet by himself, so he began to recruit other NorthWood members. Now dozens of adults work in this program, teaching Bible studies, mentoring, and facilitating recovery in many other ways. Today, this has become Mark's primary ministry.

Mark is a persuasive guy. He shared the good news of Jesus with one young man he was mentoring, and while the boy wasn't quite ready to commit to Christ, he remained willing to be mentored by Mark. Four or five weeks into the process he told Mark that he had given his heart to Christ. He had been at the NorthWood-led Bible study when the dots all connected, and suddenly it all came together for him. At that moment, he opened his Bible and out fell a sheet of paper Mark had given him weeks earlier that described how to become a follower of Jesus. He couldn't believe it. It was like a sign. Right then and there, this young man gave his heart to Christ. He didn't suddenly became a model teenager, and in many ways he's still a rebellious kid, but he's serious about changing his life now, and by God's grace he's making headway.

I mention Mark's experience with this young man because it brings up something important that we must accept. Sometimes the guys at the youth rehab center accept Christ, but they still have a lot to learn about what real discipleship means. They will often tell you what they think you want to hear instead of revealing their real inner struggles. We do not give up on them or judge them for having inner issues that don't resolve immediately. Many of them have been through a kind of hell that we cannot imagine.

By far the biggest issue with most of them is their dad. Not a single one of the boys at the TYC has had a positive relationship with his father. Most of them don't even really know their dad because he is either in prison, is an alcoholic, has skipped out on the family, or is dead. Those who volunteer to mentor these young men are often the first positive male role models they've ever had. We've learned that you can't give up on these boys just because their conversion to Christ doesn't immediately turn them into model teens. You have to persevere, continually praying for them and feeding them a steady diet of truth.

One Sunday I had Mark come to the stage and share his story. He brought three of the young men they've been working with who have truly changed. At the conclusion we had them kneel and we laid hands on them. It was such a moving testimony that a dozen people volunteered that morning to join Mark in his ministry. We live in an affluent area, and it's hard for some people to picture businessmen and community leaders in an area like Keller, Texas, serving at-risk youth. But it's happening. And once these men serve, it triggers something deep within them that inspires a passion to continue. They are bringing help and hope to young men who desperately need it.

I asked Mark how his ministry with the TYC has changed him. His answer is a sermon in itself:

> This is where I see God. As Christ said, those who have done good to the least of his people have done it to him. When you serve others, God is present and alive. You can be drained from a hard day of work and it's hard to get up there to the TYC. It doesn't matter, you go, and when you do it's a joy. People who just go to church on Sundays are missing the boat. They're not getting the abundant life.
>
> You know, I've read all the books on seeking God and spiritual disciplines, and they have their place. But it's not until you engage others with no motive other than to bring God to them that you actually witness God. You see him in their eyes and hear him in their voices. There's nothing better than hearing a kid say, "Thanks for coming. No one ever visits me or cares." How do you put a price tag on that?

As you can see, there have been several connections throughout his life that have allowed Mark to link his skills, passions, and sense of calling with God's work. Mark's story puts flesh on some of the principles I outlined in the first chapters of this book. I believe that it is our responsibility, as a church, to make disciples. We did that with Mark, teaching him and equipping him with the understanding and skills to serve others. But it's the responsibility of our members, as disciples of Christ, to engage the community. Mark did that when he organized and participated in the ministry to the TYC. I think it is significant that Mark — *not the church leadership* — took personal ownership and responsibility for the TYC program. He started doing it on his own, and it was up to him to keep it going. He recruited the volunteers and developed the programs.

Don't get me wrong — church programs are fine, but processes created and driven by church members are usually much better because the members own them and take responsibility for the results. Church-sponsored events have their purpose, and they are usually worthwhile ministries. But a church is truly "missional" not because they are engaged in official, corporate projects, but when their members are personally following Christ's call to engage with their neighbors and bring healing to hurting people.

You may look at your own life and think, "I don't have the initiative or creativity to do what Mark did." Maybe not. Not everyone does. But notice that Mark needed fifty volunteers in three or four specialized areas to make the program work — Bible teachers, mentors, and assistants to teachers. None of these roles require extraordinary organizing or initiating skills. There are always jobs for everyone to get involved. Even if you can't work at the top as the one who initiates and leads the ministry, there's still a place for you!

I'm convinced that it's only when ordinary Christians get their hands dirty and get involved in the communities, meeting the needs of our society and sweating it out in the trenches, that the church will really make a difference. It's time for the churches in America to empty the pews and start getting involved in the community!

SHOWING INSTEAD OF TELLING

Today there are over six billion people on the earth living in more than 220 nations. What difference is Christianity making to that six billion, to those nations? Again, I'm not asking about the number of converts we've made in those nations, but the quality of life. Is the life of a person in Syria or Cambodia or Vietnam better because of Christianity? Some will disagree with me on this and say that winning souls is far more important than improving the quality of life in these places, but I would argue that thinking about priorities this way is like putting the cart before the horse. I've found that people are typically no longer interested in hearing arguments about which religion is right. They want to see and witness the actual difference that your faith makes in your life. Disciples of Jesus should be bearing the real fruit of a transformed life. I believe that if we show others that God has made a difference in our lives by the way we act and by the way we love people, we'll start seeing more than "conversions"; we'll start witnessing true discipleship.

Our typical method of engagement with non-Christians has been limited to a verbal gospel presentation. This approach can lead to converts, but discipling followers of Christ requires much more. Verbal engagement can give us converts to a set of beliefs, but we will not necessarily have disciples. To put it simply: all disciples are converts, but not all converts are disciples! There are many people who are willing to nod in acceptance to a set of beliefs or a statement of doctrine who have no practical understanding of what it means to live it out. Biblical discipleship is more than just an acknowledgment of what the truth is; it involves the practice of that truth in daily life and relationships. Discipleship is about obedience to King Jesus — whatever that means given our cultural context. It means rolling up our sleeves and getting involved in the messy work of sacrifice and suffering, of reconciling broken people and broken institutions with God. Work like this requires sweat and persistent engagement. Only a committed disciple is willing and able to hear what God is saying.

Over the years, as I've served as a pastor, I have found that it's a lot easier to get people to come to my church than to get them to follow Christ with abandonment. I've wondered why this is true. I believe that this disconnect, between those who come to church as converts to the Christian faith and those who seek to follow Christ where he leads them, goes back to the actual decision that people are making for Christ and what it means to follow him on a daily basis. Does the decision to follow Christ go beyond reading our Bibles, praying before meals, and going to church on Sunday mornings?

To make disciples, the church must learn to engage the city and the world in a different way than we have in the past. Let me be clear:

I am not suggesting that we throw out the whole notion of conversion. I believe that the answer involves pulling everything together into a comprehensive process that includes verbal proclamation and compassionate witness; it's about engaging the culture by meeting needs *and* using the "four spiritual laws" to share the gospel with people.

Engaging the culture means that we serve sick people just as Christians did during the medieval plagues; we serve poverty-stricken people as Albert Schweitzer did in Africa; we learn to relate to different religions as Francis of Assisi related to the Muslims in his day. Today we have the benefit of history, the blessing of communication, and the opportunity of travel. What is lacking is the will to sacrifice our time and comfort for the sake of serving others. God help us if we fail to follow Christ into the world because we are too comfortable in our churches.

When I meet someone, I may not know where they stand with God, but I can see when there are obvious needs in front of me. If I respond to that immediate need and model the love of Jesus Christ along with a verbal witness to Jesus and his life, then I've provided a holistic message of hope for that individual. As I see it, disciples don't need to live in the tension of the either-or, we can embrace the beauty of the both-and; we can share the gospel and serve our communities!

When I speak of sweat, I'm talking about engagement — working side by side to serve the common good of society. All the while we look for opportunities to share why we do what we do. We are eager to talk about what the love of Jesus has done for us, what it can do for them, and how it can change the world. The problem with our mission and outreach today is that it is largely a religious response to the world, isolated from the context of actual relationships. While there are a few churches here and there and some mission organizations that recognize the need for change in our approach, more change is needed.

I remember a few years back when I was starting in ministry, most pastors were not trained to lead churches of several thousand people, manage staffs of hundreds, or administer budgets of millions. There weren't really any books by other pastors on "megachurch management theory." So many pastors began to aggressively read books by successful businessmen. They read these books because these leaders specialized in what these pastors needed to learn.

Let me say up front that as followers of Jesus we must read the Bible first and foremost. The church of Christ is *not* a business, nor should it be, and business principles may not always directly apply to ministry. But there is still value in learning from the skills and experience of people outside the church. And I would suggest that the same principle applies to the church as we seek to educate ourselves about serving locally and globally in cross-cultural ministry. Today, some of the most helpful mission books aren't being written by the religious guys (though there are some wonderful resources out there) but by sociologists, anthropologists, and urbanologists. The writers may be Jews, Hindus, Muslims, or even agnostics. In many cases, it doesn't matter what the religious perspective of the author is.

These resources are helpful because when I want to do mission work in an urban community, I need to really understand that community. So naturally I turn to an expert who has studied it. If I want to understand a certain foreign culture, a Christian pastor writing mission theories about that culture won't help me nearly as much as an expert on that culture, regardless of whether he or she is a Christian. Basic cultural information is the same for everyone, regardless of religion.

That's why I read both Christian and non-Christian authors. I've enjoyed books like Os Guinness's *The Case for Civility*, Jonathan Sacks's *The Home We Build Together*, and Fareed Zakaria's *The Post-American World*. Other books of interest are Hernando De Soto's *The Mystery of Capital*, Peter Berger's *The Decentralization of the World*, and Richard Florida's *Who's Your City?* I find that books dealing with current affairs and biographies are particularly helpful for keeping abreast of today's world. I try to follow Barth's advice to read with the newspaper in one hand and the Bible in the other, but sometimes I put down the paper for a helpful book!

That said, while reading is helpful, it's merely the means to an end. The vital thing that makes all the difference is our choice to *engage*.

Getting out into your community and sweating with the people you serve will change your entire paradigm for missions. There are plenty of experts who have read a lot and developed elaborate theories for mission engagement. But theoretical processes rarely fit into a given context. They must be developed on the ground and learned through trial and error in the context of actual engagement.

At this point, you might be wondering: What do I mean by "engagement"? I'll put it simply: getting your hands dirty in the soil of life wherever people are suffering. I mean using your job, your mind, your skills, your passion, and your love of Jesus to serve society. I mean staying somewhere long enough to build real relationships so that people can know you love them regardless of the religious, racial, political, or whatever differences you might have. What matters is that you are committed and involved long enough for them to see the light of God's love shining in your life. You're there long enough for them to see how you respond to difficulty. You're around long enough for them to know that you care and will stick with them even when the going gets tough.

Once I was with some leaders from a country where the political climate was such that they could not officially admit that I was working with them. They told me, "Given your religion and ours, and given your government and ours, we don't understand why you would work with us. But you do. We value what you do so much that we would like to give you and your church an award. But you understand that we can't do that in our current context." For me, it was reward enough that they knew of my love for Jesus. Our service in his name was a seed planted in their lives from which God can grow a huge and fruitful tree. Many people come to find Christ through seeds like this. I'd love to share some of them with you, but many of them cannot be written about without getting certain officials in trouble with their government.

I will say this. Stories like the ones I've shared about Rusty and Peter are happening all over the world. These are the stories of disciples who roll up their sleeves and sweat. Their faith is viral and deeply relational.

BUILDING SOCIETY

In my first book, *Transformation*, I wrote about nation building. I don't use that term anymore. It has too much baggage now, having become associated with war, political coercion, and a host of other negative concepts. Instead, I like to talk about society building. Whereas nation building implies government-initiated activity, society building is something done by individuals, nongovernmental organizations (NGOs), and other religious organizations.

A society is part of a nation, but it's also a community. As I said in a previous chapter, the template for engaging a society or a nation is its domains — the areas of trades and professions in which the citizens work. Domains give us natural points of engagement in any society. We all work in a trade or a profession, which means we can effectively engage society by using our vocations. We take our natural abilities and expertise into another society and put those talents to work in the corresponding domain. When we serve in this way, our differences in religion or race or politics don't matter. Our work together is based on what we have in common — our vocational domains.

That's what we are doing at NorthWood in our local context. It's Rusty using his skill at hospitals to build a clinic in a Fort Worth suburb. It's Peter using his skills as a contractor to make over homes of disadvantaged families. And it's happening globally as well. It's Andy setting up water treatment plants in Vietnam. This is "glocal" ministry — disciples of Jesus linking their job skills to God's global work.

In the United States, I sometimes wonder if Christians have retreated from service to others partly because the U.S. government has decided to make human welfare its own responsibility. While that may be true, I believe that we must not just concede this responsibility to the government. The church in America and around the world must learn to step in and engage the society. Government care is often impersonal and lacks the transforming power of God's grace.

In fact, government care sometimes has the opposite effect on people. Recipients of government assistance can become dependent on that assistance and lack the internal motivation to change. They settle into a perpetual state of hopelessness. That's where disciples of Jesus Christ can really make a difference. When followers of Christ get involved in caring for people, the engagement is personal. And when Christians serve in the name of Christ, the recipients of this care see the power of Christianity not just as a theory, but they witness the love of God in action. They experience the love of the Christian, and from that reflection they gaze up the beam to the source of the light — Christ himself.

God can use them not only to bring transformation to the lives of individuals; he can use them to change an entire society. At its best, the government of a nation is a reflection of the society to which it belongs. If the society is passive and docile, the government can take advantage of the people and rule by an abusive exercise of power. If, however, the society is vocal and engaged, it has the power to change the government so that it becomes more responsive to the voice of the people. When we start at the bottom of society among the common people, the influence for change can even percolate upward to the leaders of government. Jonathan Sacks explains why this works:

> The problem we face is about society, not the state. It is not about power but about culture, morality, social cohesion, about the subtle ties that bind, or fail to bind, us into a collective entity with a sense of shared responsibility and destiny. It is just this that many political thinkers tend either to take for granted or to dismiss as irrelevant. Yet it is clearly not irrelevant. If society fragments, politics will lose its legitimacy. Why should I honor the laws and government of a society to which I do not feel I belong?[35]

Sacks is telling us that a government that wants to retain its power will be responsive to the voice of the people. Therefore, the key to changing the government is not through a regime change, but by changing the society, and this happens one person at a time. Changes in the broader society can either improve a responsive government or give people hope under an unresponsive or tyrannical one. As

Sacks reminds us, "Social covenant creates a society. Social contract creates a state."[36]

As we noted earlier, social contracts are dependent on the rule of law and emphasize the rights of individuals. Social covenants are more about the intangible things like relationships between people in a community, our sense of responsibility, and the overall morality of the society. Since most of us are not lawmakers, we typically influence society in these ways, through the power of a social covenant rather than enforcement of a social contract. We bring change, not by demanding our rights as individuals, but by demonstrating responsibility for others through our care and compassionate service. Our social responsibility is expressed through personal engagement — getting our hands dirty and sweating alongside our neighbors.

As we begin to touch those with needs, individual lives will be changed. And as more lives are changed, the influence of the gospel will spread. Soon movements will begin to grow. Eventually, these movements will draw political attention to problematic issues, and the government will feel the pressure to do something.

I have seen this in the example of Saddleback Church and the work of Rick and Kay Warren. Throughout the 1990s we saw little government emphasis on caring for those suffering from the AIDS epidemic in Africa. But through the involvement of leaders like Rick Warren, with his intentional focus on Africa and his wife Kay's focus on AIDS, the issue moved from a local church concern to the level of our national consciousness — eventually getting the attention of government leaders. His work, ministering to those in Africa, brought Rick Warren together with Bono and President Bush — the pastor, the rocker, and the president — in an alliance that is bringing real and lasting change to the continent.

Jesus has created a new society among his followers, a society that transcends national boundaries — the "Society of God." It's a covenantal society where we live out our created purpose to love God and others — often at the same time. After all, Christ tells us in Matthew 25 that service to those in need is service to him. That's why engaging society is simply an authentication of true Christianity. But what if we choose not to live out our faith? What happens in a society when Christians do not engage? Valuable institutions can decay, due to the lack of involvement by principled citizens.

I believe that this is what we are presently seeing in the American public schools. As American society has become more affluent, self-focused, busy, and career-oriented, parents have left the PTAs, reduced their involvement with teachers and school administrators, and lost their influence on values in the schools. This parental pullout from public education ended up hurting the schools and frequently isolated Christians from the public square. The resulting decline in education and values in schools became so acute that many Christians gave up on government schools altogether, turning to other options like private schools or homeschooling their kids.

But Christians should not throw in the towel and retreat from the public schools; they should actively engage them. Because the masses are being educated in the public school system, public education programs have a large impact on society. As followers of Christ, we have a duty to participate in improving our society and moving it toward a positive future.

I suggest that it's time for us to step up and be responsible. If we don't, the government will step in to fill the gap, and we may not like the result. When the government bears the burden of the society, you typically get fragmentation and tribal politics. We are witnessing this in America with an increasing fragmentation among diverse groups, each group wanting more rights in the social contract but becoming less willing to assume the covenantal responsibility.

I recently visited a brilliant man in Kenya whom I greatly admire. I reflected that there were no architectural or monumental ruins in Kenya like the pyramids of Egypt, Ankor Watt of Cambodia, or the Mayan ruins of Central America. I asked him why. "Because of tribalism," he answered. "Being nomads before colonialism, we could never stay in one place long enough to develop anything." Having a stable society means planting our feet and digging in for the duration. The future of a society depends on covenantal responsibility, and that means engagement by people who can make a difference.

FINDING THE COMMON GOOD

One of my neighbors is a Mormon and another is a Catholic. A Muslim lives just down my street, and a gay couple lives down another street. Scattered throughout the neighborhood I know of Buddhists, Cambodians, African Americans, Koreans, Africans, Middle-Easterners, and whites. Their occupations are just as diverse: preachers, plumbers, doctors, builders, engineers, and teachers. What do we all have in common? The answer is simple: We all live here.

I believe God cares about all these people. And I believe he has placed me here to be a witness to them. I also believe that in spite of our differences, there are many things that matter to us all — good schools, good jobs, good roads, low crime, high morals, and civic duty. How, then, can we work together to realize these concerns?

I find that many Christians think of societal engagement in a limited sense. Engaging society involves pushing a political agenda. It's true that Christians should be involved in the world of politics; however, our politics should flow out of our servanthood and not simply depend on legislative or judicial agendas. Political agendas lower us to the level of the world, turning our focus on rights and protecting privilege instead of pursuing the covenantal approach of responsible service to our community. Christians will not transform society by becoming like the world. The answer is not for Christians to push a political agenda, but to live out the truth and share it one-on-one, first through deeds, then through words. As Saint Francis said, "Preach the Gospel at all times, and when necessary use words." Unless we get off our blessed assurance and engage society at the elementary level, we are in danger of contributing to the decline of the nation.

SIDE-BY-SIDE SERVING

Over six billion people, over two hundred nations, and thousands of languages — despite the increased connectedness we see through communications, we live in a world that is increasingly fragmenting and coming undone. Why? The answer is that electronic and relational connectedness are two different things. We can be connected to sites on the Internet around the world and yet fail to connect relationally to the family next door. In fact, our electronic connections may actually inhibit our personal connections. Many people have become so enamored with internet relationships that this electronic interface has effectively replaced personal, face-to-face relationships. The result is tragic: at a time when so many people are looking to connect in meaningful ways with other people, we find ourselves living in the same city but separate, segmented, segregated, and distant from our neighbors.

Few things divide us more today than religion. The more religious groups grow in number and size, the more they seem to retain their separateness, which breeds distrust and hostility. This growing separation of people and groups leads to the fragmentation of society. Is there any way to reverse the trend? Until recently many believed that open communication and dialogue between groups was the best answer. The thinking was that if we could all just sit down at the table and talk it through with each other, we could work anything out.

But in many situations, this dialogue among disparate groups seems to generate more dissension than harmony. The more words we utter, the more polarized we become. The rise of globalization and the potential for better communication among different cultural groups doesn't necessarily lead to reconciliation and unity. In fact, the opposite is happening in places all over the world. As people experience rapid changes, they are turning to the past, looking for their roots. Tribalism is dramatically on the rise in the world. These tribes can be ethnic, cultural, philosophical, or racial.

We cannot control what other people do or think, but we can work to make sure that our own faith does not become isolationist or divisive. There are three basic models for integrating groups into a society. One is *assimilation* — the melding of everyone into a single homogeneous culture holding the same basic beliefs. The second is *segregation*, where differing groups keep to themselves and refuse to participate in the common culture. The third way is *integration without assimilation*. This involves holding to one's own beliefs while still participating in the common good of building society. I believe that this is the model Jeremiah gave to the Jewish captives as they went into Babylonian exile.

> Thus says the LORD of hosts, the God of Israel, to all the exiles whom I have sent into exile from Jerusalem to Babylon, "Build houses and live in them; and plant gardens and eat their produce. Take wives and become the fathers of sons and daughters, and take wives for your sons and give your daughters to husbands, that they may bear sons and daughters; and multiply there and do not decrease. Seek the welfare of the city where I have sent you into exile, and pray to the LORD on its behalf; for in its welfare you will have welfare." (Jeremiah 29:4 – 7 NASB)

Integration without assimilation is a valid model for us as Christians. We must continue to be people with strong convictions, and we should never compromise the truth of what we believe. But we must also learn to handle that truth in a way that does not build walls between ourselves and those with whom we live. Our lives should reflect our commitment to the truth, even as we seek the good of the society in which we live and work.

The solution to this cultural isolation and fragmentation involves rediscovering what we all have in common. What is so valuable to all of us that preserving it is worth abandoning our separateness? The answer is society itself. All people, regardless of personal or religious differences, want to live in a stable, productive, prospering society in which they can raise their families, preserve their relationships, and pursue their goals. When we engage society at the level of its domains, we find true commonality in spite of all our differences. There is something about sweating side by side with other people that breaks down the barriers and differences. We may have disagreements about what we believe or how we practice our faith, but we also have something in common — and that's where we start.

When I listen to the news and read blogs about Muslims, I can easily become fearful and develop a distrustful attitude toward them. But I find that when I work with them on water projects, education projects, and other social goals, they lower their guard and become less defensive about their beliefs. That's when I discover that there are many things we have in common. Working with them I have come to admire and respect them as individuals, and I empathize with them for what they've been through as a people.

When I work with Muslims, I learn things about their faith and their view of God. As I noted earlier, the best way to understand Islam is to read the Koran and to talk to Muslims. In that way I can see the differences between Islam and Christianity for myself; I don't have to depend on secondhand knowledge. Moreover, I've also learned that when I develop a close relationship with a Muslim, he will openly answer my questions about his religion. If we disagree, we disagree. Relationship removes the fear of differences and opens hearts for honest, respectful discussion.

I believe that one of the reasons we have so many arguments in the American church over doctrine, practice, and worship style is that Christianity has long been the dominant religion in America. External differences with other religions have been so uncommon that we've had the leisure to turn inward, debating differences with each other. I've found that Christians in other parts of the world have a more realistic view. Since they must live their faith in the context of Muslims, Jews, atheists, Hindus, Sikhs, animists, and Buddhists, for them the central question about us is truly the central question: Who is Jesus and how does he live within us and make all things new? All other differences are secondary.

I have become friends with a Syrian Muslim leader named Mustafa. Mustafa just received his Ph.D. and he enjoys talking about religion. Because we have spent time together and have developed mutual respect, we can ask one another sensitive questions about our faith. We certainly don't agree on religion, yet because of our relationship we are looking at ways of working together in the future. Yes, he has tried gently to convert me to Islam. It's very interesting being on the other side of the conversation!

At this point in our friendship, Mustafa and I retain our separate faiths. Perhaps we always will. But as we have developed a trusting relationship despite our differences, we have begun to find common-alities that enable us to serve together. When we work together, even our differences can become assets. As Sacks puts it, we are "bound by commonalities, but enlarged by differences."[37] The advantage of having differences is that we bring to the table our uniqueness and diversity, which enables each of us to see things we would not other-wise see and thus learn from one another. And yes, in case you're wondering, I have told Mustafa about Christ. He hasn't come around, but because we have a trusting relationship, all things are possible.

BRINGING HOPE

Not only do we live in a world of fear and distrust; we also live in a culture of "victimhood." Victimhood denies personal responsibility for mistakes and encourages people to harbor resentment from their past. Victims tend to look backward instead of forward. If we are to have any hope of integrating the disconnected tribes of our society, we must move forward toward a solution, shedding the lingering burden of blame, and begin to shift the responsibility for change to our own shoulders.

Nothing will destroy a society as quickly as a culture of victim-ization. And it's not unique to American culture. Talk to a Jew or a Palestinian and you'll likely find that both parties in the conflict feel like victims. Why is victimhood so dangerous? Like a deadly virus, it spreads "from individuals to groups, and from there to the public square. In every age there are victims and we must help them ... What is new and dangerous is the culture of victimhood. It involves the blurring of the boundaries between the personal and the political."[38]

As Christians, we have a solution to the culture of victimhood. While others are focused on protecting their rights and privileges and on blaming others, we are motivated by a Christ-centered com-mitment that emphasizes responsibility to others over the rights of self. Christians have a message of hope to bring to the world. We have the love of Christ in our hearts, which flows outward toward others — not only those of our own family or church, but a genuine love for our society and our community, for people of all faiths and nations. The challenge for the church is to begin putting that love into action by identifying the needs of people and meeting those needs in service.

Connection Steps

⊙ What is the biggest issue in the community needing reconciliation?

⊙ Name one place in the world in dire need of reconciliation.

⊙ "To be a part of reconciling this I could . . ."

⊙ What lessons have you learned from another culture or country that has enriched your life and understanding of God?

Making Space
for Everyone

I have always been careful to avoid anything even vaguely political in the work I do in Vietnam. As a pastor and a guest in that country, I am always concerned about having problems with the government — or rather, I'm concerned that the government might have a problem with me! When you're an American pastor working in a country known as one of the world's top ten violators of religious freedom, you don't want to do anything to attract negative attention.

Over the years many people have pressured me to get involved in political issues in Vietnam, and they often get upset when I decline. The issues are incredibly complex, and even more so for an American working in a culture so unlike our own. For one thing, a lot of falsehood is reported regarding religious freedom on both sides of the issue. And not every issue regarding religious freedom is a governmental issue. Some of the conflict is culturally related, involving family reactions and pressures over people changing religions. It's not always as clear-cut as we think; the problem is related to the whole order of society.

No one can deny that serious violations of worship freedom have occurred in Vietnam, but as a pastor trying to serve a nation, if I get involved in that fight I defeat my whole purpose. Because we have approached our work in Vietnam with the biblically based philosophy of serving the society at the point of human need, we are often able to work in societies that do not promote the freedom of religious expression. If we were to shift our philosophy and focus on getting converts to Christianity or begin pushing for the freedom of religious expression in every country where we work, we would likely be barred from entering many of these countries and our opportunities to affect change in that society would be severely limited.

When you travel to a foreign country, it's appropriate to remember that you are there as a guest. You have been graciously given a visa, and it is your responsibility to obey the laws of that country and respect their culture.

In this chapter I hope to outline some of the complex issues relating to religious freedom and how our understanding of the concept in America differs from what we find throughout the world. Those interested in working in other countries should have a basic understanding of this issue and possess a certain amount of wisdom and discernment. I will share some practical examples of how we, at NorthWood, have been able to work in the religiously restrictive culture of Vietnam, and then I will give you a sketch of the basic philosophy of religious freedom and how it is understood in nations outside the United States.

THE CHRIS SEIPLE STORY

My friend Chris Seiple is president of the Institute for Global Engagement (IGE), a nongovernmental organization (NGO) founded by his father, Robert Seiple, former president of World Vision and the ambassador-at-large for religious freedom under President Clinton. Chris is a former Marine with an M.A. and Ph.D. in international relations from Tufts University. He is classically trained in diplomacy and has coined a term that he calls "relational diplomacy."

Chris and I met in May of 2005 and discovered that we shared a common interest in Vietnam. Because the organization Chris leads is involved in work in Vietnam, I wanted to meet Chris to see if the IGE was interested in coming alongside us to share in the opportunities we had developed. Our work has never been as large as that of an organization like World Vision, but we had done enough work in Vietnam that we now had a visible profile in that country. After all, it's not every day that a local, American church is able to work so openly in a "closed" country.

Chris asked me if I would participate in the first set of a series of conferences on religion and the rule of law. My initial sense was to decline, but a friend who serves as a leading Vietnamese diplomat urged me to accept the invitation. He felt that my firsthand knowledge of the country and the connections I had developed could be an asset to the conference. Given the political nature of the conference, he also urged me to be extremely careful and wise. International diplomacy can be a minefield! I agreed to attend the conference, which was held at George Washington University in Washington, D.C. There were people attending from the U.S. State Department and the Vietnamese State Department, several university professors, heads of NGOs, as well as other interested parties.

To my great surprise, I found that I already knew many of the people in the Vietnamese delegation. At the start of the conference, several of them came over and greeted me by name. Then, when it came time for the meeting to begin, protocol prevailed over personal relationships. The Vietnamese took their seats on one side of the room and the Americans were on the other. Everyone wore headsets through which they listened to an interpreter render the speeches in their own language. But during the breaks everyone took them off and spoke in English. I was learning a lot about protocol! I've heard a lot of boring preachers in my lifetime, but let me tell you: nothing is more boring than a gaggle of diplomats meticulously mapping out their positions.

I was among the last of the presenters. I started out by saying that I understood that Vietnam is not actually opposed to religious freedom; they are simply concerned about the destabilization of their government. I reminded everyone that it is widely known that Vietnam has not always had a good experience with Christianity as a religious movement. The French had used Christianity to colonize the country, and there were lingering questions about American involvement as well.

Still, I urged everyone to keep in mind that religions are growing all over the world and that they will continue to grow in the future. Like it or not, the government of Vietnam was going to have to deal with the issue of religious freedom. I suggested that the Vietnamese have two options on the issue: they can become a narrow, totalitarian, communist state, or they could work on becoming a progressive, socialist state that respects the principle of religious freedom. I reminded the Vietnamese delegation that Ho Chi Minh had admired Thomas Jefferson and had even patterned Vietnam's Declaration of Independence after our own. At the conclusion of my talk, I laid out several issues and proposed the following solutions:

1. One of the biggest problems concerning religious freedom in Vietnam is that while the laws have changed for the better, not all government officials understand the new rules. I proposed raising money for an information campaign to make sure that officials at all levels are taught the laws and their intended application to ensure consistency throughout the country.

2. Since Vietnam is making progress in religious freedom but the perception is still bad in many regions, I recommended that they allow our church to work in the areas most criticized for repressing religious freedom.

3. I recommended that the Vietnamese government allow Vietnamese pastors to convene with pastors from around the world. Christians like to meet with other Christians from around the world, just like any other group would (communists included).

4. I urged them to let us connect with churches in Vietnam, to serve these churches, build relationships with them, and learn from one another. As a church, we had been engaging person-to-person with individuals in their society, but we had never worked directly with churches. I clarified that we would never do this without the proper government permission. A church-to-church connection would go a long way toward demonstrating religious freedom by showing cooperation between church and government. I asserted our premise that people of faith should serve others and urged them to help us find ways to partner together to serve the people of Vietnam.

5. I suggested that they allow our media to come into Vietnam to prove that they have made big changes.

6. I told them that we would be willing to allow the police to accompany us on any of our activities. After all, if we are following the law, why should we be bothered by police presence?

As I was speaking, I noticed a lot of head nodding and expressions of agreement. Afterward I received much affirmation to my proposals. But as we all know, agreeing on ideas and acting on them are two vastly different things. Talk is cheap, but turning ideas into reality — that's a long road to travel.

After the conference, several delegates gave me their cards and asked to visit with me sometime. Chris invited me to be a part of a small delegation to visit some of the areas in Vietnam that have faced persecution and to meet with key leaders to set up the first conference on religion and the rule of law. I agreed to go.

OUR VIETNAM "RELIGIOUS FREEDOM" TOUR

Chris and I headed off with a small delegation to Vietnam, where we attended several meetings (all quite boring, to be honest). We accompanied a few Vietnamese government officials on a hike way up into the northwest provinces. On our visit I met a young Vietnamese man who had become a Christian pastor and who had seen the majority of his village come to faith in Christ. He told us that there were several house churches throughout the region and explained that they were trying to get these churches registered for the sake of protection. Chris interviewed this young pastor openly with government officials present. I told the young man, "Your faith has been heard around the world and it is an honor to be with you. Keep living the Christian life as you have." It was an incredibly moving experience for me.

The next day we were taken to Sapa, Vietnam, to meet Father Peter, the first full-time Catholic priest to minister in that city in fifty years. I enjoyed our meeting and prayed that God would continue to use him and bless him in powerful ways as he proclaimed the good news of Jesus Christ.

From there we traveled to another village and entered the home of another young pastor. It was evident that his home was really a house church. Pews were stacked against the walls, along with a makeshift pulpit. Printed on the wall was the law granting free religious worship so people could see that what they were doing was legal. This man couldn't have been more than twenty, and he told a beautiful story of how he came to Christ.

Leaving the northwest provinces, we went down to the central highlands, where we met with the region's government leaders and several pastors. Our host and guide in this area was Mr. Thuy, the General Secretary for the Vietnam – USA Society. He was very cordial to us. I completely understood his role in being with us, and he did too. Along with being our host, he was also there to keep a watchful eye on what we said and did. But he was a genuine man. He loved to sing, and strangely, he made sure that we prayed at every meal. I found this interesting. I didn't often pray publicly in Vietnam out of sensitivity to the culture and to avoid raising eyebrows. Yet here I was, praying out loud with one of the nation's leaders!

As we continued our tour, we met with several Christian groups. This was the first time I had ever had that much contact with Christians in Vietnam. At one point I sat in a real "house" church — a small house that had been converted into a worship center. The kitchen and small living quarters were in the back of the worship area, and the bedroom doubled as a Sunday school classroom for children. I listened as three men told us what it was like to follow Christ in Vietnam. These men had paid a price, as their conversions had been strongly opposed. They told their story as the government officials with us listened passively. It was a surreal experience.

It was clear to me that the church is really growing in the central highlands of Vietnam. As I sat in that house, one of the church leaders told me why: "For many years we've been working with our bare hands to do the work of God. But today we are growing primarily through the young people. God is always with us. He is active in helping us and his power is working in light, right now and forever. Thank you for your prayers. We must have faith and unity."

In Vietnamese culture, it's not a good thing for a man to cry in public. But after witnessing the courage and dedication of these men, I couldn't hold back; I excused myself, went to the bathroom, and sobbed. These Vietnamese Christians were real heroes, authentic followers of Christ. Even allowing us to meet with them was an act of courage. It raised their profile with the government leaders, which could have negative consequences.

These Christians continued to share openly with us, and then we knelt with them around a pulpit — Christian pastors and communist officials alike — and we prayed. I know such a scene would have been utterly confusing to most outsiders. As a matter of fact, it was confusing to us too! But God was present, and when he's there I don't engage in second-guessing. I simply accept the blessing of the moment.

Later we visited a Rai Catholic church, which met in a building elevated on stilts. We attended Mass, and despite the fact that I'm a Protestant, I felt the presence of Jesus in that place. Later we witnessed a special celebration in which several people beat drums while others played instruments. At one point they stopped and sipped some kind of beverage as part of the ritual. I had my suspicions about the beverage they were sipping, so I passed. After all, I am a Baptist!

During the celebration, one of the government officials, a young man who had frequently tried to engage me in dialogue about my belief in God, began to sing and beat the drum, really getting into the spirit of things. "What are you doing?" I asked him. "I thought you didn't believe!"

"Bob," he replied, "I don't understand this much, but at some point I became one with them in the celebration. We feel this deeply, very deeply, in all our hearts. When I stand here with these people, I am one of them." At that moment I was reminded that our longing for God, however we understand that, is bigger than the things that divide us. God's witness is always present to each person at the right time and in the right place. This young man was not a believer, but something in that worship experience spoke deeply to his heart.

As recently as ten years ago, no one seriously focused on religion as a factor in foreign policy and diplomacy. That has left us woefully unprepared for the world we find ourselves in today. Today, religious faith is exploding all around the world. Ignorance of the religion factor — a failure to understand who believes what and why it matters — continues to cause confusion and prevents leaders from truly understanding the problems and underlying causes of conflict.

A BRIEF HISTORY OF RELIGIOUS FREEDOM

Unlike Islam today or Judaism in the Old Testament, Christianity is not aligned with a national government. There is nothing in Christianity that parallels the Islamic Sharia Law or the Judaic Law of Moses. In the past there was what we might call the rule of Christian law, of course, during the time of Constantine and much of the Middle Ages, and this continued throughout much of the Reformation and post-Reformation period. People who were not the "right brand" of Christians were indeed killed. But no country today has established theocratic punishment for failing to believe or practice the Christian faith. Our situation is very different from the experience of those living in ancient Israel. In Israel, anyone who turned from the true God and worshiped idols could be executed. As a theocracy, belief in God was mandatory for every Israelite. But the Christian faith is not tied to a single nation or culture. Believing in Jesus is a decision that every person makes of his or her own free will.

In the founding of the United States, the concept of religious freedom went through a process of growth and development. In John Winthrop's famous sermon, *City on a Hill*, delivered to the Puritans in 1630, he said that the community they established in America should become a model of Christian charity because people would be watching their New World experiment. In America, people would be free to exercise the Christian virtues of love and mercy, the two things that all law should be built upon. But when the Puritan community was founded in America, the only freedom that was guaranteed was the freedom to practice their own religion. The early Puritan communities were not interested in granting religious freedom to other religious groups. They banned those who didn't believe as they did and were no more tolerant of diverse religious practices than the Church of England from which they fled.

The real shift in the history of religious freedom in America came when Roger Williams, a Puritan himself, founded Rhode Island and the first Baptist Church in 1638. I don't mean he just raised some sprawling building on a prominent street corner of his community with a sign reading "First Baptist Church"; I mean he established the *very first* Baptist church in America.

When Williams came to America in 1630, he pastored a Separatist church at Plymouth. He became good friends with the Indians and insisted that any land taken for use by the colonists should be fairly purchased from local tribes. His view of the Indians was considered too advanced for the time and drew considerable criticism. Yet because of his knowledge of the Indians and their ways, he was often called to settle disputes between Indians and settlers.

Among the radical ideas that Williams proposed was the notion that civil judges shouldn't adjudicate religious matters. Williams advocated complete separation between civil and ecclesiastical courts. He was the earliest proponent of the principle of separation of church and state and the first to coin that term. He also espoused an idea that he called "soul liberty," or the right of each individual to follow his own conscience in matters of faith. This idea, along with his opposition to the charter that established a theocracy in Massachusetts Bay, resulted in his banishment from Plymouth Colony in 1635.

On leaving the Massachusetts Colony, Williams established the town of Providence in the unclaimed area outside Massachusetts. Williams then returned to England to get a charter to establish the colony of Rhode Island, which he set up as a fully democratic province. In 1652 Williams passed the first law in North America that made slavery illegal. As a result, many Baptists, Jews, Quakers, slaves, and others who had suffered oppression made their homes in Rhode Island.

In those early years Williams pastored the church in Providence, but he eventually abandoned all forms of organized religion and started calling himself a seeker. Williams felt that it was impossible to suppose that any single church could claim to have all truth. He believed that every church had some truth in it, but none of them could give you the full picture. Without a doubt, Williams' thinking helped pave the road for our founding fathers to build into the U.S. Constitution the concept of freedom of religion. They understood that when a state supports a given faith, conscience can be stifled by the majority imposing its beliefs on the minority. The power of religious freedom lies in the protection it gives to the minority religions. John Leland was a Virginia Baptist, which was a minority faith in the time of our nation's founding. He wrote, "Let every man speak freely without fear, maintain the principles that he believes, worship according to his own faith, either one God, three Gods, no God, or twenty Gods; and let government protect him in so doing."[39]

Despite these powerful voices and early precedents, freedom of religion was far from a slam dunk for the framers of our constitution. In his book *Founding Faith*, Steven Waldman writes:

> The birth of religious freedom was not inevitable. The Founding Fathers contemplated the approach taken by their grandfathers for more than a century — and rejected it. Through a variety of battles, some local, some national, some born of enlightenment and some of parochialism, these men and women helped create a radical new three-part creed:
>
> ⊙ Religion is essential to the flourishing of a republic.
> ⊙ To thrive, religion needs less help, not more, from the state.
> ⊙ God gave all humans the right to full religious freedom.
>
> The Founding Faith, then, was not Christianity, and it was not secularism. It was religious liberty — a revolutionary formula for promoting faith by leaving it alone.[40]

THE IMPORTANCE OF RELIGIOUS FREEDOM

Freedom of religion protects *minority* religions from the religious intolerance of the majority; but is freedom of religion ever in the interest of the *majority* faith? I argue that it is. Christianity has never been the official religion of the United States, but in the early days of our nation it was so widely believed and the government was so closely aligned with its principles that it was greatly favored over other religions. In our current culture, however, that condition has been largely reversed. The explosive growth of diverse religions in

America has led institutions cautiously to avoid anything that even hints of a preference for Christianity. While some decry the loss of national alignment with the principles of Christianity, we must still remain thankful that the concept of religious freedom remains intact. Constitutional protection of religious freedom means that Christianity cannot be legally prohibited, even when there is growing intolerance toward it.

Freedom of religion sometimes presents believers with troubling philosophical questions. Jesus makes it clear that Christianity is the only way to God. "I am the way, the truth, and the life," he says. "No one comes to the Father, except through me" (John 14:6). How does such a narrow and exclusive statement fit with the concept of religious freedom? How should Christians view other religions if Christ is clear that they do not offer salvation? Should we respect other religious perspectives or view them as enemies to the Christian faith?

At the heart of the concept of religious freedom is the recognition that the human being has a conscience, and they must have the freedom to follow where their conscience leads, *even if it leads them in a wrong direction*. Without that freedom, faith is forced and becomes a societal obligation imposed on everyone. When this happens, true faith loses its power and no longer has the ability to engage individuals at a meaningful level or to produce the personal transformations that will, in turn, transform the culture.

How essential is religion in shaping the culture of a nation? One way to answer that question is to examine what happens when governments try to adopt a purely secular ideology and reject outright the concept of God. The Soviet Union and other communist bloc countries took a hard line against Christianity and effectually denied themselves the leavening power of a cultural force that has inspired, encouraged, and benefited millions of people. Religion provides a perspective that gives rise to industry, cooperation, and mutual support among people. Communist societies have now, for the most part, collapsed, and though it is difficult to locate a single source for the collapse, it is certain that the rejection of religion as a cultural unifier has had consequences. In China, a similar approach has been taken, as the government has tried to legislate God out of existence, denying its citizens the freedom to believe in Christ. But unlike what happened under the Soviets, the church in China went underground, and today it is the largest church in the world.

Governments can make religion illegal. They can deny people the freedom to believe openly. But they cannot legislate the heart. To underscore the importance of finding the correct relationship between church and state, I want to address three key questions about this relationship.

WHY DOES FAITH MATTER IN SOCIETY?

On Friday, June 23, 1775, George Washington left Philadelphia to take command of the Continental Army. On that same day Rev. William Smith preached a sermon at Christ Church in Philadelphia in which he said, "Religion and liberty must flourish or fall together in America. We pray that both may be perpetual."

Why would Smith link religion with liberty? Research indicates that economically and socially, religious freedom and liberty have more to do with a nation's development than one might think. I was at a meeting in Washington, D.C., with the prime minister of Vietnam and several other government leaders. In that meeting Thomas Farr, a professor at Georgetown University, drew our attention to an article by Brian Grimm titled, "Is Religious Freedom Good for Us?" In this article Grimm wrote:

> If religious freedom is an integral part of the bundled commodity of human freedoms, religious freedom should be closely associated with the general betterment of people's lives. The Hudson Institute data again confirm just such a correlation. The study found that wherever religious freedom is high, there tend to be fewer incidents of armed conflict, better health outcomes, higher levels of earned income and better educational opportunities for women. Moreover, religious freedom is associated with higher overall human development as measured by the human development index.

… Our research on 143 countries finds that when governments and religious groups in society do not erect barriers to
religious competition but respect and protect such activities as
conversion and proselytism, religious violence is less. A further analysis of the data shows that countries with no restric-
tions on conversion, in particular, tend to have higher levels of
fundamental freedoms, better lives for women, and less overall
armed conflict.

… In sum, religious freedom promotes stability, helps to
consolidate democracy, and lessens religious violence. Based
on our analysis it is much more than an American pet peeve;
religious freedom is a universal aspiration.[41]

Jon Meacham summarizes the many societal benefits of religion
in this line from his book *American Gospel*: "The great good news
about America — the American gospel, if you will — is that religion
shapes the life of the nation without strangling it."[42]

Of course, we cannot deny that there are risks in allowing religious
freedom. There is the risk that respected leaders may hold distorted
beliefs, and their example may lead people into erroneous views of religious truth. Franklin, Adams, Jefferson, and Washington, for example,
believed that Jesus was a great moral teacher but not the divine Son of
God. Yet despite the lack of control over religious teaching and expression, Meacham believes it is worth the risk: "The benefits of faith in
God have outweighed the cost."[43] So what are some of these benefits?

1. Faith Is Necessary to Form the Character of Society

In a letter to Thomas Jefferson, John Adams wrote, "Without religion
this world would be something not fit to be mentioned in polite company, I mean Hell."[44] Adams recognized that law itself is not enough
to govern human passions. Law may enforce obedience by the impo-
sition of coercive power, but religion influences the human heart to
willingly curb individual passions and look to the good of others
instead of self. Morality makes obedience to law a matter of individual conscience, and without the broader perspective of religion,

morality loses its authority, leaving individual passions ungoverned except through the coercive power of law.

In a society without religion, the laws must be more restrictive, and the society will chafe under governmental control. Where there is religious freedom, the laws can be more relaxed because the individual is accountable to something other than one's private conscience or the law of the state. The relaxation of law allows for greater freedom, encouraging creativity and initiative.

Now because religion has benefits to society, some are inclined toward adopting a mandatory faith into the laws of the state. Meacham warns governments against taking this step: "The distance between a culture informed by religiously inspired values but governed by civil institutions that respect personal liberties to a kind of theological totalitarianism is a short one." Later, he goes on to say, "the founding Fathers made the choice to link liberty and the idea of God together while avoiding sectarian religious imagery or associations."[45] In other words, the genius of the way American government was set up was to recognize the high place of faith in a stable society, but to refrain from making faith mandatory. This is freedom of religion.

2. Faith Is Necessary for the Spirituality of Society

Vietnam is one of the most spiritual societies on the earth today. Even the general secretary has in his home an altar to his ancestors. Of course, as Christians we believe spirituality has an altogether different meaning than worshiping the spirits of our ancestors. We believe that God imparts his Holy Spirit to us, giving us a connection to him that transforms our lives and guides our actions. This leads us to love our neighbors and to serve them in their needs.

This recognition of a living reality beyond what we experience with our senses enables us to live in this world with more confidence and gives us a reason to look beyond ourselves and to care for the needs of others. Freedom to worship as we please — whether we worship the spirits of our departed ancestors or the Spirit of the living God — enables us to experience life in another dimension, which improves life in the temporal realm of world societies.

3. Faith Is Necessary for the Conscience of a Society

The wise and witty Englishman G. K. Chesterton once said that America seemed to think of herself as "a nation with the soul of a church."[46] Indeed, it seems that this soul was infused into our heritage by our founding fathers. Benjamin Franklin, while debating the shape of the constitution in 1787, replied to an opponent during a fierce moment of the debate: "I have lived, sir, a long time; and the longer I live, the more convincing proofs I see of this truth — that God governs in the affairs of men! And if a sparrow cannot fall to the ground without his notice, is it probable that an empire can rise without his aid?"[47] Throughout America's history this "soul of a church" has acted as the nation's conscience, righting wrongs and alleviating suffering wherever it has been found.

On September 22, 1862, President Abraham Lincoln explained why he was issuing the Emancipation Proclamation. On the previous Wednesday his Union forces had won a decisive victory at Antietam, Maryland, in a battle that would go down in history as the bloodiest of the war. "When the Rebel Army was at Frederick," Lincoln said, "I determined, as soon as it should be driven out of Maryland, to issue a Proclamation of Emancipation ... I said nothing to anyone, but I made a promise to myself, and to my Maker."[48] It was his conscience that drove him to this decision.

In our own century the Rev. Martin Luther King Jr. awoke the Christian conscience of the nation in the 1960s by his activism, which called attention to the poor treatment of blacks that still lingered a century after the freeing of the slaves. I could point to hundreds of instances where Christian men and women acted on their consciences and brought about great improvements by correcting the ills they found both in America and abroad. This sort of social activism would be impossible without freedom of religion, which allowed them to act on the dictates of their conscience and speak freely of the need for reform.

4. Convictions Become the Basis of All Behaviors

Laws regulate behavior, but they do not motivate good behavior. Punishment for disobeying the law can be a motivation for a person to toe the line, but negative consequences do not necessarily inspire good, moral behavior. That is another reason why faith is such an asset to society. Faith provides positive motivation for good behavior — not only minimally good behavior but behavior that reaches outside the self and exhibits concern for others. Faith often becomes the glue that holds a society together. Faith can actually do much of the government's work for it by creating an atmosphere where obedience to law and loyalty to fellow citizens is motivated from within, eliminating the need for coercive measures.

WHY DOES FREEDOM OF RELIGION MATTER IN SOCIETY?

1. Freedom of Religion Allows Healthy Expression for Diversity

The founders "were politicians and philosophers, sages and warriors, churchmen and doubters."[49] They knew history and literature, politics and philosophy, theology and business, statecraft and soldiering. In other words, our founding fathers were a diverse group of men. They were a microcosm of the diversity from which our nation derived its strength. The only way to accommodate this kind of diversity is to allow freedom for each person to exercise his gifts, express his opinions, and act according to his own beliefs.

2. Under Religious Freedom, Conscience Cannot Be Bullied or Bought

The alternative to freedom of religion is political coercion that forces all citizens to adopt the same religion or to have no religion at all. This course may seem to stabilize a society by fitting everyone into the same mold, thus preventing the frictions that come from diversity. But that is not what really happens. A government may restrict a people's freedom to act on their beliefs, but it cannot restrict their freedom to think. It can repress external activity, but not the inner heart.

Political coercion, therefore, creates two problems. First, it affects only the surface. Beneath the appearance of unified activity lies the reality of diverse ideas, hidden in the recesses of the heart. This produces a nonintegrated person who must act in conflict with his beliefs and thus diminishes his loyalty to the state. Second, politically forced ideologies often create not only diminished loyalty; they can trigger outright resentment as the true beliefs of the person boil beneath the surface and build pressure that can explode into rebellion.

3. Freedom of Religion Keeps Evangelism Pure

Freedom of religion has another benefit for Christians. It keeps our evangelism pure. Pressuring people to accept faith does not produce true converts. Religious freedom ensures the choice of one's religion to be authentic by eliminating the pressure to convert that could be imposed by a state-sanctioned religion. Freedom means that when a person is converted, the change is of his or her own free will. There is no point in forcing people to practice rituals from a religion they would never choose for themselves.

4. Freedom of Religion Allows Investigation of Alternatives

Truth is found not by isolating one's belief and protecting it from all challenges, but by open investigation and observation. If one's faith cannot stand on its own feet in a room with other faiths, it should be abandoned. In the arena of competitive beliefs, truth will prevail. What is true does not need the protection of the state, nor can it be smothered by repression by the state. A society wants to see truth prevail among its citizens; it will do all it can to assure that freedom of religion is not abridged and that no single faith is allowed to impose its belief on others.

WHY IS SEPARATION OF CHURCH AND STATE IMPORTANT?

If there is no separation of church and state, then the religion most favored by the state is dominant, and other religions must reshape themselves around the dominant religion. When there is no separation of church and state, the state-favored religion may become coercive, using the power of the state to enforce its tenets and practices. In many cases such religions use the power of the state even to enforce universal membership in the favored religion. Just as the religion can use the power of the state, the state can also use religion to justify its restrictive policies.

The principle of separation of church and state has prevailed in the U.S. since the founding of the nation. For much of that history, Christianity has been so prevalent among the population that it has not been politically expedient to be something other than a Christian. When Lincoln was campaigning for Congress against Methodist evangelist Peter Cartwright, the future president attended a revival to hear his opponent preach. At one point Cartwright asked all those in the audience who did not wish to go to hell to stand. Only Lincoln kept his seat. Mr. Cartwright asked, "May I ask where you are going, Mr. Lincoln?" Lincoln replied, "To Congress."

Although Lincoln's speeches and behavior indicate a strong belief in God, Lincoln never publicly revealed his religion. And in America that was his right, though it may not have been expedient. Anyone who runs for office has the constitutional right to believe in any religion he chooses or to have no religion at all. The laws of the nation neither favor one religion over the other nor require any citizen or officeholder to hold to a particular faith. This principle is explicitly stated in the First Amendment to the U.S. Constitution:

> Congress shall make no law respecting an establishment of religion, or prohibiting the free exercise thereof; or abridging the freedom of speech, or of the press; or the right of the people peaceably to assemble, and to petition the government for a redress of grievances.

The incredibly talented and influential Thomas Jefferson wanted to be remembered for three things, which are inscribed on his tomb: the founding of the University of Virginia, his authorship of the Declaration of Independence, and the Virginia Statute of Religious Freedom. His draft of the bill proposing the statute, which he wrote in 1777, is so profound that I want to include a part of it here:

Well aware that the opinions and belief of men depend not on their own will, but follow involuntarily the evidence proposed to their minds; that Almighty God hath created the mind free, and manifested his supreme will that free it shall remain by making it altogether insusceptible of restraint; that all attempts to influence it by temporal punishments, or burthens, or by civil incapacitations, tend only to beget habits of hypocrisy and meanness, and are a departure from the plan of the holy author of our religion, who being lord both of body and mind, yet chose not to propagate it by coercions on either, as was in his Almighty power to do, but to extend it by its influence on reason alone; that the impious presumption of legislators and rulers, civil as well as ecclesiastical, who, being themselves but fallible and uninspired men, have assumed dominion over the faith of others, setting up their own opinions and modes of thinking as the only true and infallible, and as such endeavoring to impose them on others, hath established and maintained false religions over the greatest part of the world and through all time ... that our civil rights have no dependence on our religious opinions, any more than our opinions in physics or geometry; that therefore the proscribing any citizen as unworthy the public confidence by laying upon him an incapacity of being called to offices of trust and emolument, unless he profess or renounce this or that religious opinion, is depriving him injuriously of those privileges and advantages to which, in common with his fellow citizens ...[50]

Jefferson recognized that even God does not coerce people to follow him. Freedom of religion is not, as many believe, a principle invented by America's founding fathers. Jefferson believed that freedom of religion is something given to us by God, an intrinsic right. It's a freedom that is not only basic to our American identity; it is basic to our humanity. It was something given to Adam and Eve in the garden when God allowed them freedom to choose between good and evil. That freedom validates our status as moral agents before

God who can choose to love him or reject him, even though the latter choice is to our peril.

THE CRITICAL IMPORTANCE OF RELIGIOUS FREEDOM

It is true that freedom of religion can be abused. One can use his or her freedom to choose faith and then use a distorted version of that faith as a justification for doing evil. Former slave and social reformer Frederick Douglass saw this kind of abuse up close. In the summer of 1832 Douglass's master was converted at a Methodist revival meeting. The event brought hope to Douglass, who expected it would result in a gentler life for the slaves. But as Douglass wrote, "It neither made him to be humane to his slaves, nor to emancipate them. If it had any effect on his character, it made him more cruel and hateful in all his ways; for I believe him to have been a much worse man after his conversion than before. Prior to his conversion, he relied upon his own depravity to shield and sustain him in his savage barbarity; but after his conversion, he found religious sanction and support for his slaveholding cruelty."[51]

Reading about that one abuse of "religious freedom" changed my entire perspective on the subject. I realized from Douglass's account that freedom to choose one's religion is something deeper than what it appears to be on the surface. His master ostensibly made a choice to become a "Christian," but in reality that was a camouflage for a deeper, darker choice. This realization taught me five things.

1. It taught me that religious freedom is about something far greater than simply being allowed to worship whom and how one chooses. At the core of religious freedom is the right to determine what you consider your ultimate authority. We build our very lives on that foundational choice. In reality, freedom of religion is freedom of thought — the freedom for a person to choose the basic foundation on which he or she will build one's entire being. If a person is denied that primary choice, then no other freedom has meaning. Those who are denied the right to make this choice for themselves become the puppets of those who impose their own foundational

decisions on others. This is why freedom of religion truly is the first freedom.

2. Religious freedom is important because any religion that must use coercion and force to spread itself is a weak faith that denies the God-given dignity of a human being. Such a faith is not worthy of survival. It may survive as long as the government has power to enforce it, but it will not survive forever. For a religion to have power, it must penetrate the human heart. The power of faith is not demonstrated by our willingness to kill for it, but by our willingness to die for it. It is better to die for what you believe than to reject it under force and affirm something you do not believe.

If Christianity cannot win because of its message, winning by the sword will be futile. What we would force, we cannot hold forever. What we believe and accept willingly in our hearts will last beyond our life on earth. Christianity should be accepted on its merits, its message, and its love demonstrated in the activity of Christians. If it cannot spread on that basis, it doesn't deserve to win. This is why, though I passionately want the whole world to be Christian, I would never force conversion on anyone. I would fight for someone else's freedom to choose another religion even if I believed that religion was hopelessly wrong.

The right of a person to choose, even wrongly, is important because in the long run, it benefits Christianity. I know religious freedom is working when a person can be a Hindu in Jerusalem. That shows me people are granted the right to choose, and when that right is granted, the message of Jesus has a chance to prove itself.

When teaching the people at NorthWood about our work and service with people around the world, I tell them, "We do what we do, not *to convert*, but because we *are converted*." This is an important contrast. If I am serving others just to make them into Christians — as wonderful and important as that is — my motive is impure and I'm using my act of service to get converts. As some of our youth would say, I'd be "pimpin'" Jesus.

One principle we must remember here is that *we* cannot save people; only *God* does that. As the apostle Paul said, "I planted. Apollos watered. But God gave the increase" (1 Corinthians 3:6). So I serve, not knowing who will follow Jesus and who will not. I try to do what God asks me to do, but then I must leave the results to him.

People generally live out this principle better than they think they do. Most Christians who see someone bleeding by the side of the road will stop to help without thinking of using the incident as an opportunity for conversion. "Uh, sir, now that your broken leg is set, your punctured lung is inflated, and your concussion is taken care of, don't you think you should consider saying the sinner's prayer and making Jesus your personal Savior?" No, we don't do that. Each of us exercises the compassion for the suffering that God has built into us. We abuse that passion when we train ourselves by a misguided standard of manipulation to see every occasion of human suffering as an opportunity for conversion. We must be willing to do our part and let God do his.

I can't tell you how many people have "volunteered" to convert because we helped them in some significant way. I always explain that if they follow Jesus, it must be only because they believe in him, they want him as their Lord, and they are convinced that his way is true and right. They should never convert out of gratitude, obligation, or anything less than true belief and a heartfelt willingness to follow him. And whether or not they convert, our relationship will not be affected. I'll serve them anyway, love them anyway, and continue to be their friend. It's a great tragedy when we create an atmosphere in which we cannot serve people without their wondering what strings are attached. There are no strings attached to God's love ... only a cross.

3. Religious freedom is important because it enables us to apply kingdom theology. We have been called to reconcile "all peoples" and "all things" to God. This reconciliation is not only a future hope to be realized in eternity; it is a thing of the moment to be realized both in individuals and in the structures of society. But

if we do not have the freedom to serve and operate, we cannot engage the whole of society. As Chris Seiple told me, "When the church has the freedom to gather as two or three in his name, it has the opportunity to disciple transformed lives and equip ambassadors for Christ. Only then is it ready to transform culture and society."

Although we encounter varying degrees of religious freedom around the world, I have found that as long as you respect the religious laws of a country, even if you disagree with them, you will be able to serve the people in the domains of society. In time this will gain the country's trust, and you will be given permission to speak to the issues that matter in regard to religious freedom.

4. Freedom of religion is central to the fulfillment of God's law. Love God and love your neighbor summarizes the essence of the Ten Commandments. God grants our neighbors the same right to choose that he grants to us. If we love our neighbors, we must love them even though their choice may differ from ours. We can't love without respect, which means we must learn to disagree but still respect their choice. To respect or tolerate those with whom we disagree means we must acknowledge them as human beings of value and worth. It is never my place to strongarm anyone. If I love my neighbors, I must allow them freedom to choose.

   I have come to love many non-Christians as my own family. Some of these people are often in and out of our home. We run around with them; we celebrate holidays together. When we dine together, I pray over our meals "in the name of Jesus" and we talk about our faith. If I were to push Christianity on them, some perhaps would convert out of sheer friendship. I want them to become Christians, of course, but when they do, I want them to mean it. Many of them, I might add, have in fact become followers of Jesus; but that story is theirs to tell, not mine.

5. Freedom of religion is important because it eliminates the suffering caused by religious persecution. As I write this there are

people held in jails who are going to lose their lives for one simple reason: they are Christians. As Christians we should challenge this deplorable fact because we have a responsibility to alleviate suffering wherever we can. I know people say that the gospel spreads through persecution. That is historically true. But notice that it's only those who are not being persecuted who can make such an objective observation. I've yet to meet a Christian who was suffering who didn't want it to end as quickly as possible.

We must also remember that just because God can bring good out of an evil does not justify the evil. We've been commanded to visit those in the prison and to stand for justice. If we have the power to bless someone and fail to do it, we sin.

FREEDOM OF RELIGION IS FOR EVERYONE

The overwhelming consensus globally is that freedom of religion is something Christians focus on for their own benefit. It's largely viewed as an American thing. When the world understands that religious freedom is good for everyone, individuals and nations alike, it will be a huge step toward enabling all nations to hear and receive the faith.

Although religious freedom is not presently common throughout the world, it is possible for people to change when they understand the advantages it brings. Even the most hardened religious enemies can learn this lesson, if not by coming to an intellectual understanding of it, then by the harsh reality of experience.

For example, not long ago I had the privilege of meeting James Wuye, a leader of the evangelical church in Nigeria. He and a Muslim imam had been fighting one another, killing one another's people and burning down each other's places of worship. In one of those attacks James had his arm cut off. He began to ask, "What am I doing in the name of God?" The answer convicted him. He realized that force was not a legitimate way to spread Christianity, and killing another person because of his faith could hardly be called loving one's neighbor. It dawned on him that God created men and women free to choose him or not, and whether or not James agreed with their choice, he must respect it and love them.

James met with the imam, who was receptive to his change of heart. The two asked each other's forgiveness and started a reconciliation ministry between Muslims and Christians in Nigeria. James's story is a living example of the power of freedom of religion and a testimony to the validity of the message of this chapter.

Connection Steps

⊙ How are you using your religious freedom to bring about transformation?

⊙ Whom do you know who has been persecuted by being beaten, put in jail, or killed simply for being a Christian?

⊙ Pretend God is calling you to work in a place where there is no religious freedom — what would you do?

CHAPTER 10

Stop Subverting the Message

C hristianity began as a Jewish movement to Christ, but I believe it will end as an Islamic movement to Jesus. Several decades ago, China was one of the largest frontiers for the Great Commission, but today China is spiritually awake, and Chinese disciples of Jesus are taking the gospel all around the world. Africa, once the "dark continent," now boasts more Christians than the United States. Among the existing cultures that remain unreached by the gospel, the Islamic nations make up the largest bloc.

It's no secret that Muslims now see America as a field ripe for harvest. Islam is making inroads into Western cultures, particularly in cities and urban areas. As a result, in many parts of the American church there is widespread fear and distrust toward Muslims. Some of this distrust comes from a lack of understanding about the religion of Islam — a fear that was there even before the events of September 11, 2001. But the events of that day heightened our awareness of Muslims and intensified some of our existing prejudices and misunderstandings. As followers of Christ, the church should be the last place where fear, prejudice, and distrust form the basis for our relationships with other people. We should not fear Muslims, or people of any religion for that matter. Instead, our calling as disciples of Christ is to follow the teachings of our faith, serving those who different from us and sharing with them the good news about Jesus. And when we disagree — which will certainly happen — we must resolve our differences with respect and courtesy.

This principle has not always been on my radar screen. I grew up not knowing any Muslims. In the small East Texas towns where I was raised, the biggest religious difference was between a Protestant and a Catholic. In my denomination we were heavily steeped in evangelical end-time theology. I grew up in a culture of dispensational premillennialism — our charts were incredible! We could outchart anyone with explicit details about how Jesus was going to come back and tell you exactly when it would happen. Though no man could know the hour of his return, we could certainly know the date! Even though Jesus said he could come back at any moment, we knew he wouldn't come until certain events occurred that were necessary to fulfill prophecy. Of course, the fact that many of those prophecies were not clear didn't faze us. We had our prophetic experts to give us their explicit meaning.

This was the insulated environment I grew up in — an environment permeated by settled convictions about how godless people would be destroyed and Christians would rise up triumphant at the return of Christ. In such an environment, I rarely thought about showing love toward those of other religions. In my mind, they were the enemies of God.

It's funny how things change. Those I feared the most in my youth have now become those I love the most. In this chapter I will share with you a few stories about my friendships with those of other faiths, especially with Muslims, and what a difference these relationships have made in my life. These experiences have helped me to see that the church needs to develop a new way of relating to people with deep religious differences. When those of other religions are able to observe our faith in action on a personal level, it will make our witness to the world and our work of living out God's kingdom principles even more effective and powerful. Most important, I believe these examples will give us clues as to how we can bring the kingdom of God to the very people we tend to fear — our Muslim neighbors.

CHANGING MY THINKING ABOUT THE MIDDLE EAST

As I thought about engaging Muslims, I realized that I needed to start by looking at the things that matter to them. What do they care about? What are their concerns, needs, and priorities? For most of the Muslims I have talked with, their top concern is the Arab–Israeli conflict. At one point in my life I would have just said: "Forget the Muslims! They are God's enemies because they hate the Jews!" But I have found that the answers of my dispensational premillennial days aren't helpful here.

As I began to visit Islamic nations and to get to know Muslims on a personal basis, for the first time in my life I felt conflicted over my attitudes and prejudices toward these people. My eschatology was directly conflicting with my love for them and my desire to tell them the good news of Jesus. Why didn't my understanding about the Great Commission harmonize with my end-time theology, which favored Israel over other Middle Eastern nations? I realized that something was wrong. And it wasn't just me. It was affecting our nation and our foreign policy.

Many of the theological convictions I had been raised with gave the Jewish people a privileged position in the purposes of God; as a result I had been taught to be sympathetic toward our religious forerunners, the Jews. In many areas of the American church today, support for the nation of Israel is strong and is driven by theological convictions about God's purposes in the end times. As a predominantly Christian nation, some of those *theological* convictions have also spilled over into our *governmental* support of the Israeli nation.

Now personally, I don't believe in jihad (holy war) as a means of resolving religious differences; jihad is an Islamic concept taught in the Koran. So you can imagine my surprise when I heard a well-known televangelist on a Christian television network call for the bombing of Iran. I wondered if this approach was a good reflection of the Great Commission, if bombing our enemies was really the best way of sharing the gospel with them. If that's our approach as Christians, then what real difference is there between a fundamentalist Muslim jihadist calling for war against Christians and a fundamentalist Christian pastor calling for the bombing of a Muslim nation? My expanding vision of the kingdom of God was undermining all my previous understandings and creating some real conflict for me.

Often, when your thinking begins to change, you begin to ratio-nalize things in order to look for something that can rescue your former beliefs. I thought, "Who knows for sure what God's intent is for the Jews and Palestinians in Israel? Since the Jews and Mus-lims are both there, both wanting the same land, maybe it's better to side with the Jews and not upset the applecart." At about that time I stumbled on a book by Brother Andrew called *Light Force*. In this book he articulated the very same questions I had been asking, and his answers did not endorse the typical pro-Israel attitude that was so prevalent in my upbringing.

Still, I wasn't entirely satisfied. So I contacted an evangelical Pal-estinian pastor, a resident of Bethlehem named Bishara Awad, and I arranged a meeting with him. At our meeting, I found that Bishara loved God deeply and was a strong believer in fulfilling the Great Commission. He believed that to fulfill it we would have to engage the entire Middle East, and that he and his friends in the Middle East were being called to that very purpose.

I immediately sensed a great irony in what Bishara was telling me. While most American evangelicals are passionate about their support of Israel, I found it strange that they tend to forget about the Palestinian evangelical Christians, their true brothers and sisters in Christ. Wouldn't it be just like Satan to prod evangelical Christians in America to rally to the support of Israel, a nation that has rejected Jesus, and ignore the very people indigenous to the land who for centuries were eager and willing to fulfill the Great Commission? I'm now convinced that it is a strategy of the enemy to marginalize the very people who have the potential to impact the Middle East more than any other people group — Palestinian Christians.

When my new friend Bishara Awad shared his personal story with me, my eyes were fully opened to the falsehood of my former preju-dices and understanding of the Middle East. Bishara was raised in a small, peaceful Palestinian village where Jews, Christians, and Mus-lims all lived together. He was still just a little boy when the Israeli tanks came to his village. Bishara and his family fled their home in terror, like many other Palestinians, and as they were leaving a stray bullet hit his father and killed him. The family buried his body in the backyard and continued their flight from the Israelis. Bishara's mother did her best to raise the children, but eventually she had no choice but to put them in an orphanage. At the orphanage, Bishara and his brothers Alex and Mubarak accepted Christ as their Savior.

When Bishara told me his story I was heartbroken. Keep in mind that his family had lived on that land for *centuries*. I wondered, was it right for the Jews to take over their nation and control it? By supporting Israel, was I saying that I supported actions like this? Don't mistake what I am saying here. I have always been disturbed by what the Jews suffered in the Holocaust, and I continue to recognize that as a great evil. But does the evil of their suffering justify their present treatment of the Palestinians — confining them with walls, requiring special identification, restricting access to jobs, and pushing innocent families out of their ancestral homes? Is it ever right to respond to one injustice with another? As a Texan, I know that we Texans would fight like Crockett at the Alamo if another nation tried to take away our land. What justified the actions of Israel? Was it somehow acceptable for them to do this because they were God's "chosen" people?

At that point, I again recognized that there was something wrong with my theology. The Great Commission teaches that God has no longer confined his redemptive work to a single nation — he loves people from every nation, tongue, and tribe. God wants every nation and people group to be reconciled to him. If that is true, then any end-time theory or doctrine that excludes specific people from the reach of God's love is necessarily flawed. The clear teaching of the Great Commission should trump any notions or theories we may have about God's attitude toward nations in the end times.

PUTTING MY NEW THEOLOGY TO THE TEST

In early 2002 I was asked to assist with some humanitarian work in Afghanistan. Even though I agreed to go, I must admit that I did so in fear. With the events of 9 – 11 fresh in my mind, I was not sure that a Muslim nation was the best place for an American evangelical to be traveling. Through my experiences in Vietnam, I had come to love "communist atheists" and had learned not to fear them, but Muslims — well, that was another story!

Despite my initial fears, within a short time I fell in love with the Afghani people. Their radically different culture intrigued me — the food, the smells, the landscape, the clothing, the sound of the language. At one point during my trip to Afghanistan I was in the Afghan desert with a group of imams (I'll spare you the long story of how I got there). They began asking me questions about my religious beliefs. In the midst of our discussion, we came to the time for prayer, and the imams began spreading out their rugs on the desert floor to pray. Since it was prayer time, I followed suit and took to my knees, praying to Jesus while they said their prayers. In many ways, this was a turning point for me. Back in the United States it was easy for me to fear these people, but after living with them, talking with them, and praying alongside them, my fears began to evaporate. I can now honestly confess that I love and care deeply about the Afghani people.

I've found that real love motivates us to seek understanding. When you truly care about someone, you do whatever you can to understand them. For the first time in my life I was actively trying to love Muslims. And as I sought to love them, I began to see these supposedly fearsome Muslims in a different light, the light of God's kingdom. I saw them not as fearsome, angry people, but as people whom God loves and wants to reconcile to himself. I began to see that God is not just interested in individual Muslims, but that he has a love for them as a people, that his goal is to redeem and reconcile "all things" to himself.

The kingdom of God is a reality that transcends national boundaries and political parties. It's a kingdom of the heart, a gracious movement of God's love that transforms people in all societies into one unified body. The New Testament affirms that the gospel is for every tongue, tribe, and nation. Practically speaking, that means that the gospel is for the Afghani Muslim, and it is for both the Jew and the Palestinian.

For many Muslims, the conflict in the Middle East between Palestinians and Israelis is a key concern. They want to know and understand our thoughts on this issue. It's not something we can simply ignore and hope it goes away. Those who work with Muslims in the Middle East need to be informed, and they need to have thoughtful opinions on the subject. Personally, while I support the existence of Israel, I do not offer my support because of a promise in the Old Testament. I support the people of Israel because they are a people without a land, a people in need of a place to live, and because they are a people with a deep and rich history in God's Word.

Since the Jewish people, as a nation, have rejected the Messiah, they stand in need of the gospel just as much as our Muslim friends and neighbors. As evangelicals, the political alignment of our nation in the Middle East creates problems for our witness in that area of the world, problems we need to thoughtfully consider and be ready to address. If we wish to fulfill the Great Commission in the Middle East, we must recognize that American support for Israel and policies that exclude the Palestinian people put us at odds with the majority of the people we are trying to reach in the Middle East.

Obviously, American foreign policy is largely driven by political realities. But it is dangerous for us to formulate American foreign policy on the basis of speculative theology, and I am convinced that this is happening. Many of these end-time ideas about Muslims and the Middle East have been so pervasive among American Christians that they have covertly influenced government policy for decades.

As a church, we have a responsibility to prepare people with a kingdom perspective and equip them with the understanding they need to be disciples of Christ. As the bride of Christ, the church also has a responsibility to prepare things so that all is ready for his return. Our task is a positive one, motivated by the commission of Jesus and the love of God, not a negative one. We are not called to cringe in fear and adopt opinions that perpetuate prejudice against particular people groups. We are not called to declare God's wrath against a particular ethnicity or culture. We are called to invite people and nations to reconcile to God before Christ comes, to find the source of joy and peace in Christ that transcends the turmoil that leads to his second coming.

How can we reach the Muslims? We take a lesson from the apostle Paul and reach them the same way he reached the rabbis and the

Jews. When Paul came into a city, he went straight to the synagogue and engaged the people there on their own terms. Instead of thinking of Muslims as our enemies; we must learn to engage them on their own terms, on their own ground — not as antagonists, but with respect and humility.

I confess that I had failed to view Muslims in this way. For many years, I had viewed those who followed Islam as my enemies. I saw imams as false prophets, forgetting that Christ tells us that false prophets are deceivers within the ranks of the Christian church and not practitioners of other religions (see Matthew 24:24). But it occurred to me that if God is going to move through Islamic culture in a massive way, will he just bypass the religious leaders? As the religious gatekeepers of their culture, I'm convinced that imams hold the key to seeing the gospel spread in the Islamic world. We see evidence of this approach in the book of Acts. Despite the fact that a majority of the Jewish leaders rejected Jesus, Luke tells us that a great number of them came to faith in Jesus and became his disciples (see, e.g., Acts 21:20).

So how can we reach out to these leaders, especially if they are entrenched in their religion? Aren't they the most difficult ones to lead to Christ? The key to effectively reaching people in these settings is establishing relationships where we live out our lives in front of them as witnesses to God's love. Muslim leaders may choose not to accept what we believe or to agree with what we say, but we love them anyway. At the very least, even if I don't win them with my argument, I have been a responsible witness for Christ. And even when we fail, there is always the possibility that God will work beyond our abilities, entering the heart and doing what we could never do.

THE MUFTI AND THE WEST BANK

Several years ago, I called my friend Bishara and set up a trip for my wife and me to visit Israel. We flew to Tel Aviv and were picked up by Bishara's brother, Alex. He took us straight from the airport to a kibbutz where a congregation of messianic Jews was holding a Christian worship service. Alex, a Palestinian Christian pastor, was preaching that day. Nikki and I found it deeply moving to worship with people from all over the world who had two things in common: they were both Jews and Christians.

In the midst of that worship service, I had a thought: Could the answer to the conflict in the Middle East be for these messianic Jews and the Palestinian Christians to lead the way? As both Christians and citizens of the Middle East, they seemed to have all the relational connections necessary to make them the natural spearhead for a movement to Jesus. Sadly, as I talked with many of them after the service, I found that these Jewish Christ-followers are frequently isolated from their neighbors, often because of the policies and attitudes of Western Christians.

Later in the day Nikki and I arrived in Bethlehem, where we had to go through all the military checkpoints you hear about in the news. I was shocked at the massive wall being built around Bethlehem, separating the Israelis from the Palestinians. The machine-gun turrets staring down through their black glass encasements made us feel as if we were in a prison camp. The place where Jesus was born is quickly becoming a museum, and among those shut out by the wall are the Palestinian Christians.

For most of my life I'd heard about the injustices experienced by the Jewish people during the Holocaust of World War II. As I stood inside the massive walls surrounding the checkpoint at Bethlehem, I was struck by a sad irony. The very people who know what it means to be oppressed are now inflicting oppression on the people of Bethlehem.

We saw all the sights that tourists normally see in Bethlehem, Jerusalem, and Galilee. Later in the week, Bishara introduced me to some of his Muslim friends, including Abdul Rachman, the Supreme Islamic Scholar of Palestine. He set up a meeting for me with the Grand Mufti of Jerusalem. At the appointed time Abdul took us to the top of the Mount of Olives to the Grand Mufti's apartment, where I met the Mufti himself.

The Mufti is a fair-skinned man who looks like just about any sixty-year-old Baptist preacher I ever knew back in East Texas. I told him so, and he asked if that was good. "Oh yes, of course," I lied.

I explained that I was an evangelical pastor, but that while I supported the right of the Jews to Israel, I also supported the right of the Palestinians to the West Bank. The Grand Mufti hadn't met many evangelicals who held that position, so he began to quiz me about many of my beliefs. At one point in our conversation I told him, "Here we are, Christians, Muslims, and Jews. This country is the heart of the three Abrahamic faiths, and for us to be fighting all the time is a slam against all three religions. It makes all three faiths look like a joke. We should do all we can to promote peace." He agreed with me. I took the agreement as an opening and asked, "What if we did some humanitarian projects together, enabling Christians, Jews, and Muslims to work side by side and build positive relationships?"

This is an idea I had been keen on for a good while. I had encountered the idea while I was a part of the Brookings World Islamic Forum. At that forum I spent time visiting with the Grand Mufti of Bosnia, who told me that he had talked of peace for sixty years and had little to show for it. He said the best way to engage is not through more talks, but by doing something positive together.

That's the idea I shared with the Grand Mufti of Jerusalem, and he liked it. Then I took the next step. "If I brought some church leaders over and found some willing rabbis, would you be willing to engage with us in such a project?" He affirmed that he would, but he wasn't sure about the other Jewish leaders.

Nothing certain had been established, but it was a start. In spite of our differences, we had found common ground and learned to be comfortable with each other. Comfortable enough, in fact, to start talking about theology. I looked out his window and was overwhelmed at what I saw. Here I was at the top of the Mount of Olives in the Grand Mufti's apartment, looking out at Jerusalem's Eastern Gate. I told him, "You know, some Christians believe when Jesus returns he will literally go through that gate."

He responded, "Yes, and if that happened, I would be glad of it."

"Really?" I asked, shocked at his positive reply.

"Yes," he assured me. But I was pretty sure his reasons for being happy were not the same as mine.

When we returned to the U.S., I contacted Kensington Community Church, a church with an attendance of over 10,000 in the Detroit area — the Arab capital of America. I challenged the pastor, Steve Andrews, saying, "What if your church were to engage Bethlehem and we mobilized your members to focus on that spot?" That challenge led to an invitation for me to speak at his church. As a result, in February of 2008, I was on a plane to Israel with Chris Seiple and Don Anderson, one of the pastors at the Kensington Church. In Israel we met again with the Grand Mufti and other Islamic leaders, but also had a chance to meet with Palestinian President Mahmoud Abbas and heads of the Israeli State Department to explain who we were and what we wanted to do. We were received with grace and courtesy, and at the time of writing this book we are developing a unified project that will bring together people from these three diverse religions, focused on working together in one of the most volatile religious settings in the world.

When I tell people about this venture, I am sometimes asked if there is any possibility that some of these groups may be using me politically. Certainly, that is true for some people. There is always a chance that when we do something, others will use our good intentions for their own gain. But when you follow Christ, you take chances like that. While we need to be wise in the choices we make, ultimately we should care more about seeking opportunities to be used by Christ rather than worry about whether others are using us for their purposes.

WHAT I LEARNED FROM BISHARA AWAD

I am deeply indebted to my Palestinian friend and brother, Bishara Awad, not only for putting me in contact with people who led to this three-way connection between Jews, Christians, and Muslims, but for many other reasons as well. I have learned much from him about what it means to be a Christian in both Jewish and Islamic cultures — things I could not have learned from any other source. Knowing he would have much of value to share with readers of this book, I interviewed him after our Jerusalem trip. Here are some of the highlights of that interview.

BR: *What is it like being a Christian in an area controlled by Muslims?*

BA: We've lived side by side with them all of our lives. We've considered them our neighbors, and good neighbors. We never thought of each other as different, but as being part of the same society. They are Palestinians just like us.

BR: *Did you ever face difficulties from Muslims because of your faith?*

BA: I have never hid my beliefs, nor have I faced difficulties. Muslims have always had respect for my beliefs, and their attitudes have never been against what I believe.

BR: *Did you ever feel left out, shunned, or looked down on because you were a Christian?*

BA: No, I never felt that way either. At an early age we lived together in the same orphanage. In fact, I took classes from Muslim teachers, and I know many verses from the Koran by heart even now. And I'm proud of all of that. Once you fellowship and eat bread together, then you are friends together.

BR: *How do you account for Muslim persecution of Christians in the world?*

BA: I hear stories like anybody else. Burning, murdering, destroying churches, etc. I recently heard of Muslims murdering Christians in Egypt. In one instance, masked men entered a jewelry store and killed the owners. These are unfortunate things and we are saddened, because deep inside I know that these are not the Muslims that I know. What happened in Gaza is an indication that the violence isn't caused by the Muslims who have lived with other Christians for years and years. It is obviously caused by Muslims from outside the communities or by extremist Muslims. That's not indicative of most Muslims I know.

BR: *How do you account for those Muslims who are extremists?*

BA: The whole world is changing. The political incidents and events that have taken place in the world have increased the violence, especially toward Muslims — the wars in Iraq and Pakistan and other places; America supporting Israel whether right or wrong. Unfortunately, people don't look at America merely as a nation, but as a Christian nation. Many of them can't understand America. How can they be a Christian nation and yet engage in wars against Muslims? This causes them to react with violence.

BR: *Would you say that there was as much Muslim persecution fifty years ago as there is in the world today?*

BA: Things were calmer and easier than today.

BR: *Can Christians today, in your opinion, have a healthy relationship and dialogue with Muslims?*

BA: I believe they can sit down with them and have a very healthy dialogue. I have yet to meet a Muslim who refused to have dialogue with Christians.

BR: *What is it like being a Christian living in a predominately Jewish state?*

BA: The Israeli government does not treat Palestinian Christians any better than the Muslims. Both are Palestinians, and as far as Israel is concerned both are terrorists. Unfortunately, that is the word they use to refer to all of us. So we are not being treated in a better way at all. No permits to travel. Being a Christian does not grant you any special status or help at all. Basically, Israel is against both Christianity and Islam.

BR: *How difficult is it when a Jew becomes a Christian?*

BA: He is persecuted by his family and also by the government. The antimission law in Israel says if you even give a Jew a Bible, it is considered a crime because it means you want to convert him.

BR: *What do you think is the best way to engage Muslims?*

BA: Take away the fear and reach to them in love. I also believe we should be open and not hide our agenda, whoever we are. If we make our agenda clear to them, they will give us respect even though they do not agree with what we want to do.

BR: *What is your opinion on doing humanitarian projects together?*

BA: I have no problems with that. The Shepherd Society and aid given to Muslims and Christians are very helpful. There are several organizations like World Vision that hire Muslims to do the development to get the work done. So we have no problem with that.

BR: *What is your opinion of Kensington Church and Steve Andrews and their desire to come and serve the people of Bethlehem?*

BA: We welcome the Kensington Church to be involved and engaged in the work we are doing in the Bethlehem community. I believe they can be a great blessing. I've met Steve Andrews and Don Anderson personally, and they understand the need and the situation. We welcome them and we will work with them. It's always good to work through the local church to spread the blessings to the rest of the community. This way the church can have respect in the whole community.

BR: *What would you say to others who want to work in Bethlehem?*

BA: We welcome anybody and any church that wants to be involved in the ministry and the work, be it spreading the gospel or humanitarian and relief work. We'd like to see these groups work through the church so the church can get the credit. We welcome every church that wants to work to be a part of the community. Some people come and work on their own, and after they leave the church has to pick up the pieces.

BR: *What was your opinion of our meeting with the Grand Mufti?*

BA: It was a great meeting — a meeting among friends, a meeting between religious people that have respect for each other. I love being a part of that. I have met with him on many different occasions.

I hope that in this interview with Bishara Awad you saw not a Palestinian, but a person and a dear fellow member of the body of Christ. I hope his responses have given you new insights into the problems, the attitudes, and the needs of Christians and Muslims living in a culture hostile to them.

In fact, that is my hope for you in this final chapter. Many times, we as Christians are afraid of the unknown. We have an image of Muslims that makes us afraid to talk with them and share with them. One of the most significant lessons I've learned about engaging people of other cultures and nations is that when we isolate ourselves from them, we tend to fear them. And when we fear them, our attempts at evangelism will be ineffective or even destructive. Unless we really get to know and love people enough to wish their good above all else and to serve them in their need, we cannot effectively speak to the issues that concern them.

In my experiences working with followers of Christ around the world, I have learned that the kingdom of God is not only for the Americans and the Jews; it is for all people. God loves Palestinians, Jordanians, Arabs, and Iranians every bit as much as he loves you and me. Muslims may worship Allah, but God dearly desires to reconcile the people of these nations to himself.

Connection Steps

⊙ List all of the non-Christian religious places of worship in your community.

⊙ List one friend you have who is of a different religion — not just a different Christian denomination.

⊙ List three practical ways you can serve people of other religions.

⊙ How have you seen speculative theology and political bias undermine the Great Commission?

I Have a Dream

Researchers and analysts have observed and documented that different generations of people in the U.S. tend to have their own unique outlooks and tendencies. The attributes of one generation tend to differ from those of the next generation. Despite cultural or economic differences, people of a given generation often have specific attitudes and outlooks in common with most other members in their generation. As we consider the work of linking our jobs and callings with the work of God throughout the world, I believe that two generations in particular are poised like never before to come together and effect change. They are the Baby Boomers and the Millennials.

THE BOOMER

Boomers is shorthand for Baby Boomers, those Americans born between 1946 and 1964. One of the most incredible Boomers I've ever known is Al Weiss, president of Disney Theme Parks Worldwide. Al is humble, unassuming, and incredibly sharp and savvy, as you would expect in a man in his position. In my mind, Al Weiss is the quintessential example of a Boomer. He's a man who has been highly successful in his field and has reached the point where he has the resources to reach out through his skills and passions into the wider world.

Here is how Al describes himself:

I often say I grew up in a very privileged home; and when I do, people automatically wonder what my dad did. What kind of cars did we drive? What was our house like? They are always surprised when I tell them, "My Dad was a church planter." Because of that I learned so much.

My dad was the kind of man that would start a church from scratch, get it into its first building, on its feet, and then after about six years he would come in and say, "Okay kids, it's time to do it again," and we would pull up stakes and move. Moving often was financially challenging, so to make everything work my dad had to be careful and organized in what he spent. I saw people knock on our door needing money for groceries, and my parents would help them out, even when it meant doing without themselves. But God always provided.

That's how we wound up in Orlando: it was Dad's final church. When I was eighteen I got a minimum wage job at Disney to help me through college. Little did I know that I would wind up doing what I do today. But my dad prepared me, partly though his excellent counsel and wisdom, but also because what he had learned from starting churches from scratch had made him a great business manager. He had only had so much money available, and so how he used it was extremely critical. I learned a lot from watching him.

About three years ago, God began to speak to my heart about doing something for him. So I partnered with Steve Johnson, a pastor and church planter, to start Vision360, which is a plan and a process to start new churches. At first the target was just Orlando, but a year later after getting Orlando up and going, we began to think about planting in the fifty largest cities in America. Then a couple of years ago I was promoted to the position of president of Disney Theme Parks Worldwide, and I heard God calling me to the world as well.

God's vision and our dream is to plant churches in the 500 most influential cities of the world. But it has to be the right kind of churches — churches that are engaging the domains of society and seeing the transformation of their city.

Al is well on his way to seeing the Vision360 dream fulfilled. He has put together a team; he has started raising the necessary resources; and he is moving toward the goal. I am happy to be a part of the project, and I am amazed not only at what God has said to him, but also at his ability to inspire businessmen to get on board. As he speaks across the country and connects with these people, they start chompin' at the bit to be a part of it. It's turned out to be about far more than planting churches; it's about calling businessmen to engage the world, not just with their money, but also with their time and skill as well. I know of at least three highly successful business owners who work full-time on the church-planting project — without pay! His dream is to find dedicated businessmen in each target city who will raise the resources to start churches through a self-perpetuating fund.

Because NorthWood starts a lot of churches people often ask me, "Why have you partnered with Al Weiss and Vision360? There are other denominations, networks, and organizations you could choose." I tell them that he's the only businessman I know in the U.S. that has felt called to start churches. Many preachers have felt that call, and they answer it by working through these other organizations. But how many businessmen can you point to who have been inspired with such a mission? Al is the only one I know. I've run across many businessmen who want to give or raise money and then let others do the work, but Al wants both feet in the ministry — the giving and the doing.

THE MILLENNIAL

In addition to the Boomers, social scientists have termed the generation born between 1980 and 1994 *Millennials*. Among the many people who attend our church and belong to this generational group, I'd like to focus on the story of one exceptional young woman, Paige Kimmel. I believe Paige illustrates the characteristics that define this generation, and she gives me great hope that God will use this generation, along with willing Boomers, to revolutionize our understanding of the Great Commission.

In 1992 Mark and Valinda Kimmel moved back to the U.S. from Eastern Europe, where Mark had been training pastors. Soon after their return, Mark joined our staff at NorthWood to head up administration of the church. While Mark himself is an exceptionally gifted and capable individual, his greatest accomplishment may be the raising of a son and a daughter who love God deeply and have a genuine heart for serving others.

When Mark's daughter Paige was fifteen, I still remember sitting with her and some other students from the youth group on a bus. I was asking her questions about her future and what she was planning to do with her life. What I remember most from that conversation was what she said about her dad: "He's one of the greatest men I've ever known and I've looked up to him all my life." Paige recently graduated from Texas A&M with a degree in English. She is currently working at Thompson-Reuters as a copy editor.

Having grown up in the middle-class suburbs of Fort Worth, Paige now lives in inner-city Fort Worth in an economically disadvantaged neighborhood. Many minority families live there, including a high percentage of single moms and their kids. The house Paige shares is a small, decades-old frame structure, but it's in pretty good shape. Things break down, but the landlord helps with the repairs. There's crime and other challenging issues, but Paige feels called to be there.

Paige shares the tiny house with several other girls. Two guys their own age live next door in a duplex. I wondered why Paige, with a successful job and a good income, and her friends live in this environment. All of them have made an intentional choice to live in that area because they love the community. They have built relationships with the people who live there, and living in the neighborhood has created opportunities for them to serve in ways that would have been impossible living in the suburbs.

These young men and women have chosen to live together in this inner-city neighborhood, not only to serve others, but also to express their core convictions. Part of the motivation for living in community with one another is a desire to live simply and concentrate on what is essential. "It's been really beautiful," Paige told me. "Many Scriptures come alive when you live the way Jesus taught. It's also been hard, which is strangely comforting to me because it means it's real. When you live simply and share responsibility with others, you have to work through issues such as who does what chores, how we pool our money, and how we use our gifts."

Many of their activities are done together as a group. On Thursday nights they have a meal with everyone they serve with, both those in the suburbs and the inner city. On Sunday nights they worship together, read, pray, teach, and celebrate. People from the community are invited to attend: sometimes they come, sometimes they don't.

Since these young people have their own jobs, they set aside Saturday as a day for serving the community. Typically, they either serve on Lancaster Street, in the shelter, or they help people with groceries and take care of kids. They spend considerable time both on Saturdays and weekdays fostering relationships with the other people of the community. Part of the motivation for living in this environment is to model the type of engagement that Jesus did — incarnational living. Jesus didn't just talk at people or throw resources at them; he lived among the people and reached out to those who were disadvantaged and those who were suffering.

After Paige had lived for almost a year in the inner city, I had an opportunity to talk with her, and I was able to ask her some questions. "Are you glad you decided to do this?" I asked.

"Yes," she answered, "It's been life to me. It's the gospel not in words but in life. It has taken the truth in Scriptures and made it alive, so that faith, grace, mercy, and forgiveness are not just words but a way of living."

"What lessons have you learned from your experience?"

She replied, "Sacrifice is hard, but it's worth it. Real love is hard, but it's worth it. I've come to understand I can't live out the kingdom of God without a community of people. I can't do that on my own. To find satisfaction and fulfillment in my future means serving God by giving my life away in an inner city or wherever there is a need."

Paige then shared with me an experience that demonstrates the practical impact their presence is having on the community. "At the women and children's shelter we met a single mom with two small boys. She wasn't born in poverty, but her circumstances drove her there — out of a job, no home, no car, living on government assistance. One of the issues at the shelter is the lack of laundry resources. So we girls let the women use our washer and dryer, and this young mother came and hung out while her clothes were washing. After several such trips, we became close. She grew up in a religious family, but faith didn't 'take' in her. She was dealing with difficult issues involving her ex, and so we asked if we could pray with her. Through a combination of her persistence, our help, and God's provision, she managed to get an apartment. She's now working part time and looking for jobs on her own.

"It is significant that this woman now invites us to her apartment to cook for us, because it shows that we have a mutual relationship. Many of us have had conversations with her about God, and we can see her attitude changing. She told me recently, 'As I was growing up, I'd heard about God, but I didn't really believe anything I heard. But I'm starting to believe it now.' Some people come to know Jesus in an instant, while others have to experience him through other people before they can come near him."

Then I asked Paige, "Are examples like you and your friends unique?"

"I can't speak for everyone in my generation," she responded, "but in the Christian world people of my generation want what we're experiencing — action that mirrors Scripture. We don't want a disconnected faith, and so we try to connect theory with practice. And when we do, we see the Scriptures come alive, which makes us willing to take the risk and jump right into it. Having ties to a local church means a lot. It's real life here on earth, not just waiting for a real life to come only after we die."

Paige believes her experience has made her a different person: "The best part," she explains, "is that it gives you a platform to work out your faith. I know Christ more intimately than I did in the past. It's not really because of what I'm doing; it's because I'm trusting him and letting him work in me. I think I'm being helped more than I'm helping others. Just as we are discipling people, God is discipling me. Faith comes into play at every minute. Through this experience I've learned that God is in control. We say that all the time and think little about what we mean. But in our environment, you see that he really is in control. You encounter so many circumstances where you have no experience or answer that you listen for his Spirit speaking to you. And when you hear it you say, 'God, I hear your voice and I don't know the way, so I'll do it as you say.' That's faith. It's the most awesome thing about all this."

Paige grew up going to NorthWood, and on Sunday morning she still joins us for worship with several of her friends. NorthWood is a megachurch, a far different experience from the house church in downtown Fort Worth where she worships Sunday night with her inner-city group. So I asked her, "What do you feel about the difference between the two churches. Has being a part of NorthWood helped you or hindered you in your inner-city ministry?"

Paige responded by telling me how her thinking had changed in this area. "I'm such a black-and-white person that when I started on this road, I went to the extreme and felt I had to get away from an established church with a big building. In the inner city, I grappled with questions such as why have a building, a big organization, and all the things that go with it, and as I did so, I began to be less critical. The headaches and difficulties I've encountered with a house church of a handful of people have led me to appreciate the beauty of an organized church. The most awesome thing is what NorthWood teaches about the DNA of who we are as believers and the core things about what it means to be God's children. That has been the foundation, the mindset, and the worldview that has pushed me into the place where I am today. There I learned that missional living is every day — at work, at home, and in the community. Now the only thing that scares me about organized church is the danger that it could stop being the people and start being the institution — a bureaucracy." I think she's right.

I wanted to hear Paige's take on ministry to the world, so I went on to ask, "How do you see that issue? What is your thinking about local and global mission?"

"It's hard for me to keep things in balance," she replied. "I want to take on everything. God in his sovereignty and power is turning hearts and minds to himself through his people wherever they are all over the globe. Not only in Vietnam, but also in Haltom City or Keller or wherever. He is raising up a generation that cares. I used to be scared about what's happening in the rest of the world, but now I can see that he loves this globe a lot, and he is showing his care by using people from my generation with a heart for God."

"THE JILL"

Just to make sure that Paige was not the only person of her generation with these convictions, I turned to another Millennial named Jill, who also attends NorthWood, and as it happens, is my daughter. But Jill is her own person. As a small child she grew up working with us in the inner city and traveling around the world. At the time of writing this, she's a junior at Baylor University studying social work. She has big dreams, but hasn't quite figured out what she is going to do with her life. One day she wants to establish orphanages all over the world, and the next day she wants to work at a community center. Nothing she does will shock me.

Jill has an incredible heart for people. She spent a recent summer at a ministry called Mission Waco. In the mornings she taught a class of at-risk children. In the afternoon she did projects at the center. In the evening she checked in homeless people to the shelter. While working at the mission she lived with a group of girls, and my wife and I sometimes went down on Saturdays to hang out with her. As her father, I admit that what she's doing makes us a little nervous at times, but we are incredibly proud of our daughter and have encouraged her to pursue God's leading in these areas.

Since Jill is clearly focused on doing ministry and is already pursuing opportunities to be trained and put her knowledge into practice, I asked her where this interest and passion came from. She answered, "I think a big part of it was the natural passions and heart that God gave me. But it flourished and developed with the way I was raised and the things I was exposed to, whether it was going to Vietnam or just going to get clothes for someone at the homeless shelter. Growing up in a family involved in ministry and serving under privileged people put me around such ministries most of the time. I suppose it got into my blood."

When I asked Jill how it made her feel to see hurting people in the shelters or in places like Vietnam, she said, "It breaks my heart. I think one reason I don't fear being in the inner city of Waco is because of my love and desire to help them. Whenever I check people into the homeless shelter or serve them breakfast in the morning, I try to picture my parents and my friends going through the line.

That personalizes what I do and makes me more compassionate. It makes the situation more real and relational because those people are somebody's parents and friends and not just faceless people from whom I can totally separate myself."

I wondered if Jill thought her generation was different from other generations in its thinking about helping people with hurts and problems. Her answer was, "I think the mind-set of today's students is changing from focusing only on the practical goals of a future career and how to support themselves and their families. Today they are taking bigger strides toward finding what their passions are, the gifts God has given them, and how they want to impact others."

"What do you see for the future of faith in America?" I asked.

Jill responded, "I think there are different categories for the way people are practicing their faith today. Whichever way young people choose, they tend to be extreme. Some are totally turned off by God and don't even consider faith. Others are raised in the faith and consider themselves Christians, but they are spiritually stagnant and care little about religion and tradition. Then there are people on fire for God, living out their passions and submitting their will to him. In each category there are extremes. Whichever choice my generation makes, God isn't an in-between thing or a flippant thought. They go all out one way or another. I think attending a Christian school and being saturated with highly active Christianity makes it easy for me to see Christian leaders rising up from my generation. But I don't know if they are representative of it."

When I asked Jill what kind of impact she hoped her generation could have on the world, she replied, "If we can maintain a good work ethic, we can turn the world upside down, because there are a lot of innovative young people who want to impact nations and make a difference. We are passionate, but our work ethic isn't as good. Vision is a good thing, and we've got it, but you have to work to make it happen."

Finally, I asked Jill what her dream for the future would look like if she could have it just as she wanted. "I want to be able to look at my life and see that I'm making a difference with my career and that in everything I do I'm helping people. And I want to see people my age work together and use their different strengths and God-given abilities to change the world. Oh yes, and I want a 'hottie' of a husband!"

Well, I hope she's not in too big a hurry to fulfill that last wish, but aside from that, I heartily approve of her hopes. And I believe that she, like Paige, is expressing an outlook common to many of the young people in her generation.

Though they are far from representing everyone in their age group, I believe these two young women give us a fair picture of the concerns and perspectives that shape many in Millennials. My reason for sharing these stories is simple: each generation has its own way of seeing the world, a unique perspective that God can use to bring the world to him. Now that we've encountered some stories, let's dive in for a little analysis of each generation, exploring the way their differing perspectives can balance our own sense of calling.

BOOMERS AND MILLENNIALS

Boomers Have ...

Time. Many have retired, and some have retired early. With time on their hands, they are looking for ways of making a difference.

Money. We are currently in the greatest transfer of wealth in the history of humanity. Literally billions of dollars are accumulating in the bank accounts of highly successful Boomers.

Skills. I've been amazed to watch the Boomers of NorthWood use their jobs and skills in glocal service. Boomers tend to be go-getters — largely college educated, highly motivated, and with a strong work ethic. These attributes have served them so well in their careers that many of them are wealthy. And many of them have been managers who not only have their own skills, but also know how to bring the skills of others together in a unified effort.

Experience. The top end of the Boomer generation is just now graduating from the level of middle age into — what shall we say — elder statesmanship? Spending a lifetime accumulating experiences builds wisdom, if you learn from those experiences.

We can glean great counsel from our elders. When it comes to working globally, older generations have an advantage. While youth culture is worshiped in the United States and other Western cultures, the rest of the world maintains a greater respect for the wisdom of elders.

Desire to make a difference. The Boomers were raised with a sense that they would make the world different. In the 1960s, as turbulent and troubled as they were, it was Boomers who made an idealistic statement as to what the world could and should be. Somewhere along the way many gave up on those dreams and entered their fifties and retirement by settling into the status quo. But the desire is still alive in the hearts of many.

Millennials Have ...

Youth and energy. Because they are young, Millennials are filled with endless and boundless energy. They can get by on little sleep and they can sleep in tough places that would make me wake up with aches and pains that would last a week. You can never underestimate youth.

Idealism. Millennials, like the Boomers of the 1960s, believe that anything is possible and that they can be a part of it. They are overloaded with optimism. They have dreams, and not just dreams about serving others, but also dreams of creating the kind of world they want to live in.

Vocational opportunities. Partly because of their idealism, Millennials are more inclined to pick jobs that match their passions and to choose vocations that can make a massive difference in society. Because of their youth, they have an entire life ahead of them to give to that job, increasing the likelihood that they will succeed in making a difference.

Ability to connect technologically. Millennials grew up on computers. I heard someone say that they are the first truly global generation. According to some analysts, the Millennials in their early and mid-twenties are significantly different from those in their late twenties for one simple reason: the older group remembers when they got the internet, and younger group doesn't remember a time they weren't on the internet.

Ability to travel geographically. I'm all over the world, sometimes in really wild places. But no matter where I go, I'll meet some young Millennial guy or gal backpacking. I often warn them of the places where they need to be extra careful. They look at me and grin, and I suddenly realize I'm no longer twenty. These kids may be young and inexperienced, but they quickly learn how to travel and take care of themselves with less preplanning and scheduling than people like me require.

What about the Busters?

I want to give a quick nod to the Baby Busters. Busters are people born between 1965 and 1980. Busters are currently in the years when career and growing families dominate their time. This is important, and it often fills so much of their time that they have little left for service or mission. But Busters still have enormous amounts of energy and can take on many things at once. We have a church full of Busters at NorthWood who engage in many of our projects.

It's true that the Boomers, who are over forty, generally have more time and money, yet we have many Busters heading up initiatives, both local and global. We even have several with high family demands who get involved part-time or for specific projects or travel. So while we find generational tendencies, it's a mistake to prejudge and lump everyone into the mold of their peers. Ultimately it's not what our generation does, but what we do as individual people that really matters.

GOHUB — LINKING YOUR JOB WITH GOD'S GLOBAL WORK

As I've already mentioned, our church has been working in Vietnam since 1995. As the years have passed and God has blessed the work, many other churches and individuals have asked us for help. Some of these requests come from pastors who want to lead their churches to engagement. Others come from individuals who read or hear about us and want to participate in the type of things we do, but whose own churches don't engage globally or locally.

A few years ago, as I began to help others connect globally in other countries, mentoring them to do what we've done in Vietnam, I began to dream about how every church and every believer could engage in glocal ministry. I knew that in some way the internet was a key for connecting people together for engagement in the Great Commission. I dreamed of an open website where a person could log in to see the needs across the domains of society at locations all around the world. Users would be able to connect to organizations and individuals who could help them use their skills and passions to develop solutions to problems and meet real needs. My friend Al Weiss and I put together a few rough ideas for a website, but since neither of us is technologically gifted, we connected with computer whiz David Grubbs.

David is twenty-three, a 2007 graduate from Baylor University with a BBA in finance. When I met with David, I found that he was immediately tracking with our ideas. David was working out some ways of using the internet to sell products from indigenous peoples. His vision was to help bring people out of poverty by giving them the means and the tools to sell what they were producing on the global market.

David's thinking seemed to match our vision for a global connection point that would link job skills and passions with the needs of people all over the world. Since I didn't know David very well, I began asking him some deeper questions. What made him care about the poor? Why was he motivated to do all of this?

"I think it's inherently in you," he said. "It comes up from inside. The primary questions in all of life are how to find fulfillment, discover your purpose, and uncover what is meaningful. These were the questions I found people asking in college, and they're also the questions people everywhere are asking. I believe that the only true source of meaning, purpose, and fulfillment is Christ. And what does he call us to do? Clothe the naked, feed the hungry, and meet all those other needs that hurting people tend to have."

In the mysteries of God's ways, we discovered at that meeting that the vision for our network gave form and substance to some of the vague ideas that David had already formed. From the meeting, Gohub.org was born. Through Gohub, we hope to remove some of the barriers that keep people from answering God's call upon their life. Gohub.org connects people with other people who have resources and similar interests. Ultimately, its purpose is to network people together, matching gifts, skills, and calling with specific people and places where God is at work.

Recently, I had a chance to sit with David and asked him to describe Gohub.org: "You go on the internet to our website, Gohub.org. You log in and upload your skills, interests, and abilities, which means that basically you create a profile of yourself. From there you can search needs based on your profile, and when you find matches you can make contacts and go from there."

"But," I asked, "what if a person wants to serve in a specific community or a specific place in the world?"

"Gohub is geared to handle such preferences," David replied. "You can filter your preferences in many ways," he said. "You can base it on locations, types of groups, or types of needs to be met. You can do it by date range and the time you would be available. You can even choose to affiliate with any particular group you wish. In other words, you can base your search on your own set of circumstances.

"For example, let's say you're going on vacation and you have an extra day or two that you want to devote to some kind of ministry. You can use Gohub to find the needs in that area and learn whom to contact at that location so that you can get involved in serving right then and there. Or, let's say you're on a business trip and you have a day off. You want to know what you can do to help the local community where you'll be. On Gohub you can find everything you need to know. You don't even need to be traveling. If you want to serve locally, you can find ministries and needs right in your home community. The purpose of Gohub is to help people make engagement and service a lifestyle — not separate from who you are — but something that is integrated into the everyday course of your life."

Gohub can also be used by churches and people who want to do more than just make an occasional trip. It's also for those who may want to connect on a long-term basis, doing work as doctors, dentists, architects, engineers, professors, businessmen, or any other profession. Gohub is a huge platform that connects you to many different missions groups and related websites.

I asked David if there was anything else I should tell the readers of this book. "Yes," he replied, "let them know that Gohub is a not-for-profit organization, and we need the help of everyone who can join us, contributing their support and help and expertise to keep us going. The more people who join up, the more resources we have, the more needs we can identify, and the more valuable Gohub becomes."

As you can see, Gohub provides people wanting to serve with a valuable resource that will do much to enable them to put their faith into action and make a difference. Essentially, Gohub is a social networking site for people who want to work together to engage the world. It's about volunteering our time and gifts and connecting with others who share our passions. Its purpose is to provide a flat place for people of faith to come and sweat together, serving Christ.

"GOHUM" — WORSHIP WITHOUT ACTION

Isaiah ends his worship in chapter 6 by saying to God, "Here am I, send me." Many Christians today don't think of worship as being sent. They think of it as assembling in a place, listening to a message, and meditating on some ideas. This leads to a passive, lethargic, and uninspired faith. That's why I call it "GoHum" (it rhymes with "ho-hum").

Worship is about more than an event — it's about all of our life! It's about how we do our work, how we engage in our relationships, how we go about our day, and how we engage in service to others. Our greatest act of worship is not in sitting in the pew; it is in serving other people and living an authentic Christian witness in the world.

"GOPRAY" — MEDITATION WITHOUT ENGAGEMENT

I fully believe in prayer. Nothing great was ever accomplished or born without prayer and dedicated time spent in serious meditation. For those who don't make this a regular part of their day, take some time to get on your face before God. Open his Word. Open up your journal. Sit quietly and let God speak to you. Write down what he's saying to you. But don't let prayer turn you into a bystander; authentic, Spirit-led prayer should turn you into a participant. Prayer must move our feet to action.

"GOSERVE" — INTENT WITHOUT ACTION

Dream as big as you can possibly dream; God will always outdream you. Many people hear a message or feel inspired to do something, but never take the first step. Many have good intentions, but they don't do anything because they are waiting for a perfect action plan that never materializes. No matter how much you plan and strategize, you will never have a perfect action plan where every detail is worked out. It's impossible to plug every hole and prepare for every possible contingency. Don't wait until everything is exactly as you want it. If you have a sense that God is calling you to do something, make a reasonable plan and push your boat into the water!

As you serve, know that God will provide the resources in ways that you could never foresee, and the act of moving forward will bring greater clarity and insight to your existing sense of calling. Clarity rarely comes to those who stand still. It's impossible to test the wind on the open seas if you remain tied to the dock. Sometimes, to find the wind, you have to pull up the anchor and start rowing.

START ENGAGING THE WORLD

Neither David nor I present Gohub as the only way to follow through on the message of this book. But I have introduced Gohub here because I believe it gives you an idea of one way that you can take that first step. Even if you don't use this service, you will still need to seek out ways you can connect with the world. Look around and you may find that God has already opened doors of opportunity through your current job, the church you attend, or a friendship that you have.

The primary purpose of this book has been to encourage you to do something with the job skills and passions that God has developed in your life. Christians have a call from God as individuals and disciples of Christ to engage the world and expand his kingdom by serving people. My hope is that you have been inspired by the examples and stories of people who have heard this call and responded. As you have seen, there is no model or pattern that is typical for every person. Each story is unique, and God uses each of us in ways that fit our gifts and passions. I hope that these examples will motivate you to put your own faith into action, and that you will take that first step by finding a place for your God-given skills and talents to make a difference.

There are many other places where you can discover the mechanics of engaging the world. For example, you can go to northwoodchurch.org and see how one local church puts all this into practice, or you can go to glocal.net and find resources, curriculum, and training offered to individuals and churches. Glocal.net also helps connect churches, nonprofit corporations, and individuals globally. (This is also where you can read my blogs from NorthWood and all over the world.) The training you will find on this site will lead you through the various ways you can identify your talents, locate a ministry or a need that matches them, arrange your time in such a way that you can engage, find methods of funding your ministry if needed, and many other useful bits of information that will help you get your feet moving.

I've just talked a lot about methods, websites, training, and connections. But I don't want to minimize the crucial and vital role of faith when it comes to glocal engagement. At NorthWood, we are doing what we do today not because we had a manual, a mentor, or a model to guide us. We are where we are today because God broke the hearts of our people, and we began to move forward wherever he opened a path. The greatest stories told are not about what someone did because he followed a manual or devised a method, but because someone was obedient to God and moved out in faith to pursue a dream, a vision, or a passion that God had given them.

In the end, it's really about abandonment to God, recognizing that the work is his, from beginning to end. And that means leaving everything in the hands of God. We don't read about Moses asking Aaron to develop a purpose statement or a ten-point strategy document when God told them to stand before Pharaoh. God gave them their strategy as they needed it — in this case, it came in the form of plagues! All Moses and Aaron were asked to do was to move in obedience to God's calling upon their lives.

If you want to change the world and see society transformed, your ability to do it won't come from a book, but from being broken — from falling on your face before God. It will come from an idea, a thought, an impression, or a call from God that urges you to step out and do something. Give me a man or woman with faith and courage to obey God's voice over one who has a foolproof strategy.

This doesn't mean that we should neglect careful reading and clear thinking. Certainly, you should read a lot, follow the manuals, use resources like Gohub, and be grateful for any help you can find. But these are all secondary things. The first step, and certainly the most essential, is to get on your face before God. Then, when you've met with him, make sure that you get up and follow his call. Welcome to the adventure of a lifetime!

MY DREAM

I have this dream deep in my soul that I cannot let go.

It's a dream that sees men, women, boys, and girls, sweating side by side.

It's a dream where followers of Jesus hold tightly to their faith but don't fear or ignore the Muslim, the Jew, the Hindu, the Buddhist, or the atheist. They are secure in their faith and are neither intimidated nor quickly confused, because they are tied to the Author of life. They can discuss their faith openly and without hesitation, and they can live it out in the presence of other faiths because their own faith is secure.

It's a dream where followers of Jesus are known more for hope, love, and service than for fear, doomsday pronouncements, and isolation from the rest of the world.

It's a dream where not only individual lives, but also entire communities begin to undergo transformation because followers of Jesus are serving without expecting anything in return.

It's a dream where people follow Jesus, not just because of our logic but because of our lives.

It's a dream where people want churches in their community because the disciples who make up those churches love others more than themselves.

It's a dream that the world can be changed.

Haven't I been given the Holy Spirit? Didn't Jesus say we would do even greater things than he did? Didn't his disciples in the New Testament turn the world upside down? Didn't Jesus command us to do the same thing?

Nowadays, everyone seems to be trying to change the world, and many for less than noble purposes. As a Christian who has received God's mercy and been given the hope of the world, should I not try to change it? I certainly won't be the first. Others have had great ideas and we live in the light of their impact on history. But I believe that Jesus has something that no one else has. And if Jesus lives in me, shouldn't we follow in his footsteps, dreaming the dreams that motivated him?

So I dream to see this world transformed. Maybe I will die trying. Maybe I won't see the result of my efforts. But it doesn't matter. If I walk by faith and not by sight, Jesus can make of my small effort something wonderful. He can take my sack of loaves and fishes and multiply my meager efforts and resources into something that gives nourishment to many and satisfies their hunger. Even if I contribute that small part, my life will be worthwhile. The fact that I lived will have meaning.

What about you? What will you do today, no matter how small it may seem, that God can use to change this world?

Connection Steps

⊙ Make a list of your Boomer and/or Buster friends and have coffee and see if you can partner to do something together in engagement.

⊙ Visit Gohub.org and explore opportunities and post a comment.

⊙ Get on your knees, pray, and get up and GO!!!!!!!

NOTES

1. C. S. Lewis, *Surprised by Joy* (New York: Harcourt Brace & Company, 1955), 16.
2. Maurice Merleau-Ponty, *The Visible and the Invisible, Followed by Working Notes* (trans. Alphonso Lingis; Evanston: Northwestern Univ. Press, 1968), 215.
3. Edward Hopper, quoted in Rolf G. Renner, *Hopper* (Los Angeles: Taschen, 1999), 11.
4. Winston Churchill, quoted in Os Guinness, *The Call* (Nashville: Nelson, 2003), 79.
5. Søren Kierkegaard, *Journal and Papers* (Bloomington: Indiana Univ. Press, 1976), quoted in Guinness, *The Call*, 3.
6. Guinness, *The Call*, 4.
7. Dietrich Bonhoeffer, *The Cost of Discipleship* (New York: Macmillan, 1959), 18.
8. www.wikipedia.org/wiki/Node_%28networking%29.
9. Don Tapscott and Anthony Williams, *Wikinomics* (New York: Portfolio, 2008), 19–26.
10. Ibid., 83.
11. Fareed Zakaria, *The Post-American World* (New York: Norton, 2008), 2–3.
12. Colorado Springs is the home of several megachurches and influential organizations such as Focus on the Family and NavPress.
13. Zakaria, *The Post-American World*, 37.
14. Ibid.
15. Ibid., 47.
16. *Glocal* is a coined word, combining "global" and "local" to convey the idea of total ministry at all levels.
17. C. S. Lewis, *Mere Christianity* (New York: Macmillan, 1943), 119.
18. Os Guiness, *The Case for Civility* (New York: HarperOne, 2008), 31.
19. Ibid., 84.
20. Ibid., 21.
21. Jonathan Sacks, *The Home We Build Together* (London: Continuum, 2008), 141–42.
22. Ibid., 66.
23. Guinness, *The Case for Civility*, 96.

24. Patrick Devlin, *The Enforcement of Morals* (Oxford: Oxford Univ. Press, 1965), 10.

25. Sacks, *The Home We Build Together*, 84.

26. Ibid., 85.

27. Ibid., 132.

28. Ibid., 56.

29. Joseph L. Allen, *Love and Conflict: A Covenantal Model of Christian Ethics* (Lanham, MD: Univ. Press of America, 1995), 17.

30. Sacks, *The Home We Build Together*, 110.

31. Guinness, *The Call*, 98.

32. Ibid., 101.

33. Bob Buford, *Halftime* (Grand Rapids: Zondervan, 1997), 161.

34. Guinness, *The Call*, 106.

35. Sacks, *The Home We Build Together*, 94.

36. Ibid., 106.

37. Ibid., 230.

38. Ibid., 53.

39. Quoted by Jon Meacham, *American Gospel* (New York: Random House, 2006), 32.

40. Steven Waldman, *Founding Faith* (New York: Random House, 2008), xvi.

41. Brian Grimm, "Is Religious Freedom Good for Us?" in the *Review of Faith & International Affairs* 6/2 (Summer 2008), 4 – 6.

42. Meacham, *American Gospel*, 5.

43. Ibid., 31.

44. John Adams, Letter to Thomas Jefferson (April 19, 1817), available at nationalhumanitiescenter.org/pds/livingrev/religion/text3/adamsjeffersoncor.pdf.

45. Meacham, *American Gospel*, 48, 75.

46. G. K. Chesterton, quoted in Sydney E. Mead, *The Nation with the Soul of a Church* (Macon, GA: Mercer Univ. Press, 1985), 48.

47. This quote from Benjamin Franklin is available at www.americanrhetoric.com/speeches/benfranklin.htm.

48. John G. Nicolay, *A Short Life of Abraham Lincoln* (New York: Century, 1902), 339.

49. Jon Meacham, "God and the Founders," *Newsweek* (April 10, 2006); online at www.newsweek.com/id/45970/page/1.

50. See www.geocities.com/Athens/7842/rfindex.htm.

51. Frederick Douglass, *Narrative of the Life of Frederick Douglass, an American Slave*; see www.sunsite.berkeley.edu/Literature/Douglass/Autobiography/09.html.

INDEX

The Multiplying Church

The New Math for Starting New Churches

Bob Roberts Jr.

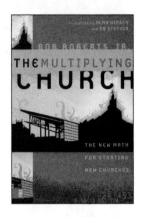

The Multiplying Church is a primer for pastors and lay leaders involved in, or wanting to learn about, the church multiplication groundswell in North America. It shows how multiplying churches should be a natural, regular function of every church to reach the 70 percent of Americans who have no meaningful church relationship.

Detailing the stories and guiding principles of this dramatic growth, this guide offers insight on:

- Why churches are multiplying in the East but not in the West
- Keys to church multiplication
- The missing link—pregnant mother churches
- Antioch vs. Jerusalem: Which got it right?
- What kind of churches should we start?
- What is the end game of church planting?
- How big does a church have to be to start multiplying churches?
- Church planting movements or Jesus movements?

Bob Roberts helps us return to an early-church model of multiplication, where a single church sent laypeople out to plant other communities of believers.

Hardcover, Jacketed: 978-0-310-27716-3

Pick up a copy at your favorite bookstore or online!

ZONDERVAN®
.com

Glocalization

How Followers of Jesus Engage a Flat World

Bob Roberts Jr.

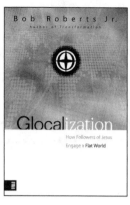

If you want to know where and how the church is going to grow, think local and global. Think glocal.

Glocal is Bob Roberts' term for the seamless connectedness between the local and global. That connection is affecting the church in ways that never could have been imagined in the first-century church, or even the twentieth-century church. And it's creating unprecedented opportunities for individuals and churches—for you and your church—to live out their faith in real time across the world.

Glocalization offers a vision of the unprecedented changes of our times and how they are impacting the church. Discover how these changes will transform the way churches define their mission and how Christians relate to one another and to the world. This provocative book turns the traditional mission-agency model upside down and shows how transformed people and churches can make a glocal (global and local) impact.

Glocalization offers an exciting vision for churches and individuals who want to reach this changing world for Christ.

Hardcover, Jacketed: 978-0-310-26718-8

Pick up a copy at your favorite bookstore or online!

ZONDERVAN®
.com

Share Your Thoughts

With the Author: Your comments will be forwarded to the author when you send them to *zauthor@zondervan.com*.

With Zondervan: Submit your review of this book by writing to *zreview@zondervan.com*.

Free Online Resources at
www.zondervan.com

Zondervan AuthorTracker: Be notified whenever your favorite authors publish new books, go on tour, or post an update about what's happening in their lives at www.zondervan.com/authortracker.

Daily Bible Verses and Devotions: Enrich your life with daily Bible verses or devotions that help you start every morning focused on God. Visit www.zondervan.com/newsletters.

Free Email Publications: Sign up for newsletters on Christian living, academic resources, church ministry, fiction, children's resources, and more. Visit www.zondervan.com/newsletters.

Zondervan Bible Search: Find and compare Bible passages in a variety of translations at www.zondervanbiblesearch.com.

Other Benefits: Register yourself to receive online benefits like coupons and special offers, or to participate in research.

ZONDERVAN.com/
AUTHORTRACKER
follow your favorite authors